Dirty Living

By
Sierra

Sierra

STREET KNOWLEDGE PUBLISHING

Note: This novel is a work of fiction. Any reference to real people, events, establishments, or locales, is intended only to give the fiction a sense of reality and authenticity. Names, characters, places and incidents are products of the author's imagination or are used fictitiously. Any resemblance to actual events, locale, or persons living or dead, is entirely coincidental.

Published by: Street Knowledge Publishing

Street Knowledge Publishing
P.O. Box 345
Wilmington, DE 19899

Copyright date: 2016
ISBN: 978-1-944151-00-3

Dirty Living by Sierra
Edited by Street Knowledge Publishing Services
Cover design by Street Knowledge Publishing Services
Formatted by Krystol Diggs
Typed from handwriting to text by Vanessa Cooper

All Street Knowledge Publishing titles are available at special quantity discounts for bulk purchases for sales promotion, fund-raising, educational, or institutional use and book clubs.

www.streetknowledgepublishing.com

Printed in Canada

CONTENTS

PROLOGUE

The #1 prostitution strip in Delaware is route 13. Up until three years ago two motels, the Delaware & the Red Rose Inn were leading the state in soliciting, but have since been demolished to be turned into Wawa's, scattering the working women and men throughout the city.

New Castle Avenue is the second-largest hoe strip in the suburbs, which earned itself the street names 'Trick City or the Triangle.' Not only are the Days Inn, Super Lodge, and Motel 6 homes to the night life, located conveniently yards away from each other, but the Gulf Station is located in between the three motels, with a little alley of bushes running behind it called 'Pick-Up Strip.' It's where the low-level dealers catch the whores before they can cop from the rooms.

On any given day you can buy anything from heroin, down the north end of the avenue from the South Bridge projects, to ecstasy, marijuana, or crack cocaine from the in between neighborhoods along the avenue called Rose Gate, Oakmont, Dunleith, or Arbor Place. But by far the motels are the most lucrative spots on the avenue, because the freaks truly do come out at night. And what only women possess, all men need.

"Psss!" Kasi called out from the bushes to his runner as soon as he saw a potential customer.

"Yo! We got that drop over here!" Tranz called out.

A suspicious looking white man came staggering out of the Super Lodge entrance, tilting a brown paper bag to his

4

lips. Kasi's touter dashed over to see if the man wanted to spend.

Tranz could hear the two men negotiating as they approached, so he darted over to his Chevy Malibu, parked in the nearby McDonald's parking lot. Looking around the lot for anything out of order before he went into the stash spot, Tranz asked himself, *where did all the bitches go?*

"What you working with?" Kasi asked the dusty looking man, after he removed the bottle from his lips.

"A eight ball," he responded groggily.

"A eight ball? Why'd you just ask me for a forty then?" the Touter asked.

Kasi gave the touter his "shut up" look without saying anything.

"Man, I better be getting more than one from this cracker, because I made this deal happen." the fiend demanded.

"What's taking Tranz so long?" the fiend asked.

"I don't know?" Kasi said, and then looked back over his shoulder to see for himself.

Pop, pop, pop! Gunshots rang out within seconds, destroying the overhead street lamps in the parking lot.

Deafened by the loud blasts, Kasi turned back around to see what had happened. That's when he saw that the shooter had him at gunpoint.

"That was your warning shot," the perpetrator announced as he shook off the paper bag that concealed his weapon. "Now lay down on the ground, or you'll never move again."

Kasi looked over in Tranz's direction for help, but three masked gunmen were manhandling him.

"Help! helppp!" Tranz screamed after each skull-shattering blow to the head. Realizing that no help was coming to aid them, the touter began to plea for his life. "Please, don't shoot me."

"Where's your stash at? This can't be everything?" One of the masked men asked Tranz after grabbing a zip lock bag, containing $1,100 in cash 131 dimes from the armrest.

Just as the man was about to smack Tranz with the butt of the gun again, a familiar sound came echoing from a nearby bush. *"Clack-clack!"* Was the sound of a shell being loaded into a shotgun.

"Wait. Did you hear that?" One of the men asked.

At that moment two of the three men called out to the man holding Kasi at gun-point and then turned towards the bushes.

"On three, run," Kasi whispered to the whimpering fiend beside him.

"I'll check it out boss," one of them called out as they made their way over to the other men.

The lead man gave the go-ahead nod. Once the man got close enough to see through the shadows sparks lit up the bushes, sending pellets everywhere. In all the confusion Kasi and his friends got up and started to run in opposite directions. And just as quickly as the gun battle started, it ended, but with bloodshed.

CHAPTER 1

About 25 miles north of Bayside State Prison, in a McDonald's parking lot, Deshonne "Magic" Robinson was reborn. With a newly found lease on life, and a fresh look, he was ready for whatever would come his way, dressed in a white t-shirt, tan prison-issue khakis, and the same rundown gray and white Reebok Classics from four years earlier. With only one thing on his mind, he anxiously dialed up the only female he knew who would break speed limits for a drop of his backed up jizm.

"Hello?" a soft voice answered on the other end.

"Can I speak to Desiree?" Deshonne asked with a strange look of confusion on his face because he didn't recognize her voice at first.

Excited to hear the gentle voice of her first love and best friend, Desiree's eyes lit up as she whipped her $200 dollar micros away from her right ear. "This is she. What's up boo?"

"Yo, it's finally over, Dee. I'll see you in a little while, okay?" he stated while waving at his two sons through the restaurant's storefront glass doors.

"Wait! Don't hang up on me like that," she yelled. Remembering her lunch date with Alex, she quickly asked, "Where are you at now?"

"I'm still over in Jersey somewhere. So I'll call you back when I get over the bridge because I'm eating up my mom's minutes. And I ain't even trying to hear her mouth already."

"Tell her I'll buy her some more minutes."

"Nah, it's cool. I was just calling to let you know that I was on my way so you wouldn't make any plans. That way I can be the main topic of your thoughts and hopefully your friend for the night," he hinted. "I'm trying to caress those Victoria's Secrets. So I'm putting my bid in now, because I know you got a friend," he said with a devious smirk on his face.

"Boy, I know you ain't worried about me having no friend, so stop it with the games. And just make sure you don't make no stops on me, if you really want the night to be yours." Her breasts were pulsating with anticipation of his delicate touch. She unconsciously touched herself as she spoke until her nipples were fully erect. "As long as I can taste you first, Magic, you can stay for breakfast," she promised.

He was in a hurry to hang up the phone because his family was returning to the car with his number 3 quarter pounders with cheese meal and acknowledged the look from his mother that he knew meant, *get off of my damn phone!*

"That's all I needed to hear, Dee," Magic replied. "I'm about to call Kenny, so I can get a couple outfits and some Air Ones."

"Okay, boo, I'll be waiting for your call. Bye!"

"See you later, Dee."

*****

The young saleswomen hawked the only two customers' inside the store, hoping for a good commission. Deshonne and his childhood friend aimlessly ransacked the tables of City Blue for a bargain.

"Magic, it's so many different styles of jeans in this store. Why do you want me to take you back in town to buy them played-out-ass Silver Tabs?" Kenny asked in disbelief, picking up a pair of Enyce Jeans for himself while eyeing another. "It's 2003, cousin. 1999 played out like Prince's last album. I'll buy you them whack-ass jeans if you want me to, but I'm telling you, the only throwbacks niggas is rocking are by Mitchell-n-Ness," his lanky friend stated confidently.

Kenny was Deshonne's right-hand man growing up in New Castle, in the suburbs of Delaware. At one time they were flipping fifty-dollar double-ups for outfits and basketball kicks. But in Deshonne's absence Kenny had blown up a hundred times over. And now he had his own block, with his own workers. And Deshonne had quickly caught on to how much his ego had changed with his new status.

"Yo, why don't you just grab up a pair of Akademics and I'll grab you some white tees from rashes on Market Street, cause that's what it's hitting for anyway," Kenny suggested. Then he turned in the direction of a saleswoman, smiled, and asked for assistance to prove his point. "Excuse me, shorty. Can you let my peoples know what's hot right now on the streets because he's been away for a while and his taste for fashion is a little stale?"

She instantly caught on that his friend must've been fresh out of jail. With a heavenly smile on her unblemished face, she eagerly walked over to help them. "Of course those Akademic jeans you picked up earlier are hot, and not to mention new in style."

Deshonne followed her movements with his eyes, paying very little attention to her sales pitch.

"We also have Roc-a-Wear, Sean John, Phat Farm, and Enyce Jeans, khakis, or sweatsuits over there," she informed them as she pointed in the opposite direction. Trying to catch her first sale of the day, she quickly bent over to refold a unneeded pair of jeans that were barely wrinkled, knowing that her tight-fitting, size 6 Capris would cause lust and almost certainly seal the deal. "I can pick something out for y'all if you want me to," she suggested to Kenny.

Eyes glued to her 36Cs, Kenny said, "I'm cool, shorty. It's his day today." Then he shoved Deshonne forward. "Magic, don't get shy on her. Go ahead and tell her what size you wear so we can bounce. I got somewhere to be."

Feeling embarrassed by his boy's suggestion of shyness, Deshonne seemed to stand a little taller than his 5'8", 189lb. frame. "I ain't never been the shy type, so don't let these new glasses fool you, cause I'm still the shit," he stated in a matter-of-fact manner. "You just kick out the change so she can get me out of this jail shit."

"It's crazy that your style is stuck in the 90s along with your good eyes," Kenny said over his shoulder jokingly as he turned towards the cash register.

"Keep it moving, clown boy. We don't need your corny ass jokes back here!" Deshonne complained. *Let shorty with the donkey on her back pick my shit out in peace*, he thought as he walked off in the direction of the dressing rooms.

"Yo, I'ma give Kia $300 for whatever you pick out. I have to go out into the hall so my Nextel can pick up a signal because I have to make an important phone call, okay?" Kenny yelled back towards the dressing room.

"Who in the hell is Kia?" Deshonne barked over the short wooden door.

"My peoples up there at the cash register," the five-foot-two helper said while passing him another pair of overpriced jeans.

"What about my feet?" he yelled out, praying that he wouldn't have to go another day in his bad-luck Reeboks.

"Don't worry, I got you covered! The sooner we leave, the sooner you can retire those Classics. L.D. will be on the Ave. he got your size," Kenny yelled as he walked out of the store to dial back his last missed call.

*****

Riding down Philadelphia Pike, the longest route to Wilmington's north side of the city, coming from Tri-State Mall, Deshonne sat back in Kenny's new, pearl-white 2003 Lincoln LS, feeling like a brand-new man. As bad as he wanted to drive, so he could stunt for the up-and coming ghetto queens of the inner city, just to let them know he was back, he quietly enjoyed the scenery.

"So, what's next?" Deshonne asked out of curiosity, still anxious to toss the four-year-old prison shoes.

Kenny drove with both knees steering the car while he searched through his CD case for the *Best of Freeway*. "We're about to go through Market Street so I can catch L.D. before he leaves this girl's house. He got some Air Ones for you. But don't worry, if we miss him, I'll just shoot out to Christiana Mall and grab you some," Kenny promised.

"That's what's up, Kenny! Thanks for everything, fam," Deshonne replied, grateful that his boy was looking out for him. He swiftly rubbed his hands together as if they were itching, as if he was over-anxious.

"Ah, don't worry about it. It's nothing. We're practically brothers, Magic," Kenny replied without looking up, as if his charity was out of love.

Knowing that his funds were limited to the gate-money check the prison cut him, Deshonne kicked out hints to his boy. "Yo, you know I hate this being broke shit, right?"

"You've only been home half a day Magic. Being broke should be the farthest thing from your mind right now," Kenny said, while finally putting in the CD he wanted to listen to. "You should be focusing on trying to smut one of these phat-ass hood rats walking up and down Market with nothing to do." Kenny simultaneously waved at a female as he backed into the O.K. Discount Store parking lot, on 23rd & Market. "You don't have to make love to your hand no more, homie. And these broads ain't looking for love these days, either."

"I already got that part of my day covered. As a matter of fact, as soon as you drop me back off at mommy's, it's on," Deshonne stated, reaching for the door handle.

"Do you want me to drop you off now? Because I'm going to be here for a while, and a brother needs that first shot like these fiends need my work," Kenny stated, still holding his right hand on the ignition.

"Nah, it's cool, she's waiting for my call." Deshonne smiled broadly as he remembered the soft sounds Desiree used to make during their sexual encounters. "If it's cool with you, I'm just going to hang out with you for a minute, because I got all night to be with my friend and I got 72 hours to report to probation."

Kenny shook his head in disagreement. "Ah-ight, if that's what you want to do. I'm about to go over here to my people's car lot for a minute an holler at them real quick," he told Deshonne, pointing across the street at a dilapidated building, cluttered with outdated cars and trash.

What instantly caught Deshonne's attention was the handfull of drug dealers running up and down the block, alongside the lot, making hand-to-hand sales as if it were legal.

"Do you need to go somewhere?" Kenny asked, holding out the keys.

Deshonne looked around at the changed surroundings in bewilderment before shaking his head. "Nah, I'm about to walk down the block to Jerome's grandma's house."

Kenny snapped his fingers and said, "That's right, I forgot that y'all was down together." then he forewarned his friend, "Yo, Rala's still on house arrest, and he's pumping Hydro off of his grandmother's porch, so be careful down that end."

Not knowing the first thing about Hydro, Deshonne paid the warning no attention. Maybe it was the cloudless April day that set his jail glow above everyone else's or just the muscular build that he had acquired that seemed to be attached to an unfamiliar face. But, either way, he was attracting smiles and turning heads at each glance. He just kept his eyes in amazement on all of the skirts and tight-fitting jeans walking up and down Market Street. To him, it seemed like every thick body had a beautiful face attached to it, and he loved it.

"His pop sells clothes, so see if he got something for you and I'll be in front of the car lot when you get done," Kenny yelled across the busy street.

"He told me this morning to stop by so he could hit me off with a couple of dollars."

"And watch for the D.Ts and P&P, because they stay down that end! Messing with Rala, you won't have to wait 72 hours to see your probation officer. They'll snatch you up quick."

Steadily walking backwards until the shop disappeared, Deshonne repeatedly thought to himself, *you don't have to worry about me I'm free now, and I'm staying this way.*

Even though Jerome's house was only a half a block away, the walk itself was a journey. The two-story red and brown brick row-homes were either boarded up or overcrowded. Loud music blared from a blue Ford Crown Victoria and could be heard two blocks farther down, on Carter Street every three houses or so featured individuals engaging in some type of illegal activity.

As Deshonne stepped up the three eroding steps of his friend's home, a female came flying past him, with a baseball bat, catching his attention. She was running to catch two white boys in an old, green, two-door Honda with flip-up lights. He now could see what everyone meant by *times have changed*. And he was right back in the midst of it.

*****

Standing before him, half-naked for the first time in four years, Desiree felt strange and unattractive. She knew deep down that she and Deshonne had a certain bond together, but she feared that it would fade tonight because of her newly acquired love handles.

"Magic, can we turn off the lights, please?" she asked nervously, with one of her hands on her hip and the other on the light switch.

"Why, Dee, it's not like I haven't seen every beautiful inch of you before," he said, to rebuild her obvious lack of confidence. Inside he was saying, *Damn, I hit the lottery tonight! I hope I don't cum too fast for her cause I gotta go deep and hard.*

"The last time you saw me was before I gained all of this weight, boy," Desiree responded. In the back of her mind she was wondering, *I wonder if his dick grew any since the last time we slept together? And I hope he knows how to eat pussy now because Alex's tongue game is off the chain.*

"We used to be a couple remember, Dee? You still look sexy to me, or I wouldn't be here," Deshonne told her, hoping that the compliment would ease her insecurities.

I know he can see that I'm fat now, so I hope he knows that I know he's lying, she thought to herself. "You know how

13

I feel about my body, Magic. I used to run track in school, remember?"

"Yeah, I remember. And?"

"And I hate being chunky, boy!"

The smell of her Apple body lotion was so strong that he could almost taste it. He could care less about how she felt about her body with each second passing. And though only he could tell that his heart was beating fast, it felt like all the blood was rushing into his love muscle and he felt like she knew it. So trying to put an end to all of the meaningless conversation, he gently spoke words of reason. "Dee, you just gained a little weight because of the Depo shot you used to take, remember? I could see if your stomach was hanging or you just looked busted, but you still got the whole package from where I'm sitting. Caramel complexion, still pretty, your titties don't sag, and your ass is so soft it still shakes. So there's no problem."

"I still don't like the way I look, Magic. Now, you've seen me in the raunchiest lingerie that Victoria's Secret has to offer, so I'm turning off the light."

That's when it clicked in his brain that the fireworks were about to begin. *Lets get ready to rumble!* he thought to himself as he felt around the full size-bed for his guaranteed mood-setter.

"Okay, okay, let me find the remote control to the CD player first before you cut it off," he insisted. Scanning the 20 by 12 room, from the single Cherry Oak dresser to the right, to the fully equipped electronic system located on the entertainment center lined up along the adjacent wall, he couldn't find the remote anywhere.

Desiree was a dreamer. and being forewarned by the mistakes in the countless street novels she read every day, she realized that her chances of getting pregnant by a man fresh out of jail were extremely high, especially since she was no longer on birth control. So, being always outspoken, she commanded, "You need to find some condoms before I turn off this light. And stop worrying about trying to be Romeo with the music, because I'm not trying to get pregnant anytime soon."

He pointed back towards the dresser as he leaned over to pick up their clothes, still in search of the remote. "Look in the drawer right behind me while I find the remote."

"I hope you don't have the same condoms from the last time we had sex because if you do, we're getting dressed and walking over to Wawa's."

"I bought those with the money I got from Kenny earlier, okay?"

Desiree opened up the dresser and was instantly shocked. "Who are you planning on using all of these on?" she asked as she cracked open the value size party box.

Deshonne grinned, "I can never have too many of those, boo. You know I'm backed up a couple years."

"I'm not even going to get mad at you for that ignorant answer," she said, spotting the remote in the drawer. "Here's the remote, dummy." She flung it at him, just missing his forehead.

Forgetting all about the light, she walked over and plopped onto the bed. Her heavy breasts bounced inside of the support bra as she leaned back to spread her thick thighs, revealing her un-manicured bush of pubic hair protruding outside her lace thong. "Make sure your door is locked, and cut off that stupid light," Desiree commanded.

As he reached over to turn off the light, he made one last plea to his sexy companion. "Dee, don't forget it's been a while since I-"

"I know," she said, cutting off his unnecessary speech before it turned her off. She passively patted the empty space beside her, beckoning him to come to bed.

"Be gentle," he playfully whispered.

"Come lay down, stupid," she giggled. He hit the light switch and they were in complete darkness.

Instantly the sexual escapades commenced.

CHAPTER 2

The Baby Gap was crowded with tired parents and crying babies. Marie's klepto behaviors had become a routine for her on days like this one. Her adrenaline bubbled with each boosting spree. Her lifestyle had become a form for survival that few knew about, and one that her daughter despised.

"We didn't come to the mall to shop for us, Kelia. Let's just stick to the order so we can get out of here, okay. I got somewhere to be soon, and I don't have time to do us today," Marie grumbled to her adolescent offspring.

"Mom, we never come to the store for ourselves. It's always for somebody else or their kids," Kelia stated, with disgust as she tried quietly to pop off another security button.

Easily angered by her daughter's continuous badgering, Marie chastised her. "If your dad wasn't such a fucking loser, maybe we wouldn't have to shop to eat and pay rent."

Noticing that her mother's light-skinned complexion was reddening with anger, Kelia edged her on further. "Don't you mean, if you had a real job?" Kelia mumbled back.

"What did you say girl? Don't mumble!" Marie barked, no longer paying any mind to the passersby outside of the enclosed dressing room. "Say it louder so I can smack the piss out of you in here!" she taunted to no avail. "That's what I thought, smart ass. Now fix your face, and keep putting the clothes in the back of Wali's stroller," Marie stated, holding her godson in her arms as she opened the door. "Meet me by the entrance. I'm going to get some more stuff for Zenda's bad-ass kids, so we won't have to hear that bitch's mouth," Marie ordered without looking back.

"Look at you, you so cute. Yes you are, baby. I wish I could keep you," she told Wali as they departed.

Kelia wanted to cuss her mother out as she listened to her talking to the baby as they walked away, leaving her to do all the dirty work.

*****

Kelia loathed her mother's whole demeanor. Being the spitting image of her mother had its advantages. But other than the outward resemblance, they totally contrasted.

Driving north towards Wilmington from Christiana Mall, used to be a short pleasant ride without the traffic on I-95. But listening to her mother verbally assassinating her made the ride from the mall seem like the highway had bumper-to-bumper traffic. Kelia just stared out of the Oldsmobile's window at the sun going down. She had heard the gibberish so many times before, and today's was no different, still meaningless and uncalled for.

"I wish your ungrateful behind was still Wali's size. You were the most beautiful little girl before you started looking like that sorry sperm donor," Marie told her fifteen-years-younger, mirror-image daughter. "Everybody wanted to hold you and keep you for the weekends back then because you were the sweetest little baby," she remembered.

Looking over at her daughter every few seconds irritated Marie tremendously. The passion mark on Kelia's neck incited more verbal assaults. "I tried to give you a little space because you're fourteen now, and I thought that you were a responsible girl. But now I realize that you're too damn grown to leave my sight."

"Whatever!" Kelia spat back as her mother went on.

"I can't even let you hang out with those little girls down the street because you've turned them into whores like you."

Ut oh, here this bitch goes again, Kelia thought.

"And, your stupid behind even had the nerve to come home with a hicky on your neck. Like I wasn't going to notice. Then you wonder why I didn't steal you shit. You should've asked the dirty-ass boy that you let suck on your neck for some money if you was really bright. But no, you want to be a whore and lay down for free. Dummy."

As soon as Marie veered onto the Maryland avenue exit, she looked back into the rearview mirror, at the baby's carry bag. "Look in the back seat and grab that stuff so you can count everything up real quick before I drop it off," Marie ordered.

Kelia rolled her eyes at her mother, and Marie caught her.

"Grab the stupid bag, Kelia, and don't look at me like that no more."

"Mom, Wali's sleep, and the bag is halfway under the car seat."

"You don't have to move him to get to the bag, Kelia. Now grab the bag because I need to know if we got enough stuff."

"Do you hear me?" Marie asked when Kelia didn't move fast enough.

"Yeah, Mom, I hear you."

"Good, now give me your phone so I can call Damon."

"Mom, I only got 15 minutes left," Kelia whined, knowing that she would have to go through hell to get some more.

"Girl, if you don't give me that phone, acting like I don't put minutes on it for you!" Marie commanded through clenched teeth, snatching the phone from Kelia's lap.

*****

As she displayed her newly acquired merchandise to a loyal customer, Marie's manipulative dexterity kicked in. "I know I get a bonus for same-day delivery, right?" she asked while matching up the outfits.

Damon examined the clothes and began to stick his pinky finger through holes in the collars. "Marie, some of these clothes got little holes in' em."

"Well, you know I have to pop off the beepers quick, Damon. And sometimes you have to be alright with a snag or two."

Damon pulled out a wad of rubber band-wrapped drug money. "I'm letting you know now, Marie. For my $350, I want top-of-the-line shit, not rags."

Seeing what she came for made her hands sweat. She swiftly turned up the charm. "Those snags are under the collars, boo, so it's not that serious. And besides, only you know they're there."

Damon curiously picked up another article of clothing. "Let me check out everything else real fast."

Feeling held up, she sighed. "You're only paying half price. Can you hurry this up? My babies are outside in the car, and I do have somewhere to be." She tried to throw him off because she knew there were more snags and rips. "Damn, I hate ungrateful men."

"What do I have to be grateful for?"

"Be grateful that you only have to live with a few snags and not the inked up ones. Now pay me what you owe me, boy."

Hoping that his arrogance hadn't spoiled his chances on getting lucky, Damon smiled at the eye candy. "Ah-ight, here you go, sexy. You know I was just playing with you. "Don't forget to call the number that I gave you earlier because my sister's kids need some stuff, too."

"Okay, I'll call her tomorrow and get all the sizes, but make sure she knows that I don't do credit, sweetie. I work strictly cash on delivery."

"We're far from broke, Marie, so don't worry about money because mines is long."

"I know," she stated sarcastically as she headed towards the door recounting her payment. "Bye, Damon!"

Captivated by her long Indian hair, hour-glass figure, and catwalk stride, Damon's hormones took over, causing him to grab her plump rear end. "Can I call you in a few hours?" he quickly blurted out when she stopped dead in her tracks.

She shattered his advances without arguing or even turning around. "tell your girlfriend I said hi and to call me in the morning."

Stopped cold, he stood in the doorway, fantasizing, as she bent over to tie her left shoestring before getting into the car and pulling off.

*****

Hours later, as the vehicle glided to a halt on one of Wilmington's Hilltop area side streets, Kelia's unwanted quest finally ended.

"Kelia, wake up!" Marie stated with a stiff nudge. "Take the baby in the house, and I'll be back in a little while."

"Mom, I'm hungry," Kelia grumbled as she squinted at the dimly lit clock on the sun burnt dashboard.

"Go in the house and see if Zenda cooked, cause I don't have time to go food shopping right now. If she didn't, call me on your cell phone and I'll bring you something back from Fried Corner."

Hearing that, Kelia knew in that instant that her mother was headed to their cousin's house on Concord Avenue to hang out. That meant a night filled with playing cards for money with some of their drug-dealing cousins and crackhead aunts and uncles. "I don't want to stay at this house without you," Kelia whined. "Zenda's going to want to go out, and then she's going to want me to babysit."

The woman Kelia spoke of was a 25-year-old bipolar, single mother of two demented toddlers. Being tampered with at a young age altered Zenda's thinking. Her main priorities were parties, drinking and sex. Sex was always an option to her.

"Don't worry, I'll be back tonight. So just go in our room and lock the door," Marie said to brush off her daughter's nagging.

Not satisfied with the answer she received, Kelia continued to ask questions pertaining to her hunger pains. "Mom, what time are you coming back?"

"Why, Kelia? I'm grown."

"Cause I need some pads," Kelia said as she unfastened the baby's car seat.

"As soon as I drop this car off, I'll be back. Just use my pads for tonight and I'll get you your own in the morning, okay?"

Still not satisfied with the answers she received, Kelia stood next to the car with the baby asleep in the car seat, on the roof.

"Back up so I can go. And don't try and be slick and sneak out before I come back because you know Zenda will call me if you do."

Kelia took the baby and backed up towards the stone steps, leading up to the porch, thinking to herself, *Fuck you and Zenda. I hate both of y'all!*

CHAPTER 3

While sitting at the small kitchen table with his head slumped between his hands, Deshonne drifted in and out of consciousness. He was still trying to recuperate from the physical workout that he and Desiree had engaged in for the past couple of nights.

"Deshonne, why are you up so early?" his mother asked as she came into the kitchen.

Too tired to respond, he just listened to her question, wondering why she started her day so early.

"And whose car was parked outside of my house last night when I came home from work?"

"Dee, mom," he informed her between nods.

As she hooked up the percolator for his father's morning brew, she said, "I hope she's been taking her hot ass home at night. This isn't Shady Rest Motel, so don't be laying up in here on my new furniture. You can go over her house if you need to get your little pecker wet."

Listening to his mother's words of wisdom was soothing because to him she was always right. It was all he had yearned for in prison. And now that he was home, negative or positive, he loved the attention.

"Did you sign up for probation, yet?" he heard her repeat as her voice began to fade. "Deshonne, Deshonne..." was the last thing he faintly heard her say before last night's festivities got the best of him, causing his mother's words to transform into Desiree's sporadic moans.

*****

"**Oww**, harder, Magic," she whispered into his ear with each sexual plunge.

Stroking her as hard as he could wasn't a problem because her words had him moving like a well-oiled machine. Holding onto her own ankles for support as he used his own leverage to hold up her thick, moistened thighs for more penetration, Desiree slowly moved to the rhythm of his timed gyrations.

"This pussy belongs to you, boo," she cried out as her own climax began. "Push harder," she begged, wiping the sweat away from his eyebrows.

He tried his best to live up to her challenges. Hearing her vagina make intoxicating slurping sounds tickled his mind and encouraged his body. Desiree's juices gushed out as she tightened up her pelvic muscles around the width of his throbbing shaft.

"Ah. Can you hear—her talking to you?" she gasped.

Damn, she got freakier from the last time I was home, he thought. *I'm getting tired.*

Desiree missed this type of sexual excitement. Just the thought of being satisfied by a real penis, had become a dream to her since his departure. But now, it was once again a reality, and she was taking full advantage of every minute of it. "I want you to fuck me harder, Magic," she demanded as she rolled over onto her stomach, grabbed the soaked sheets, and prepared for the onslaught.

As he banged her inner walls doggy-style, with both hands clutching her sweaty breasts, he tried his hardest to concentrate on pleasing her. Knowing that she was long-winded from previous encounters, he paced himself.

"Ouch," she whined in ecstasy. "That's my spot, don't stop."

"You like that?" he asked, pleasing his ego.

"Yeah, right there," she instructed as she grinded back towards his thrust.

Feeling her tense up, his stabbing motion quickened. "I'm about to cum," he murmured in fair warning. And so was she...

*****

"**Deshonne**, I know you hear me talking to you, boy," his mother repeated. And in a flash, he was brought back to reality.

As soon as his heavenly vision disappeared, he snapped back. "What, Mom? What! I can't even think to myself in peace."

"Oh, I'm sorry, baby. What were you thinking about?"

Embarrassed, he answered, "a job, Mom. I was thinking about a job."

She pulled his card. "Do you know that you're the sweetest little liar I know?" she said with a snicker.

"Why you say that?" he asked with a raised eyebrow.

"Deshonne, I know you like the back of my hand. You just had a silly grin on your face, and you haven't even washed it yet."

"Can't I wake up and smile sometimes?"

His mother smacked him on the back of his head. "Sure you can, baby. But remember, I had you, Negro. And I know you better than you know yourself."

"Mom, what are you talking about now?"

"I'm talking about you. You're a little freak like your daddy."

"Huh?"

"Boy, I know what you were thinking about, and you better keep a lid on that thing if you know what I know."

Damn! he thought. His dream was exposed, and his mother found it amusing. She laughed in her normal hoarse voice as he tried to backpedal. Deshonne waved the joking woman off, then retreated towards the stairs. "Mom, leave me alone. It's too early."

"I love you, too, Blinky," she said, whispering his childhood nickname.

Before he could return to his favorite napping position, the phone rang.

"Get the phone, Deshonne! And tell them girls that it's too early to be calling here. Your father needs his rest," his mother yelled.

"Hello?" he answered.

*****

Turning left onto route 13, coming from New Castle County probation & parole, headed north towards Wilmington, the silence finally broke after the initial shock of the interrogation faded.

Deshonne leaned forward from the back seat and said, "Pee-Wee, good looking out on the ride to probation. That clown said if I was ten minutes late he would've violated me."

The driver of the 2001 Toyota Avalon was a frail chocolate drop with undeniable sex appeal. She answered Deshonne's appreciating words in a squeaking tone. "You don't have to thank him. It's my car, my gas, and I'm the one driving."

Her manners were the complete opposite of what Deshonne was accustomed to seeing, making the statement *opposites attract* a reality for his friend Purnell. Dark as coffee beans, and thin as a twig, with just the right proportions of body fat, she had to be an overachiever in the bedroom. all the more reason for him to stay as far away from her as possible because he was already physically attracted to her feisty nature.

"Shut up, girl!" Purnell said in his usually disrespectful manner. He don't care whose hoopty this is."

Seeing the look of anger in both of their faces, he quickly cut in. "Thank you, Angie. I appreciate the ride."

She smiled. "It's cool, Magic. I was just playing. And as for you, Purnell," she said, cutting him with her right eye, "you need to shut up sometimes."

"What I keep telling you about using my government all the time, girl?"

"Watch your mouth then," she fired back, not willing to back down in the presence of a new face.

"Pee-Wee, have you run into Kasi yet since he came home?" Deshonne asked, just to cut off the meaningless argument.

Still looking in Angie's direction, he answered, "Yeah, I saw him and his wife the other day on Market Street Mall. I met Kenny there to talk some business, and Kasi stopped to holler at me for a few minutes while he was passing out fliers for his new C.D."

Market Street Mall is an outside historical storefront located in the center of Wilmington. Surrounded by banks, it's also the networking capital of the city.

"I need to catch up with him because he said that he was going to look out for me on the clothes tip," Deshonne said.

"Word. He definitely got it to give now, especially since he be pumping for Kenny every day on 23rd," Purnell stated, rubbing two fingers together.

Sensing the sarcastic tone in Purnell's voice, he asked, "Why you say it like that?"

"Cause he fronted on me one day last week in Shaheed's new Cadillac. I needed a ride home from the barber shop, but that lame brushed me off for a couple smuts," Purnell explained.

"Damn, I thought y'all was cool?"

"Man, Magic, that shit wasn't cool at all. I felt like fucking that clown up that day."

The light turned red at the beginning of Walnut Street, silencing their conversation. It wasn't until it changed green again that the casual talk continued.

"Anyway, Kenny ain't hit you off yet?" Purnell inquired. "Cause you know he's Shaheed's right-hand man now that the feds scooped up Marty."

"He looked out on some clothes and a couple of dollars."

"A couple of dollars?" Purnell repeated. "He should've at least hit you with a couple stacks or a big eighth. He's crushing the city."

"I don't know nothing about that."

Driving aimlessly through the main strip of the city, Market Street, through the North Side, Angie cut in on their frivolous conversation. "Where are y'all going, Pee-Wee, because I don't have enough gas to ride you around all day? I have to go pick up my son at twelve, and I have to go to work."

"You can drop me off on 23rd Street," Deshonne said, since they were only three blocks away.

"I wasn't trying to be smart, Magic, but your friend thinks that his broke ass has a chauffeur. And sometimes I have to bring him back to reality."

Purnell grabbed her by her chin and rudely asked, "Why don't you just close your trap sometimes?"

"No!" Angie snarled as she slammed on the brakes at another red light.

"Anyway, like I was saying," Purnell said, trying to ignore her. "Kenny's flooding a couple of spots on all sides of town. So just tell him to hit you with something serious."

As Purnell was finishing his statement, Angie was pulling over in front of Milton's Liquor Store, on 23rd and Market.

"Well, Kenny's supposed to be taking me up Philly on Friday to get me a linen outfit for his party at Utopia's on Saturday night," Deshonne said as he climbed out of the car. Stepping back onto the curb, he realized that he might be stranded later on, so he asked Purnell to call Kenny for him.

"Nah, cuz, I ain't calling that cat right now. I owe him some change for some bullshit cook-up that he gave me and my brother."

Deshonne didn't even inquire into why he didn't pay his bill. He just changed the subject. "Where is your little brother?"

Purnell pointed out the window. "Down the bottom of 23rd, on Jessup Street."

"Word. I might go down there and check him out later," Deshonne suggested.

"Are you gonna be okay?" Angie asked as she put the car back in gear.

27

At that second Deshonne spotted a phat flock of females coming out of Art & Trigg's car lot office and forgot all about Angie's inquiry. Brother's, Art and Trigg are Kenny's best customers and two of the biggest hustlers on Market Street. But soon they would become Deshonne's worst enemies.

CHAPTER 4

Club Utopia is also located in the center of Wilmington, on 9th and Orange Street. It is considered to be one of the most professional nightclubs' in the city. A dress code is always enforced to keep out commoners and non-ballers, which attracts a 3:1 ratio of women to men, making it the place to be if you want to be seen.

Kenny was attempting to cross over to become an entrepreneur. Few drug dealers ever make it out of the game ahead, so he was determined to be the trendsetter for the small city. Outside the nightclub he could feel the bass vibrating as he greeted each entering partygoer, known and unknown.

Get low, by Lil-Jon and the Eastside Boyz was playing. The summer's anthem emptied out the V.I.P. room, overflowing the dance floor with couples.

Kenny's i90 Nextel was vibrating in his pocket. "Yo!" he answered, covering his free ear to hear.

"Man, where are you at? I'm ready."

"It's 10:30, Magic. Where do you think I'm at? My party started at 9:00."

"I'm ready. Come and get me."

Paying his caller little attention, Kenny continued to greet people. He held his phone away from his mouth as an exotic Asian came strutting past. "How are you doing, boo?" Deshonne could hear him asking a female in the background. "Magic, I can't come and get you right now. I'm at the door by myself greeting people with just security."

"Man, who else is there?" Deshonne asked, reluctant to give up on his first real night to party.

"Everybody is here except you. You should've came with me earlier."

"You know that I had to wait for my probation officer to call me first. I told you he was an asshole."

"Yeah well, what you want me to do now? I can't leave here until I stop letting people in."

"Man, put somebody else on the phone!" Deshonne shouted into the receiver.

As he turned around to find a mutual acquaintance, Art popped out of the door with an empty 22 bottle of Corona in his hand. "Art, here the phone," Kenny said as he handed it to him.

Drunker than normal, Art greeted the caller without asking who it was. "Heyyy, sexy!"

"What's up cousin!"

"Who's this?" Art asked, confused by the sound of a male voice.

"It's me, Magic!" Deshonne said, identifying himself.

"Oh, my fault, Magic. I can barely hear you over the music. Plus, I'm sort of smashed right now. Where are you at, I thought that you were coming to the party. It's nothing but pussy up in here," art stated as he tried to lean onto a nearby light pole for support.

"Kenny forgot about me, and now I don't got no ride there. So I'm stuck now cause it sounds like you're too drunk to come and get me," he stated, looking for some pity.

"Call Trigg. He ain't here yet. I know he'll come and scoop you up."

In hearing that single shred of hope, his face lit up. "Word! What's his number?"

*****

A floor-length mirror Deshonne's mother inherited from her own mother sat in the corner of the second-floor hallway, right across from his incarcerated brother's old room. But until tonight, he never stopped to look into it.

"Damn, I'm the shit!" he said to himself as he stared into the mirror. *No more prison whites, and no more code reds*, he thought as he positioned the huge platinum chain with the diamond encrusted *Castle* charm around his neck. Retying his S-Dot sneakers, he realized that he was over-anxious tonight.

The house phone rang throughout the house while he was still admiring himself.

"Deshonne, answer the phone! And tell whoever it is, don't call my house this late no more!" his mother screamed from her bedroom.

Deshonne rushed around the corner to the bathroom, hollering to his mother, "Mom, answer it! And tell him I'm on my way out now. I have to use the bathroom first."

She took the call and did as her son had asked. But to his surprise, before he could reach the front door, she was out of the bed and right on his heels. Seeing his mother dressed in her favorite cotton robe and scarf threw a sense of guilt upon his shoulders even before she could speak her mind.

"What about your sons upstairs, Deshonne?" she asked. "You must've forgotten that you have a curfew, huh?"

With his head down he answered, "Mom, it's only 11:30 pm. I'll be back soon. And besides, both of my little mans are already tucked in and asleep."

"Deshonne, where are you going at this time of night?" his mother asked as she walked up beside him and peeked out of the closed curtains.

"Kenny's party," he said as he opened the door.

"Boy, I didn't lie for your brother, and I'm not going to start lying for you, either," she bluffed, hoping it would keep him in.

"I got my key, Mom. So just don't answer the phone or the door, please?" And with that said he stepped out and began to walk towards Trigg, who was sitting in his new black on black F150. Feeling the tension, he turned back around to face his mother still in the doorway.

"Be dumb if you want to, boy. You know you just came home last week," she reminded him.

"Mom, I got this, okay. I love you!"

31

"Whatever, boy. You better bring your ass back in here as soon as that party is over because I ain't babysitting your kids for you. And come home by yourself."

"Ah-ight!" he agreed gladly before climbing in.

*****

Florescent lighting had everyone on the dance floor wearing white glowing in the dark and looking like they were floating on air. The first glass of Long Island iced tea in Deshonne's left hand was only half empty, but it already had him mellow. His button-up linen shirt was open, exposing his muscular chest, which was bulging through his wife-beater. Almost every female in the V.I.P. room was a close acquaintance of Kenny's, so he kept his eyes on the dance floor for something special.

"What are you drinking, cuz?" Kenny asked as he sat down on the love seat next to Deshonne.

A speaker was right in front of the V.I.P. entrance, so the music muffled all conversations. Not hearing what Kenny had asked him, he looked over at his friend, who was draped in a peach-color linen and matching crocodiles and hollered, "beat it," into his ear. "You wouldn't even come and get me."

"It's my party. I couldn't just leave it."

"Man, fuck that. I'm supposed to be your peoples. You could've dipped away for 15 minutes to come and get me."

"You talking crazy, Magic. You know it takes that long to even get out of New Castle."

"Whatever," Deshonne mumbled, not satisfied with his excuse.

"Ay yo!" Kenny said as he pointed across the room to redirect Deshonne's attention. "That redbone over there in the gray dress, dancing by the picture stand told me to tell you to come over. She already knew your name, so you might as well go and see what's up, cause her and her girl is the tightest joints up in here tonight."

That suggestion eased the tension.

32

"Yo, I've been watching her shake her ass since I got here, too."

"Well, stop stalking her, and go spit that rusty 99 game you still holding onto at her," Kenny suggested before standing up and hugging a female at the bar.

Deshonne stood up and waited for Kenny to stop talking. "There you go doubting me again."

"Never that, cuz. I want you to snatch that up for the night, so I can smut her girl," Kenny informed him.

Deshonne patted his friend on the back confidently. "Don't worry, I got you," he promised, and headed towards his prey.

Just as he reached the female in the gray dress and stilettos, he spotted Desiree coming out of the bathroom. *Oh, well*, he thought. *I'm fresh out*!

*****

Their clothing was tossed around the one-bedroom apartment as if a hurricane had swept through it. Deshonne's breathing was heavier than normal and his movements more unorthodox as he tried to handle the nympho's appetite. Sucking passionately on the longest nipples he'd ever seen, he wondered, *How did I get so damn lucky*? She was one of those sex fiends who only appear in *Black Video Illustrated* flicks.

"Slow down, shorty," he pleaded. "You're good at what you do, but it's been hours."

Plop. Her sporadic movements caused his manhood to slip out. "Damn!" she whined after the third time her rough ride ended.

"Show's over," he whispered after he realized that their last condom had ruptured.

Evelyn reached between her own legs, grabbed Deshonne's still erect penis by the shaft, and slid back down onto him until her swollen lips completely engulfed him. "I'm not done with your friend, yet," she whispered into his ear.

"What are you doing?" he asked the enchanting stranger.

She apologized, "I can't help it, baby. You feel so good inside of me. I want you to fuck me until I can't walk straight." then she started to ride him again, wildly, without any inhibitions. But her vagina was so dry that her pubic hairs were almost scraping the flesh off of Deshonne's penis, making him want to cum bad inside of her just to feel the release and relief, that his juices would give him once he mixed it with the softness of her inner walls. But the liquor they had consumed made that almost impossible.

Plop. He slipped out again. This time when she reached for him, he slid back, giving her a little nudge. "Shorty, we need some Vaseline or something because you're dry and it's starting to hurt."

She just smiled. "I got another wet spot for you that will make you feel all warm inside, boo, so just relax," she said with a smile. Then Evelyn crawled backwards in the bed until her face was just above his waistline, slowly sliding the back of her hand down his stomach until his stiff, curved rod lay in her palm. Starting at his balls, she licked upwards until she reached the tip. And then she began to French kiss every inch until his lollipop disappeared into her mouth.

Deshonne's heart was beating so hard and fast, he didn't even notice her beautiful green eye's staring up at him, excitedly. "Mmm," was all he heard as she licked and sucked his most private part with the same energy she put into her earlier circular motions. As soon as he closed his eyes, the chase was over for him. But she continued to please him, anyway. And in doing so, seeing his facial expressions unfold caused her to explode with pleasure as he came in her mouth.

34

CHAPTER 5

Desiree drove for 45 minutes to and from the Pennsylvania line to work for Applied Card, a credit card company located north off of route 202. Working in the mailroom bored her on most days, but the $11.45 the company paid an hour gave her the independence she desired, so she traveled back and forth with minimal complaints.

"Hey, girl!" Iyanna yelled from the open elevator door. Iyanna Patrick was her only friend at work. She was a 25 year-old entry-level credit specialist from the 4th floor who came down every day, regardless of her own schedule, to check on her.

"Oh, hey, Yanni," Desiree said with little enthusiasm. Looking at the skimpy skirt and tight-fitting blouse Iyanna wore to work reminded her of the first time they had met outside in the parking lot. It was raining one afternoon and Iyanna had locked her keys in her 318i BMW. So, feeling sorry for her, Desiree jimmied it open with a hanger.

Their views on everything, even men, were the same, which helped their friendship develop quickly. But their methods on how to hold onto to men were different, so they shared all secrets and techniques.

"What are you up to down here in Sweat City?" Iyanna asked, walking up on her friend. "I was thinking that we could take our breaks early today and run over to Granite Run Mall to have lunch while we shopped."

"Thanks for asking, but I can't go today."

Iyanna dusted off a box and slid it into Desiree's work area to sit on. "Why not? I know you ain't trying to stay cooped up in this dump for ten hours straight when it's nice enough outside for us to break out the Baby Phat mini-skirts for the fellas."

"No, I'm not. My friend is coming to take me out to lunch today, sweetie. I have a date that I can't cancel." She explained.

"Your friend, huh?" Iyanna said sarcastically. "You would think that since Alex's wife works only a couple of floors away that he would be a little more discreet with his infidelity."

"For your information, I'm not having lunch with him. Fuck that clown," Desiree whispered.

Iyanna smiled. "You almost say that like you mean it."

"I do, girl. Alex is a married lowlife. Case closed," she stated with a wave of the hand.

"A lowlife with heavy pockets," Iyanna was happy to add.

Deep down Iyanna wished that she were in Desiree's position. Alex was a married man who paid all of her expenses and showered her with gifts, whenever possible. But Desiree didn't care about him in the least. Her motto was, "If he does it to her, he'll do it to me." So she cared for him, but only when they were together.

"So, what's he like?"

Thinking that she was still referring to Alex, Desiree said, "He's good at eating my pussy for hours. If that's what you are wondering."

"Are you still talking about Alex, Dee? Because I was referring to the new mystery guy."

"Oh, he's not new at all, girl. We have a long, ongoing history together," she said as if she was trying to downplay how strongly she felt about Deshonne.

"Well, how come you don't sound too happy about this old flame?" Iyanna asked curiously.

Still feeling bitter about their last break up, Desiree simply said, "What's there to be happy about? Some of our history was good and some wasn't."

"Hmm, sounds like I don't like this character already."

"Oh no, it's not like that. I just thought that we were meant to be together at one point in time, and he thought that the block was all that he needed."

"Well, has he changed any?"

God, I hope so. Because I just can't seem to shake that nigga loose, Desiree thought to herself.

"Dee, did you hear my question?"

"No, I'm sorry. What were you saying?"

"It doesn't matter, girl. But in case you haven't heard, thugs aren't in this season."

"He's not like that. He's different," Desiree said on Deshonne's behalf. "If you seen him, you would think that he was just a cute nerd."

"So why aren't y'all together now?"

"Because we argued about a lot of dumb stuff in the past. And when he was locked up one of his so-called boys told him a bunch of lies about me because I wouldn't give him none."

"Girl, that's why I don't like meeting a man and his boy! Because the third wheel always ends the relationship somehow," Iyanna added.

"You got that right," Desiree agreed. "That's why me and him are trying to start over now without no interference."

"Well, are y'all still close?"

"We better be," Desiree stated with a sense of entitlement.

"Girl, you've been holding back on me!" Iyanna said, sensing the steamy passion in her friend's words.

"No, I haven't. We're just close, Yanni, you know? Just like you and your friends, we ah—do things together in our free time. There's no secrets what-so-ever between us. And we have the most sexual nights two friends could possibly have without the strings of a commitment," she blurted out, blushing. "He just makes me feel ways no other man has ever come close to."

"So y'all are soul-mates, huh?" Iyanna concluded from the sincerity in Desiree's voice.

Feeling warm all over made Desiree want to talk about Deshonne. She felt like explaining everything at that moment. "It's just the little things that men won't do or don't even notice that he does constantly without asking."

"And the sex?"

"Girl, let me tell you, after all that time away he hasn't lost a thing. My baby's stroke game is still strong."

"Well, don't get shy on me now. Spit out the details girl, cause you know how I like it."

Lately, Iyanna's sex life was limited to battery-operated toys and X-rated videos. Tired of one-night stands and failed short-term relationships, she often thought about going back to her only true love. But her womanly pride kept her single and lonely.

"You know that you're going to cut into your lunch break if you want to hear about my wild nights," Desiree pointed out.

"Dee, I go all the way out New Castle to the trading post on route13 twice a week just to buy nasty movies knowing damn well that the fine brotha behind the counter is gonna find any reason he can to squeeze through the small-ass aisle I'm in, just to rub his dick up against my ass and say, "excuse me." Girl, I have no life and nothing but time right now."

They both laughed at Iyanna's honest confession, causing everyone to momentarily pause to see what was so funny. Desiree waved them back to work and began to whisper. "Yanni, you need to get help, girl, cause you are sick."

"No I'm not. I'm just sexually neglected right now. All I need is a little dick in my life and I'll be okay. Now tell me about your friend, and don't leave out the nasty parts, either."

"Oh, okay. I guess I can give you a little summary of the past week," she agreed. Desiree didn't even notice that Iyanna had begun to help her with the sorting as she started to reconstruct her memorable marathon. Turning her back to her coworker, she lowered her voice and relived the moment.

"At first, I was nervous as shit because it had been so long for us…"

*****

At five-foot-seven Desiree was stacked. She took her time in the bathroom to build up the courage to go strutting into his bedroom again after four long years.

Squeezing into a purple 38 D-cup Victoria's Secret bra, her 40DDs were begging for attention. She even brought the matching thong a size too small so that the contour of her shapely bottom would emphasize the few added pounds that rounded below her waistline. Confident that she was the classiest slut she could be, she tried extra hard not to stumble into his childhood bedroom as she strolled in wearing new four-inch Nine West heels. After posing for him, the lights went out.

Deshonne stood almost breathless between her legs while she sat on the edge of the bed and kissed from his chest to his navel. Thinking that he would feel a bit timid, she pulled off his boxers first, then proceeded to take off her own undergarments.

"Come to bed," Desiree said, gently pulling on his hand as she opened her legs and attempted to lie back.

Having other plans for her, Deshonne stepped forward. Placing his erect penis inches from her face, he gave her a silent invitation. They had never entertained each other orally, but he knew that she wouldn't turn him down. He figured that if she hadn't experimented on someone else by now, then tonight would be her first.

"Are you serious?" she asked with his swollen tip only an inch from her lips.

"Why don't you try it for me? I wanna see how it feels," he reasoned.

She was reluctant to perform on Deshonne the art that she had come to master on Alex for a fear of what his opinion of her would be. But she had promised to please him in every way imaginable, so she grasped his testicles and slowly pulled him forward to take in every inch. It only took mere seconds for his knees to get weak, and even less time for his manhood to begin jerking violently. Not wanting to appear nasty she pulled back at the first taste of precum, and his semen began to splatter all over her sexy glossed lips and plump breasts...

*****

"**Girl**, I know you was mad! Because I used to hate it when my old boyfriend used to cum in my face instead of my mouth," Iyanna bragged. "I used to tell him, you either gonna cum inside one of my holes or you gonna start using a condom! I gave him free access to all three of them, so you would think that he would've at least had enough respect to nut inside of one. That clown."

"I wasn't mad, but I would've been if he would've cum that fast inside of me without me getting my thing off," Desiree added. "Anyway, keep quiet so that I can get to the good parts for you."

*****

Deshonne's parents were asleep in the other room. Desiree tried to keep the warm, running water as quiet as possible so she could quickly wash his sticky juices off of her face and chest. He walked up behind her and slid his stiffness between her cushioned cheeks. "Stop it, Magic," she murmured. "Wait until we're in the other room." She whispered, while trying to grab one of his roaming hands. Gently pinching her left nipple until she released his other hand, he reached around her soft body and glided two fingers inside of her already moist vagina. She began to shed soft tears as he leaned her over the sink. "Magic, you gotta stop because I can't hold it," she told him.

"Just let it go," he whispered into her ear as he sucked on her earlobe.

Holding onto the sink, resting her forehead on the faucet, she braced herself and allowed the warm water running onto her tender breasts to intensify her sexual peak. Still fondling her clitoris, he thrust his aching organ inside of her from behind. She in turn pushed back onto his rod, burying him deep inside her river.

"Mmm, mmmm!" she moaned as her knees buckled, and her pulsating river slowly began to run down her inner thighs.

After having multiple orgasms she regained her composure and retook control of the situation. They finally came together in the bathroom, washed each other, and returned to the bedroom to continue the session. With crushed ice in her mouth Desiree sucked on Deshonne teasingly for what seemed like hours, from his chest to his scrotum. And in turn, he had her balled up for over five hours like a pretzel in various positions as he tried to punish her.

*****

Iyanna had developed her own vivid picture as Desiree's story unfolded. She began to erotically suck her own thumb as she listened. Desiree glanced at Iyanna and laughed once she noticed that her freaky friend was perspiring.

Once the X-rated tale was over, Desiree took a call from her mystery man. Iyanna quietly said her farewells for the day and swiftly walked awkwardly towards the elevator, her own juices seeping down through her cotton panties. She mentally thanked her friend for the overdue deed.

*****

Reclining the front passenger seat of her 96 Acura Legend all the way back, Desiree tried to rest her eyes for a moment after a hard day's work.

How was your day?" Deshonne asked as he pulled away from the security booth and headed towards the highway.

"Drive," she said, frustrated.

Damn, I was just trying to be supportive and make a little small talk," he thought.

"We just ate lunch together three hours ago, Magic. Nothing has changed since then, okay."

"Ah-ight, whatever," he said sarcastically.

Oh here we go with the attitudes, she thought to herself. "I'm sorry for the way I sound, Magic, but I'm tired and my feet hurt."

"It's cool," he said, accepting her apology.

41

"So, if you don't mind, how about telling me how your day went?"

Glad she asked, he let her choose which news she would hear first. "The good or the bad?"

"Why don't you give me the bad news first, so we can end on a good note," she told him.

"Okay, let's see. Well, I've been home almost a month already, and I'm broke. I just spent my last $10 on gas, and I'm broke. And, I was planning on taking you to the movies tonight to celebrate the good news, but…"

With a smile on her face she leaned over, kissed him on the cheek, and asked him to give her the good news.

As if it were nothing, he said, "I start a part-time cleaning job on Monday."

"Baby, that's great!" she said, with a more passionate kiss on the lips. "Let's celebrate on me!"

"Stop at the nearest liquor store so I can cash my check."

"What are you trying to do, get me drunk, lady?"

"I don't have to because you always give me what I want when the lights go out anyway, honey," she announced.

CHAPTER 6

The sun was beginning to rise, and Deshonne was just walking his exhausted body up the narrow walkway leading to his front porch.

On the nights that Desiree wasn't in his bed, he was in Evelyn's. He had been staying out later and later as the days went on, spreading himself thin between the two women. And now his carelessness was catching up with his body.

His mother was sitting at the dining room table having her morning cup of coffee when he walked in. *Shit, she's up!* he thought as he locked the front door.

"Good morning, dummy," she said cynically, to let him know that she was disappointed in his irresponsible choices. Even though both of her son's were grown, she still felt the need to be their guardian and stay on top of them as much as possible. At 26 Deshonne was her oldest problem child and also the only one home at the time. So, she was determined to keep him out of the revolving doors that repeatedly snatched him and his brother Tjuan away for years at a time.

"Hey, mom, what's up?"

"If I'm not mistaken, Deshonne, you're wearing the same clothes that you were wearing when you left out of here yesterday morning. So I'm waiting for you to look me in my face and tell me that you're not just walking in this door."

"Mom, Crissy didn't come back with eve's car until after we were already asleep. As soon as I woke up and saw what time it was, I asked her to bring me home," he explained, walking towards the steps.

"Don't let that piece of ass get you in trouble, you hear me? Because ain't nothing worth your freedom."

"Mom, I already told you that I ain't going back to jail for nothing or nobody, so don't worry, I got this," he stated, hoping that his pledge was enough to defuse a possible lecture, he climbed the steps and headed towards his unslept in bed.

"How come you can't find a part-time job to at least keep your P.O. off of your back and out of my yard?"

"Oh, damn, I forgot to tell my own mother," he muttered to himself with a snap of the fingers. Then he about-faced to tell her the good news. "Mom, I start working tomorrow at this cleaning service for one of dad's friends."

She got up from the table to hug her son. "That's good, baby. But how come you just now telling me?"

"I guess I forgot because it only pays $7.50," he said sarcastically.

"Well, at least you won't have to worry about looking over your shoulder for the police. And it's honest."

"Yeah, I guess it is."

"Now that I've lived long enough to see both of my babies grow up, I pray that I live long enough to see both of y'all become happily married and successful in life."

He hated when she talked about her own death, especially since at 48, she looked to be in the best shape of her life. But never-the-less, she always taught her sons that tomorrow wasn't promised to anyone, even her.

"I'm going upstairs to take a nap because it's too early to be listening to you talking crazy. I'll see you later."

"You need to call Shalonda and see if she'll bring your kids over for a little while after church."

"Man, every time I call to get'em, she makes up excuses as to why I can't. So from now on I'll let you call. I'm going to bed."

"Just because you don't get along with their mother doesn't mean that you can neglect your babies. Me and your father didn't do it to you, and you not gonna do it to them."

"Mom, it ain't my fault that she wants to act stupid."

"Yes, it is, because your dumb behind laid down with her in the first place after I told you that something wasn't right about that dizzy child. So now, since you done went on ahead and had two kids by the retarded girl, deal with her the best way you know how because you need to see your kids. And if she doesn't wanna act right, take her ass to court."

"Ah-ight, well, I'll call her after I take a nap."

"Call now. Here's the phone."

"Mom, I gotta get some sleep before Eve comes back to get me," Deshonne stated. "Don't worry, I'll call after I get out of the bathroom."

"See, you getting just like your brother was when he was home. He ain't have time for his daughter's or me either," his mother complained. "But now he wants to call here every hour, on the hour, just to run up the phone bill asking what we're doing. a hard head always makes a soft ass, Deshonne. And the next time you go back, GOD forbid, you're on your own."

"Mom, be easy. I'm gonna call as soon as I get out of the shower. Ain't no need to make a big deal out of nothing."

"Boy, just go ahead and take your backwards behind upstairs."

"I'll talk to you in a little while, okay?"

"I don't need you bugging me for five minutes and then leaving with them skanks. Take your shower and go about your business. Me and your dad will have breakfast together like we always do."

"Make me something to eat."

"Nope. When you get back to wherever you stayed at last night, tell her to cook for you."

"Ah-ight Mom."

"Don't ah-ight me. And don't you leave them stiff underwear in the middle of my floor, either. Bring them right back downstairs as soon as you peel them funky things off." *I can smell them from here*, she thought to herself.

*****

Twenty-third Street was a 24 hour-a-day, seven-days-a-week drug block. Business covered all age brackets and varied from hard drugs like heroin to casual drugs like marijuana. From the statue on Concord Avenue down to the Baptist Church on Pine Street, it was a recovering addict's worst nightmare. And though Deshonne was not addicted to drugs, spending the majority of his time on that particular block with Kenny and his crew was becoming very addictive for him.

Standing outside in his new work uniform he seemed oddly out of place as he watched the ballers move about the fast-paced surroundings like ghosts. He decided to take a walk back down to Jerome's until Kenny finished handling business. Repeatedly he pushed in the buzzer like a madman once he caught a glimpse of the D.T.s at the light until someone answered the door.

"Who is it?" a shallow voice asked as she slowly approached.

"It's Deshonne, ma'am. Is Jerome here?"

"Yes, just a minute," she called out as she peeped out of the mini-blinds to match the name with the face.

Five minutes had passed before the storm door creaked open. Deshonne stepped in quickly, shook his friend's hand in passing, and took a seat in one of the old wicker chairs. "Man, you took forever," Deshonne informed Jerome as soon as he finished arguing with someone on the phone.

"My fault, Magic. I was arguing with one of my baby mothers about the daycare money I already gave her slick ass once this month. Yo, get up out of my seat," Jerome said as soon as he returned from placing the phone back on its charger. "You sitting on my kitty."

Unbeknownst to Deshonne, the seat closest to the door was one of Jerome's stash spots. Under the tied-down cushion was an assortment of bagged up marijuana. And in the wastebasket beside it, covered with old newspapers, was a fully-loaded .45-caliber Colt model MK-IX series 70 automatic. Deshonne jumped up as if a snake fell into his lap and sidestepped towards the door. "It's time for me to roll, cuz. You on that hot boy shit right now."

"Me?" Jerome asked sarcastically. "I'm not the one hustling up on Market with them pretty boyz. And if I can see you from my porch late night, best believe the Jakes can, too."

"Hey, what Art and Trigg do is on them. I just be fucking with my peoples."

"Don't get me wrong, Magic. They good peoples. But they some soft niggas."

Disregarding Jerome's last statement, Deshonne switched topics. "Yo, rala, I know you got some change for me by now. What's up?"

Jerome dug his hands inside both sweatpants pockets. "Damn, I thought I had a 50 dollar bill left in one of these pockets from when I re-upped yesterday. But my B.M. probably took it last night for something. She's always grabbing shit that don't belong to her. Let me call her real quick and see if I at least got some change in here somewhere."

"Nah, you ain't gotta go through all that. It's cool. I'm about to see if these dudes up the street got something for me until payday."

Feeling bad that he couldn't make good on his promise, Jerome bent down, raised up the cushion and pulled out a family-size bag of bundles. "Yo, here cuz, you know I can't leave you empty-handed. What can you sell the fastest, crack, dope, or weed? I hear the crack is so-so because I got a shady connect. But the 7-Up goes fast, and for the tree heads I got Haze from up Philly."

"Man, what I'ma do with that shit? I ain't on that type of time no more," Deshonne stated.

"Really, you ain't gotta do shit because this shit sells itself. All you gotta do is what you been doing, sit up on Market," Jerome told him.

"Nah, I'm cool, but good looking out though," Deshonne said, turning down the offer without a second thought.

"You sure? I don't want nothing back off of it. You can do you."

"Yeah, I'm cool, cuz. I'm just gonna go up here and wait on Kenny."

Jerome put the drugs back in his hiding place. "You know that I would've hit you off if I had it, right?"

Deshonne agreed with Jerome, but deep down he thought that his friend was lying to him, and he wondered to himself why everyone who portrayed themselves to be Big Willies claimed to be broke all of the time. The doorbell rang just as Deshonne was about to open it. "You got company, cuz, so I'll just get at you later."

"Hold up, let me open up the door." Checking the window first so there would be no surprises, Jerome saw the small frame of a young boy, no more than 15. The stranger dashed in and almost knocked Deshonne down, but he said nothing.

"Slow your retarded behind down, Lil- Billy. What did I tell you about rushing in my door like you crazy?" he heard Jerome say before the door closed behind him.

Just as Deshonne reached the corner, Jerome yelled up to him, "Yo, Magic! I got $8 for you if you want that."

What the fuck am I gonna do with that? he thought to himself. "I'll come back down and get it before I go home!" he yelled back. *Maybe he'll have something to add to it*, he hoped.

*****

Squinting to see if he could see Evelyn's Honda Accord, Deshonne instructed Kenny to park four cars away from her building.

"She lives over there," he pointed out. "Blow your horn one time for me, please?"

Kenny blew the horn as if he was in a rush.

Shaking his head, Kenny said, "Man I can't believe how you is stuck on this dike broad."

"I don't know what you talking about, but as far as I can tell, she's far from a dike, Deshonne remarked. But, then again, you might be right because her girl Crissy do be acting real funny now that I be smashing eve's back out on the regular."

"Yo, where's she at?" Kenny asked impatiently, checking the rearview mirror. He was riding dirty, and just being out of his environment made him nervous. He wanted to get out of the suburbs and back into the city as soon as possible. "Man, I hope you ain't make me drive way out K-town for nothing, cause I don't see that bitch car nowhere."

K-town was another name for Kimberton, a low-income housing project located on the outskirts of Newark. It was a well-known drug neighborhood.

"She probably gave it to Crissy again," Deshonne stated as he looked up at her living room window for any signs of life.

Seconds later she appeared in the doorway, rubbing her eyes, dressed in nothing but an oversized white t-shirt. "The door was already unlocked, boo. Come on!" she yelled before disappearing.

Kenny was awestruck by the voluptuous vixen. His eyes were glued to her last position.

Deshonne got out of the car, walked around to the driver's side, and leaned over to boast. "Keep it real. She's the shit, ain't she?"

"She ah-ight," Kenny agreed.

"Yeah, whatever, hater."

"Nah, I said she's ah-ight. What you want me to say?" Kenny asked.

"Nothing, just respect my gangster, cause I'm the shit."

"Ah-ight, I'll get with you later."

"Wait, let me hold something before the hoes get it."

"Magic, I don't got no money for you to keep spending on them broads. I ain't rich."

"All that crack you pumping, and you crying broke."

"I'm about to stop hustling, fam. I need all the change I can save cause them parties are cool, but they don't pay all the bills."

"Man, I got a job now. I'll pay you back if it's that serious."

"There you go talking stupid like I'm a outsider again, Magic. If I got it, you got it. But I ain't no MAC machine for no bitches," Kenny said, as he opened up his ashtray. He peeled through the crumpled bills until he found a hundred and said, "make it last until you get paid, nigga."

The statement made Deshonne feel like a bum, but he still took the bill. "Thanks, I'll give it back to you as soon as I cash my check."

"Don't worry about it. You need it, you got it. But you missing the point of what I'm saying."

"I heard you."

Kenny's two-way pager began to vibrate. Deshonne started to walk away as he read the message. "Yo, come here real quick!"

"What's up?"

"Yo, I need you to do me a favor until later on."

"What's that?" Deshonne asked curiously.

"Man, I—um—I brought this onion out here to give to one of my young boys, but he just hit me up on the two-way and said that his money wasn't right. So I need you to hold this joint for me until he calls me back. And then I'll get him to meet you out here somewhere because I don't want to be riding back and forth with drugs on me."

Deshonne thought to himself, *Bitch, you had me in the car with drugs all fucking day long! Is you fucking crazy?* But he didn't want to say no to the only person who had his back since he could remember. "Ah-ight, let me get it. But make sure he comes to get it tonight."

Glad to pass it off because I-95 was a drug dealer's death trap, Kenny pulled one knob on his left and turned up the heat on his climate control until the ounce dropped out beneath his car.

"Oh, shit." Deshonne said.

As soon as he bent over to grab the ounce of beige crack cocaine, Evelyn reappeared, leaning halfway out of the doorway. "Are you coming to bed or what?"

"You better go ahead in now before you be sleeping on the couch tonight, by yourself," Kenny told him. At the same time, he was thinking to himself, *Damn she holding!*

Deshonne knew what the look on his boy's face meant, so he offered even though he prayed that Kenny would decline. "Yo, you wanna come up? We can try her out and see if she'll let us smut her ass."

"Nah, player, I'll pass."

Good! Deshonne thought.

"If you hear a horn out here in a couple of hours, peep out the window first. Then if it's a white pickup, go out the back door and come around to meet him," Kenny explained.

"Ah-ight, cool."

"And make sure that it's $800 first before you give him anything."

"Come on, Kenny, I ain't slow."

"I know, just call me tomorrow, ah-ight? Lunch on me."

"Ah-ight." he happily agreed and walked away.

Evelyn was waiting, completely naked, in the hallway when he walked in. "You could've left with him if you wanted to," she teased, with her hands covering only her small breasts, leaving her bulge exposed.

Deshonne smiled as he stepped in close to kiss her luscious lips.

"Nope, don't kiss me and don't touch me. You not getting none tonight," she laughed.

"Are you sure about that?" he asked as he palmed her shaved snatch.

"Say you sorry, and I'll think about it."

"Girl, you know I'm sorry," he delivered smoothly.

She kissed him on the lips. "The first one to bed gets to pick the positions," she proposed, then she ran for her door. Knowing that she loved it when he hit it from the back, he just watched her run.

CHAPTER 7

A cold shower was just what Purnell needed to wake up after pulling an all-nighter and only acquiring an hour's worth of sleep. Leaning up against the tile wall, he wondered how he was going to pay all the bills for the month with little cash and an even shorter supply of product.

"Hurry up, Purnell!" Tonya screamed from outside the shower curtain.

Tonya is Purnell's fiancée and the mother of his four children. At 32, she was six years his senior, but didn't look a day older than 21. They were childhood sweethearts, but recently the relationship had become anything but sweet. He had begun to lose interest in her once her jean size exceeded a 9-10. And that's when Angie, the third wheel, came into play.

"Don't rush me. If you wanna rush somebody, go and make sure that our rugrats are all ready to go over my pop's house," he told her. Knowing that she would come in, he pointed the showerhead towards the curtain and waited for her head to poke in.

"Ah, stop it!" she screamed as soon as the water drenched her face. "Why you always playing!"

After laughing at her for a moment, he turned the sprayer back on himself.

"Is your friend still coming with us?" she asked while drying off.

"Yeah, I think so. Why?"

"Because...don't you think that we should call him first? It is early in the morning."

He poked his head out. "Let me wash my ass first, Tonya, please. I'll call him when I get out, ah-ight?"

"You should've been done by now. You've been in here 20 minutes, like you broke a sweat last night or something," she sneered and then left him to himself.

I did, he thought.

*****

Cow Town was a 15 minute ride over the Delaware Memorial Bridge. Even though Delaware had its own Farmer's Market, a flea market out on route 13, most Delawareans frequently took the ride in search of a better bargain. Kicking up dust beneath their feet, they weaved in and out of the early morning crowd of shoppers.

"I'm going to go over to the Black Art truck to find something for our living room, Purnell," Tonya said.

Deshonne looked in the direction Tonya pointed to and saw a wide-open trailer full of artwork.

Knowing how expensive the art could be, Purnell asked, "how much money did you bring?"

"I brought whatever you gave me this morning. Why? Wasn't what you gave me for the house?"

Hell, no! he told himself. Too proud to tell her that she was holding their last bit of cash, he just said, "Don't spend it all."

"Alright, I'll bring you your change, if it's some left."

Purnell and Deshonne stopped and watched Tonya walk away. Her pink shirt and knee-length jean skirt disappeared into the crowd before they continued their stroll.

"So, what's been up, Magic?"

"Nothing. Same shit, different day," Deshonne said. Then he went into his pocket and pulled out his first pay stub to show his friend just how disgusting his check looked. "I got a part-time job working at this cleaning service because I got tired of asking niggas for money.

But as you can see, I'm still broke as a bum."

"Damn!" Purnell said once he saw what Delaware taxes did to an already sick-looking check.

"You see that shit? I made a punk ass $150 after child support and taxes were finished with me."

"Yo, this is exactly why I stay with Tonya, cuz. It's definitely cheaper to keep her."

"Man, I hate Shalonda. She's whack. All she wants is money."

"Don't feel bad. Between Tonya, the kids, and Angie, I stay broke as a motherfucker, too. At least you got Dee helping you out. She's always had your back."

"Yeah, but I hate that I gotta ask her for anything."

"Are y'all back together again?"

"Nah, we just cool, believe it or not. She got her little friend, and I got mines."

"So you and Dee are like me and Angie, huh?"

"No, we on two different levels. Y'all creeping, and we just doing us without attachments," Deshonne explained.

"Whatever you wanna call it, I'm getting the best of both worlds, believe that."

"I know. And when Tonya finds out, you gonna be getting the best park bench in Rodney Square."

They both walked and talked until they found the rotisserie stands inside one of the barns.

"You know, Kenny asked me about you the other day," Deshonne said in between bites.

"For what?" Purnell asked, almost choking on an onion ring.

"What you think? He wants his change."

"Yeah, well, I can't give him what I ain't got. We just moved out the Wilton, and most of my funds went to the house."

"Well, why don't you just call him and tell him what's what? We grew up together, so it's not like he won't understand."

"Magic, I owe him two grand, and I'm flipping a punk-ass eight-ball, scrounging to pay bills. So believe me, what I got to tell him right now won't be to his liking," Purnell stated in the most desperate tone he could muster.

"Look, I'm not trying to be the middleman, but both of y'all is my peoples. So what I'ma do is call him and see if I can give you the work he gave me to hold last week, ah-ight?"

A light went on in Purnell's head. "Yo, what he hit you with nine, eighteen?"

"He didn't hit me with anything. He gave me an ounce to hold for somebody, but they never came with the money, so I held on to it."

"That's all? So what are you gonna do with that?"

"I'm gonna ask him can you get it so you can get back on your feet. If not, I'm just gonna give it back to him."

"What you gonna ask him for? He might've forgotten about it."

That thought had crossed Deshonne's mind too, but he still wasn't going to mess with it. "I gotta ask the man, Pee-Wee. It's his shit."

The bills were already being paid in Purnell's mind. He was buying a new car after a couple flips and taking a trip to the Poconos. Not willing to take no for an answer, Purnell asked, "Is it cooked up or soft?"

"It's soft, why?"

"Because, you know you the chemist. We can stretch the 28 into 42. Bag it all up into dimes. Pay Kenny, and blow from there," Purnell plotted.

Why did I tell him first? Deshonne thought. "Pee-Wee, I'm not hustling no more. That four-piece I just did broke my black ass. Why do you think I got the corn-ball-ass cleaning job?"

"Magic, I already got a block for us to pump on and my own clientele. All you gotta do is sit in the car and watch for the jakes."

Purnell's talk game sounded convincing, but Deshonne wasn't buying it. "I'm not fucking with that man's caine without talking to him first."

"All I own is the clothes on my back. All I need is a couple good flips, and I'm back on top."

"I understand that, really I do. But it's not mines to give away."

"Magic, to be honest, Tonya's spending my last $250 right now on some ugly-ass painting. And I don't even know how we're going to pay our rent next month."

Pushing his basket of chicken bones into the middle of the table, Deshonne said, "I gotta think about it, cuz."

"Cool, that's all I'm asking for," Purnell agreed, knowing that Deshonne would help if he could. "But keep in mind that you won't have to do nothing, nothing at all. And we'll both reap the benefits. That's my word."

"You ready?" Deshonne asked.

"Yeah. Let me just get her some chicken to go and we out."

As Deshonne waited, he pondered on all of Purnell's financial burdens. And Purnell plotted his next move.

CHAPTER 8

The Robinson's home was totally silent by 1:00 am. The crickets were singing softly in the night air, alongside Mr. Robinson's loud snoring. Deshonne was in the deepest sleep he'd seen since his release until the ringing of the house phone shocked him awake. He picked up the phone after its fourth ring and rested it on the side of his face. "Hello?" he answered groggily.

"Yo, Magic, it's me. You ready?" Purnell shouted into the receiver as if he was stuck in a cave.

"Ready for what, Pee-Wee? I was trying to sleep."

"Yo! I'm over on the North Side, bubbling, and it's coming, I'm telling you. I'm about to come and scoop you up so we can get this money together. Get ready."

"Pee-Wee, please—just let me go back to sleep, and I'll talk to you about this later on. I gotta go to work in the morning."

"Nah, listen, I—I got a quarter sell waiting on me down the street, right now." Purnell stated so convincingly that he almost fooled himself.

"Ah-ight, well, go handle your business and let me get some rest. Don't let me hold you up."

"I need you. I only got four dimes left."

Deshonne looked over at the blinking radio clock before sitting up. Feeling tired, he looked for his medicated frames as if they would help him focus in other ways. "Yo, I thought I told you earlier that I was gonna ask him first. I never told you that I was gonna give you that man's shit."

"I only got four bags left, and money is coming like crazy."

"So, what you want me to do? That shit ain't mines."

"Look, Big Shane got a white boy stuck in the bathroom with almost his whole check. That's my check. I need that."

"Who the fuck is Big Shane?"

Big Shane wasn't big at all, just the opposite. Back when they were kids, Shane was a 300-pounds street bully. But now that he abused the products he once endorsed, he needed a belt to hold up his 28 slims. And the only thing big about the once well-known street baller was his habit.

"You remember Big Shane from out Garfield Park. He used to get money with Shaheed's older brother back when we was going to them parties at Rose Hill Boy's Club."

"Oh, you talking about pretty hair Marie's peoples," Deshonne said after Purnell jogged his memory.

"That's exactly who I'm talking about. He's the star touter on the North Side." Purnell cautiously stared at his rearview mirror for any signs of police as he sped through South Market and headed towards New Castle in Angie's Toyota.

"Pee-Wee, ain't nobody outside right now but you, that fool, and the P&P. Why you trying to get me caught up in your foolishness?"

Purnell was quick with every response, hoping that he gave Deshonne no reason to back down. "Magic, I don't want you to just give me the pack. I want you to come out and get this cheddar with me. And I swear you don't gotta do nothing. Me, Angie, and Shane will hug the block while you lounge in the car and listen to CDs. You can sleep in the car if you want to, and I'll just bring you the money after every couple sells."

The plan sounded so full-proof that Deshonne knew his friend had to be leaving something out. But he had already had a brief taste of what being broke felt like, too. So given the circumstances that Purnell laid out for him, he felt obligated to at least try and help his friend if he could.

"Pee-Wee, I'ma get up for you, ah-ight. But I'm telling you, it better be worth it, cuz."

Purnell looked over at Angie and smiled as they waited at the red light. "Cool, cause we're almost there."

"Whose we?" Deshonne asked.

"Me and Angie."

"Oh, ah-ight. I'm opening up the mini-blinds, then, so flash your lights as you come down the street," he instructed before hanging up.

Before Deshonne could even find a stitch of dark-colored clothing, Purnell's high beams were trained on the Robinson house.

*****

Sweating over a small antique gas stove, Deshonne mastered his technique of mixing cocaine into crack while spectators impatiently hawked him. The fresh smell of Arm and Hammer baking soda was quickly smothered by the stench inside the sizzling Pyrex.

Anxious to test the diluted product, Shane made small talk with the chemist. "So how does it feel to be home again, Magic?"

Still holding the pot over the low flame, Deshonne turned to answer. "I can't even describe it, cuz. I'm just happy that it's over, that's all."

Trying to determine whether or not he could con Deshonne out of a nice piece of rock or steal it when the right time presented itself, Shane consciously sized up his new prey. "Yo, you got big as shit since the last time I saw you," Shane said, complimenting his physique to stroke his ego.

Deshonne just glanced at him momentarily, then returned his focus to the task at hand.

"Magic, tell me you almost done. I keep seeing money walking around out there, and we missing it," Purnell exaggerated while staring out from the living room window at the deserted avenue below.

Deshonne caught a glimpse of the smirk on Angie's face as she lay on the urine-stained love seat.

"So, Shane, what's up with your peoples?" Deshonne asked, ignoring his friend's badgering.

"Who?"

"Marie. Ain't she your cousin or something?"

"Oh—yeah, that's my favorite little cousin. She comes through almost every day to see me and my mom," Shane added.

Deshonne made a mental note to stop back on another day to see if he could catch her. He had a thing for her since elementary school. "Oh, word."

"Yeah. Why, you want me to tell her something for you?"

"Nah, just um—tell her I said hi," Deshonne suggested shyly.

"What's taking you so long to cook up one ounce?" Purnell questioned.

"Nigga, if you don't leave me alone. You already got me out of my bed tonight," Deshonne groused. "Go ahead outside and see what's what. You don't gotta worry about me. I'll be done in a few more minutes."

*****

Concord Avenue was like a ghost town from the moment Deshonne stepped outside. He sat in the middle of the block, on Shane's steps, watching the street lights change from red to green to pass the boredom away. Angie was asleep in the car a block away, with the drugs tucked snugly between her legs for safekeeping while Purnell and Shane took turns running in and out of abandoned crack houses around the corner on a short street called Back Street to see if anyone had money to spend.

"I thought you said that it was a constant flow out here," Deshonne said to Purnell as he approached.

"It's always a flow. We just have to be patient and wait on it to start, that's all," Purnell replied.

"Money comes in spurts from twelve to eight, Magic. But when it comes, it comes heavy," Shane added.

"Man, it's two in the morning. And all we made besides the quarter sell was $53," Deshonne pointed out in disappointment.

"Hey, that's $253 more than you had before I picked you up."

Tired of sitting, Deshonne brushed himself off and stretched. "Pee-Wee, I owe $800 now that I don't got to give, just because you woke me up out of my sleep. I should've stayed sleep, cause this wasn't worth it."

Shane had only earned one dime bag for himself, besides the generous tester Deshonne gave him for the big first sell, which had already gone up in smoke. So he was going to keep shooting Purnell bail every chance he could until he got what he thought he deserved out of the healthy bag.

"Do y'all wanna go down to your brother's block on Jessup?" Shane asked Purnell. "The night just started for me, so I'm ready to break night with y'all, if y'all need me to," Shane offered.

"What you think, Magic? It's always money down bottom," Purnell responded, grateful for the suggestions Shane continued to shoot him every time his partner's patience began to wear thin.

"Nah, you can take me back home, cause I'm ready to call it a night. I ain't breaking nobody's night. I'm going home and getting back in my bed."

"Come on, Magic, just a little while longer. I'm telling you, it's money out here," Purnell pleaded.

Deshonne looked at his sad-faced friend. "What we don't get by 4:00 am we won't get, Pee-Wee."

And Purnell agreed because he knew once things got rolling, Deshonne would forget all about leaving. So then they all walked towards Angie and the car, each praying separately that the night turned out right for them all.

*****

To their surprise, four hours later their prayers were answered, and they were on their way home. The sight of the sun rising was once again pleasing to Deshonne's eyes when he decided to call it quits. He was thankful, things had worked themselves out through the course of the night. As they pulled up to the route 13 / Memorial Drive intersection, Angie's stomach spoke loudly, from the passenger's seat.

"Magic, can you buy me a sub outta Wawa's?" she asked without wiping the sleep out of her eyes.

"Ah-ight, I got you," he said, still counting the night's take.

"Girl, what the fuck is wrong with you!" Purnell barked. "How in the fuck is you gonna disrespect me and ask him for something to eat, and I'm right next to you?"

"Because your ass is broke, and I'm hungry, Pee-Wee. Don't trick me!"

The light turned green, but the car didn't move. Purnell sat there, staring at Angie, wondering if he should choke her out in front of his friend.

"Drive, yo, it's cool. I was gonna buy y'all something to eat anyway. She just spoke up before I could say something, that's all."

I can't stand this bitch! Purnell thought as he pushed down on the gas.

"I don't know what you acting all stupid for. I'm hungry," she mumbled as soon as they entered the parking lot.

And that was all it took to set things off. Purnell threw the car in park and jumped to her side of the car, all in one motion. "Bitch, is you crazy!" he gasped as he grasped her throat.

"Hey, hey, hey!" screamed Deshonne, leaning forward to help the defenseless woman. "Let her go Pee-Wee, the police station is right up the fucking street! Let her go!" Deshonne commanded while attempting to pry Purnell's hands loose from the poor girl's neck.

"I'm sorry," she whispered as soon as he had let go of her throat.

All three of them sat in silence for a few minutes, just to calm things down.

"How much did you make?" Purnell anxiously asked, still upset.

Deshonne recounted the total and rechecked Purnell's digital scale first, just to be sure. "Seven-seventy and some change. Plus we still got about 25 grams left."

"Don't forget that Shane owes us a buck for them 15 bags I left with him in case somebody comes through," Purnell added.

"Nah, I ain't got nothing to do with that. That's on you. I didn't give him nothing." Deshonne shot back, not agreeing with the trust Purnell had in the addict.

"Ah-ight, don't worry. I got him covered," Purnell stated confidently. Then he reached over into the glove department, causing Angie to recoil in fear. "Here, add this to it," Purnell said as he handed him a $100 dollars in small bills, which was the bulk of his re-up money.

"Cool, now I can put his money up, and we can go from here," Deshonne said, brandishing the remaining solid piece of chalky white rock.

Purnell knew it was on from that moment. Soon he would be back on top with Deshonne's help. Deshonne on the other hand was wondering how he got to this point so quick, as he tried to check his own adrenaline rush. And little old Angie was plotting on trading in the pork chop in the driver's seat for the sirloin steak in the back seat.

CHAPTER 9

As always, Kenny called ahead and had one of his lady friends circle 23rd and Market on foot, in search of marked and unmarked cars before he came strolling in. He parked his Lincoln a block away, on Tatnall Street, and slowly paced around the corner.

"Heyyy, Kasi," Kenny greeted him. "Walk with me."

Kasi's heart dropped to the bottom of his stomach when Kenny came out of nowhere and put his arm around him. The bag of heroin in his right hand smoothly slid down his side and found its way beneath his feet. *Fuck*! Kasi thought. "Ah-ight, cool," he agreed as calmly as he could. "Let me hide my pack somewhere first, D.T.s is out early."

Looking oddly at his scruffy friend, Kenny said, "Yeah, do that."

Kasi went through the motions of finding an old paper bag on the side of O.K. Discount for his crack and another for his dope while Kenny patiently watched his clumsy movements from across the street. They walked three blocks without saying a word until they reached a fast food restaurant called Fried Corner.

An old Chinese woman in a hairnet put the majority of Kenny's order on the counter. "Your shrimp will be a few more minutes, sir," she said.

"Miss, can I get a grape soda, too?"

"Yes, sir. Can or bottle?"

"Bottle," he then turned to Kasi to see if he wanted something.

"So, what's up, Kenny?" Kasi quickly asked out of guilt.

Okay, Kenny thought. "Please help me understand why you got a CD coming out in a couple of weeks, but you can't seem to stay out of the projects long enough to get a distribution contract signed?"

Kasi was at a loss for words. He just stood still with a dumb look on his face.

"I thought you told me that you weren't gonna get high no more, Kasi. Do you even know that you missed another conference yesterday?"

Kasi went on the defensive, as if he had just been wronged. "Why in the fuck do I gotta be getting high just because I like to hang in the projects? What, you forgot that that's where I'm from?"

Although it's half condemned, the riverside projects are the heroin capital of Wilmington.

"Things aren't adding up the way they should, Kasi. You missed another meeting. Not to mention, Shaheed hit you off twice without me knowing, and you got right back at him. But I hit you off and mines come back in dribbles. What's really good?" Kenny asked, feeling offended.

"Come on, now, I know you ain't acting crazy over a couple of dollars. We supposed to be better than that."

"Nah, man, I don't know which one it is, but either you think I'm soft or you fucking up. And I'm telling you now, either way we about to have problems."

The lady returned with his platters and soda. While Kenny checked his order and paid for everything, Kasi was gazing out of the window at the old gas station lot.

"Look, dawg, you don't have to come at my neck like this over a couple of dollars. As soon as I finish this pack, I'll hit you off," Kasi said as they began to walk back up the block.

"Kasi, I'm washing my hands with the game soon. I'ma stick to promoting shows and artists after I collect from everybody this go around. So don't think it's just you because it ain't."

"I'ma pay you, dawg. You don't have to worry about my end."

"See, you missing the whole principle of what I'm saying. I'm investing my money in you. You're a big part of my plans. A big part. But you can't be hiding in smokehouses, getting high on me."

"Kenny, I swear I ain't getting high no more. It's just that my bills are fucked up right now, and I'm trying not to get caught up, that's all."

"Ah-ight, well, I was concerned it was something else, but I guess I was wrong. So I'ma let you do you."

They shook hands and hugged. Kenny knew that Kasi was lying to him, but he just hoped that he would pull himself together before he took both of them under, financially.

"What you about to do?" Kasi asked, retrieving his stash.

"I'm about to go and see Deshonne."

"Tell him I said, what's up and to stop hanging down the bottom with Pee-Wee on that hot-ass block."

"Ah-ight, I will." *Down the bottom, huh? I wonder*, Kenny thought as he started to dial up his friend.

*****

The two toddlers ran around the house like Tazmanian devils. One was stark naked, leaving a trail of urine with each step. And the other was snot-nosed and heavy pampered.

"I—I can't take this shit! Sit the fuck down before I hurt both of y'all!" Zenda told them as she snatched them both up and threw them on the sour-smelling couch. "Don't be running around here, crying like no fucking sissies. And don't get up," she warned.

Zenda always fought with the kids when she didn't get to go out or have sex with a strange man the previous night. Everyone knew that she had problems, except her. The hotter it got outside, the hotter she got inside. her lay-around wardrobe was now limited to a scarf to keep up the fresh, homemade hairdo and tube socks so her feet wouldn't get cold as she walked around the house.

"Kelia!" she hollered at the top of her lungs from the front room.

66

"Huh!" Kelia answered from the bathroom.

"Can you please come and get these two stupid motherfuckers before I fuck them up!"

Kelia came out of the bathroom with a wet rag, trying to wipe a stain out of her jeans. "Okay, Zenda, don't worry, I got'em," Kelia assured her nude roommate.

"I gotta go and get dressed for my friend tonight, Kelia. I don't got time for no kids right now." holding her breath, Kelia laid the youngest boy down to remove his heavy diaper. "I'll watch them until my mother comes back from Family Dollar, okay?"

Zenda stopped short of the bedroom and turned around with her hands on her round hips. "I thought you was watching them for the night. I need you to babysit while I spend time with my friend."

"I can't because I'm about to go down to my grandparent's house for the weekend."

"I don't think that y'all going this weekend because I already gave your mother 20 dollars for you to watch them. And she said it was okay."

"Didn't she give you the money?" Zenda asked.

Obviously crushed by another one of her mother's lies, she said, "no, she just told me that she had something for me. This is crazy. First I'm on punishment for nothing and now I can't even go down Pop Pop's," she mumbled to herself.

"Well, before she walked out, she told me to tell you to call her later and to fix yourself something to eat because she wasn't coming back until late."

"Late, huh." Kelia knew all too well what that meant. She was definitely stuck for the night. "She been left, so why is you just telling me now?"

"Because I ain't know you didn't know. And, plus, you was in the shower when she called back for you," Zenda explained.

"Did she say when we was going down my grandparent's house?"

"No, but she's over y'alls aunt's house, so you can call her and ask if you want," Zenda suggested before she disappearing into her sty of a room.

*****

Marie banged on the discolored wooden door like a mad woman while the neighbors went on about their business.

"Here I come. Stop banging!" Shane yelled as he took the squeaky steps two at a time. "Oh, hey, little cousin. What's up!" Shane said.

"Shit," Marie replied simply. Shane turned to walk up the steps and Marie followed. "I just stopped by to see what y'all was doing."

"My daughter and her friends are up here playing cards, as usual. And my mom's in the basement," Shane replied.

Shane's mother rarely came out of the basement. At 67 she was a hermit, lost to the world of drug addiction. Marie was her favorite niece, but only because of what she could do for her that others wouldn't. Marie walked up to the card table, seeking out the person with the biggest money pile. They normally played Pitty-Pat every weekend for 50 cents a hand, but this week was pay week.

"Hey, Marie! Where you been at?" a dark-skinned female with bulging eyes asked.

"You late," one of her younger cousins stated after exhaling the blunt's smoke.

"It was nice outside, so I walked," Marie said with a smile.

"Bitch, stop lying," another cousin said jokingly while dealing the cards.

"Y'all ask a stupid question, so I gave y'all a stupid answer," Marie stated in her usually conceited manner.

"Your daughter called here a little while ago," Shane stated from the couch while channel surfing. "She said she was calling you on the cell phone, but you wouldn't answer."

Marie looked over as if he said something wrong. "What did she want?"

"She was mad because y'all didn't go down Uncle D's."

"Oh, well, that little bitch better get a grip. And just be happy that I haven't punched her in her face, yet."

"Why, what happened?" the poppy-eyed cousin asked as she turned down the radio.

"Because her hot ass is failing every class this year."

"Aw, I thought that Lil-K was doing good this year," Shane said.

Every time she thought about her daughter's progress notes from school it brought on rage. "Hell no. and that little bitch is gonna be on punishment for the whole summer, too. No new clothes, no phone, no radio, no nothing. She can't even walk to the corner store by herself," Marie told them.

"Well you know you did the same stuff when you were 14," Shane reminded Marie as he got up to get the blunt from one of his daughters.

"And that's why I'm trying to teach her what's important in life. But the bitch is just so damn hardheaded. At the rate she's going, I'm looking for her to end up like her bum-ass sperm donor," Marie announced.

Everyone in the room laughed except her. She just got up and went down to the basement to call Kelia back.

CHAPTER 10

A storm was brewing, so the sky was cloudy over the suburbs. Deshonne stood on the open porch enjoying the approach of his first sight of outside rain, when Kenny's Lincoln came cruising down Karlyn Drive. The sight of Kenny's 22in. Sprewell rims, slowly spinning after the car was in park, excited something in Deshonne. He took a deep breath as his friend came walking up the sidewalk, talking on his Nextel walkie-talkie. Deshonne waited for Kenny's conversation to end before speaking. He continued to rock in his father's new dynamic rocking chair while Kenny stood at the head of the porch, facing him. "So, what brings you out this late?" Deshonne asked as soon as Kenny put his phone away.

"I came to check on my boy. I even called you earlier so that we could do dinner at Seafood Connections up Chester, but nobody answered the house phone."

"I was probably at work."

"Word, that's what's up," Kenny said in an encouraging tone. "Hey, ain't that Dee's car on the side of the house?" Kenny pointed just outside the fence.

"Yeah, she's upstairs, sleep. We was supposed to be watching a movie together, but she fell asleep on me halfway through it."

Moms must be at work. Kenny figured. Because even though Deshonne was 26, she didn't play having females laid up in her house.

"So, what's been up?" Kenny asked as he sat down beside him.

70

Deshonne walked over to the mailbox on the wall, beside the front door, and pulled out a long envelope and passed it to Kenny. Holding it up with both hands, Kenny tried to look inside without opening it. He had a pretty good idea of what was inside but he asked anyway. "What's this?"

"It's two $400 dollar money orders for that pack you gave me to hold."

"What happened to the onion?"

"What you think happened to it? Me and Pee-Wee dumped it."

"Oh yeah." Kenny said with a sly snicker. "And where is good old Pee-Wee now?" he asked while checking the contents.

"I don't know. Either he's home or working somewhere on that change he owes you, I guess."

An elderly neighbor came by, tapped her horn, and waved. They both stopped to wave back before finishing their conversation.

"The next time you see Pee-Wee tell him I said to get at me because that stunt he pulled wasn't cool."

"Ah-ight," Deshonne agreed, hoping that that would be the end of it.

They sat silent for a moment. Deshonne thought to himself, *Uh-oh, here it comes.*

"So are you really still working, or is that the play off for your peoples? Because I heard that you've been spending a lot of time down on Jessup," Kenny asked.

"I was. That's how I got you your change. You got $800, I got $700, and Pee-Wee got $600."

"So why he ain't hit me with a piece of that six then if he was really trying to pay me?" Kenny pointed out.

"You asking the wrong cat that question, Kenny. I don't know. Maybe he's trying to flip a couple of times first, so he'll have something to build from."

"You don't believe that yourself, Magic, so don't feed it to me. I know he feels like he don't have to pay me because we grew up together, but business is business."

71

The look on Kenny's face said everything for Deshonne. He knew Kenny felt blatantly disrespected by Purnell, and the fact that Deshonne went behind his back to help him. But the point was, he came correct, as always.

"Look, I can't say what he's doing with his money, but I know I spent mines," Deshonne stated while simultaneously turning his pockets inside-out.

"What?" Kenny asked as if he misheard Deshonne's last confession. "What did you do with $700 that fast?"

Deshonne recounted his accomplishments on his fingers. "I paid $200 on my D.M.V. fine for my license. Me and Dee took my sons to St. Anthony's Festival, twice. And I copped a quarter pound of Arizona from Rala, for Eve to pump out Kimberton for me."

Kenny plopped back down on the lawn chair, holding his head, as if what Deshonne just said instantly gave him a migraine headache.

"What's wrong with you?"

"Man, tell me that you just didn't say that you gave that smut a quarter?"

"Yeah, I gave it to her, why?" Deshonne repeated as if he did the right thing. "You know I don't know nobody that smokes trees besides you and your squad. And that ain't enough."

"Magic, you might as well chalk that pack up as a loss."

"Shit, you crazy! I'll beat that bitch ass first."

"No you won't. Because you're not ready to go back to sleeping three in a cell."

"We'll see, watch," Deshonne stated, pouting.

"Ain't no need in getting mad cause you gave it to her. Just call her and tell her to bring you whatever's left." *This nigga's stupid! He fell in love with a carpet muncher and got worked because her pussy was tight. I bet you, he'll never catch up with her again until she's broke,* Kenny thought.

"I'ma go out there later on."

"Don't you touch that broad, Magic. It's your fault, not hers," Kenny warned.

Kenny's phone rang, cutting their conversation short. All types of violent thought passed through Deshonne's head about Evelyn while Kenny talked on the phone, down in the driveway. After a long ten minutes Kenny came and sat beside him. "You ah-ight, fam?" Kenny asked.

"Fuck, no! I'm probably fucking broke again."

Feeling sorry for his friend, Kenny dug into his sweatpants pocket and pulled out all his loose change. "Here. It's not much, but it's everything in my pockets," he stated with sincerity.

Deshonne was grateful for the gesture, but he hoped for more. As he counted up the $83, he said, "thanks, but I really need you to put me on because I'm tired of this broke shit."

"You just came home. I'm not trying to see you go straight back."

"So what, man. I'm tired of being broke."

"Magic, you get real reckless when you start pumping. Especially with them hammers."

"Nah, I got this sweet-ass block to pump on. Plus, I don't gotta do nothing really because I got Pee-Wee and Shane."

"I don't know. Let me think about it first."

They both leaned over the railing as they spoke.

"Yes or no, Kenny?"

"I don't know, Magic, it's not that simple. I'm trying to get out of the game, and you trying to pull me back in."

"Well, at least talk to your boy Shaheed for me." Deshonne suggested.

"Magic, we both know what it's hitting for if you catch another drug charge in Delaware."

"I'm telling you, Kenny. I can't take this being broke shit. I need one shot."

Knowing that Deshonne wasn't going to let him leave without an answer, Kenny agreed. "Ah-ight fam, have it your way. If I don't pick you up tonight, we'll have lunch tomorrow."

"Cool, that's all it is then. Don't stiff me, Kenny," he said as Kenny walked off the porch.

Kenny just looked back and shook his head.

As soon as the Lincoln was out of range, Deshonne called Purnell, and Kenny called Smallwood.

Smallwood made tens of thousands a week throughout Delaware, without any legitimate backing. His flamboyancy, the big house, and expensive cars were Kenny's biggest reason for leaving the game. Jail was only a matter of time for Smallwood, in Kenny's eyes. So he planned to distance himself before he, too, sealed his fate. The phone rang once before his partner picked up, reciting his ridiculous quote, "Pimps are us."

"Yo, it's me," Kenny stated, never revealing his name on phone lines dealing with business.

"What's it hitting for, babe?" He asked, as he looked around his custom-made walk-in closet for a throwback to match his new royal-blue crocodile sandals.

"I need you to do me a favor and try out my peoples," Kenny requested.

"Is his money right?"

"Nah, it's a consignment deal, but I'll cover any damages if he fucks up."

"Hey, if you say so. Just send one of your flunkies to the spot to scoop it." Smallwood stated as if four and a half ounces of powder were nothing to him.

"Ah-ight, one," Kenny said, and then hung up the phone.

Pulling up at his gated apartment complex minutes later, he wondered if he was making a mistake.

*****

Desiree's biological alarm clock woke her up promptly at 6:30 the following morning for work. The sun was already creeping into the room, so she decided to wake Deshonne up with a good morning kiss. But not just any kiss would do because she felt like waking him up in the most pleasurable way any man could think of. So, climbing out of bed, she positioned herself between his legs, on the floor. Then carefully sticking her hands into the slit of his boxers, so that he wouldn't awaken before she started, she slowly pulled out his limp dick and placed the tip only between her soft lips.

"Mmm..." he moaned as his manhood began to grow from the warmth of her slick tongue. "You sure do know how to start the day off right," he whispered while rubbing his fingers through her hair.

"You looked too at peace for me, Magic. And besides, it's time for us to get ready for work," she said with a complementary lick of his shaft.

"Why you start it if you ain't have no intentions on finishing?" he asked.

"Who said that I was finished?" she playfully asked. Then she stood up, stripped down, and laid on her back. Deshonne got up and started to climb on top of her, but she stopped him. "Wait a minute," she told him. Then while he watched, she two-finger fucked herself until she was short of breath. "Is that wet enough for you?" she asked.

"I don't know. Let me test it out." Then he rolled her over onto her stomach and slid as deep as he could inside her, in one slow thrust.

"Yes," she moaned. And he thought, It's perfect.

CHAPTER 11

Desiree came limping out of Applied Card with her hands shielding her eyes from the sun. Iyanna was sashaying beside her in a short skirt and some high heels, steadily gossiping. A black 2003 Mercedes Benz S600 came from behind a row of cars, where it was laying in wait for her. The car crept up on them so quietly that the horn startled them both.

"Desiree, can I talk to you for a minute?" Alex asked as he rode alongside them.

"Uh-oh. Look who's trying to creep around in broad daylight, like his wife don't work here, too," Iyanna chuckled.

"Mind your business, Yanni," Alex stated while driving with one hand and pointing at her with the other.

"Girl, let's just keep walking to your car and ignore him," Desiree advised.

"We're ignoring you, clown, so beat it," Iyanna said arrogantly with a flick of her wrist.

Alex knew where they were headed, so he pulled away from them and proceeded to block Iyanna's BMW. Overdressed, he hopped out of his air-conditioned car into the humid summer air, sweating in his Giorgio Armani Suit and Yohji Yamamoto shoes. The heavyset mulatto man pleaded his case.

"I promise you that I'll only take a few minutes of your time."

"We're on our way to lunch, Alex. Move your car, please," Desiree said while opening the unlocked door.

"What I have to say will only take a minute. Just one minute, please?" he begged while signaling her to get into his car to talk privately.

He looks so cute when he begs, Desiree thought.

I hope I can find a rich sucker like this lame, Iyanna thought as she slid behind the wheel of her vehicle.

"Yanni, don't leave me."

"Where am I going? Mr. Romantic has me blocked in," Iyanna sarcastically pointed out.

Then Desiree walked over to the driver's side of Iyanna's car. "Just give me about five minutes, okay?" she told her girlfriend.

Iyanna reached over into her glove compartment. "Here, Dee, just in case Mr. Suit and Tie wants to act up in that car." Iyanna said, handing over a king-size can of pepper spray.

"Don't give me that girl, I might be tempted to use it."

"Move your car out of the way!" Iyanna demanded with an arrogant wave.

As Desiree walked over to his car, she reiterated the time frame to Iyanna,"five minutes."

Alex turned on the climate control and pulled away as soon as the passenger's side door closed. Slowly he circled the parking lot in search of the right words to say. "So, how's it been? How have you been doing?"

"Alex, I know you're not jeopardizing your marriage and my job just to ask me how I've been doing."

"No, my wife's out sick today. I told her that I was going to run some overdue errands until dinner," he explained.

"Oh, that's what it is. Cause I didn't think you were that stupid." She prayed he wasn't that far gone because it would be even harder to shake a pussy whipped man with money.

"Desiree I've missed you so much these past six weeks," he proclaimed.

Oh God, he's counting! she thought. "That's nice to know, but if that's all you had to tell me, you could have just called."

"I was hoping to take you out to lunch. Your friend, too, of course, if that's alright with you."

"No, that's not alright. We don't have time to sit down and eat today, just a quick drive-thru meal."

Alex knew her schedule and could see through her flimsy lies, so he asked, "What have I done to turn you against me?"

With a smirk on her face she thought, *I should just go ahead and let this clown pay for everything since he wants to be so gullible.* "Alex, I've opened my eyes and I think it's time you did the same."

Alex gently grabbed her by the chin and turned her face until their eyes met. "Don't you mean that you've finally opened your legs?" he stated calmly.

Whack. Desiree slapped his hand away. "And what is that supposed to mean?" she asked. "If you have something to say just spit it out!"

"Okay. Where's your car at?"

"Why, Alex? My car is none of your business."

"Is he the reason that you've been avoiding me?"

A look of guilt touched her face as she spoke. "I haven't been avoiding you. I just don't see any need for us to see each other anymore, that's all. Affairs never last forever."

"But I thought we had something good going between us. You never had any problems or complaints."

"Is that what they call adultery these days, Alex, something good?" she asked. "Or did you forget that you were married each time you laid up between my legs and swore you loved only me, until it was time for you to leave?"

At that point Alex was at a loss for words, so he sat in silence. A single tear traveled down his cheek.

"If you'll excuse me, Alex, Yanni's waiting for me," she reminded him and opened the door.

"We can work this out," he said as he grabbed her arm. "It doesn't have to end this way."

"Alex, look. We both knew going into this that there was no future in our playing house together. You know what we got out of each other's company is all it will ever amount to.

I'm sorry." She got out of the car and walked around to the driver's side. "I'm moving on, Alex. Please do the same and go back to your family," she suggested and walked away.

After Desiree and Iyanna had left the parking lot for lunch, Alex remained, his tears repeatedly staining his tailor-made suit as his head rested on the steering wheel.

*****

The fresh scent of potpourri circulated throughout the Robinson house every morning. Deshonne's mother's routine seldom varied. After cooking a healthy meal for her two men, she opened all the downstairs windows and doors to vacuum as she listened to the early-morning "Tom Joyner Show" on 105.3. Hearing the faint sound of the phone ringing she cut the power to the Kirby.

"Hello, Robinson residence."

"Good morning, Mom Paulette. Is Magic there?" Kenny asked.

"Who's calling?" she asked.

"It's me, Kenny."

She sat down on the edge of the couch and talked as if the caller were one of her biological sons. "Lil-Kenny, what are you doing up so early in the morning?"

"Moms, I'm always up by sunrise, preparing for the new day. You know working people never sleep too long. That's why the early bird always gets the worm."

"I heard you finally got that business you always talked about, Lil-Kenny. I'm proud of you. You need to talk some sense into knucklehead upstairs. Maybe some of your brains will rub off on him. Because all he got on his brain is pussy. And you know where pussy always gets him, right?"

"Yes, ma'am. Don't worry, I got him."

"Good, because I'm tired of wasting my breath on him. I'm about to show him what tough love is because he thinks my house is the Red Rose Inn."

Kenny laughed at her odd comparison while she called for Deshonne. He continued to play "NBA Live 03" on the new Play Station II he had just bought.

"I got it!" Deshonne hollered down as he picked up.

"Tell your mother I said hi!" Mom Robinson added before hanging up.

"Okay, I will," Kenny agreed.

"Yooo, what's up!" Deshonne asked.

With a grin on his face, Kenny gladly chastised his friend. "Yo, I told you about having all them smuts running in and out of mom duke's house Magic. Didn't I?"

"Nigga, if you called to lecture me, call back later because I'm trying to sleep."

"Hey, I'm just giving you a little advice before you come home one day and the locks are changed on your ass," Kenny told him.

Deshonne looked over at the blinking clock on the stereo, and somehow, the time reminded him of the favor he had asked of Kenny days earlier. "Since you in a giving mood this morning, how about giving your peoples what he asked you for," Deshonne said, speaking about himself.

"That's what I called for in the first place, to see if you still wanted it."

Deshonne sat up in the bed, wrapped in the bedding, as if sitting up right made him a better negotiator. Kenny's team lost the game, so he tossed the controller onto the leather sectional. "Why you had to call? You could've just brought it over," Deshonne stated.

"Because, I wanted to give you a couple of days to think about things first in hopes that you would change your mind," Kenny told Deshonne.

But that first pack had already ignited a flame inside Deshonne that four years in prison had once extinguished. So the patience he had acquired while he was away was now replaced by his previous yearning for money. "I didn't hit the fucking Power Ball, Kenny. I'm not changing my mind. So unless you got a money tree somewhere, I'm waiting on you."

"Ah-ight, Magic. Trigg will be through to holler at you in a little while, so be ready."

"That's what's up! What's the tag?" Deshonne asked enthusiastically.

"I'm not sure yet. Ask him when he gets there. And keep in mind that it's not coming from me. So that means don't spend beyond your means," Kenny warned.

"Cool. I'm about to get dressed, my nigga. Holler back."

"Ah-ight, one." Kenny agreed and hung up.

Deshonne ran to the shower, already counting his profits in his head.

CHAPTER 12

Deshonne's whole state of mind changed once he finally got his hands on what he was asking for. He became enormously anxious and overly paranoid at the same time. So he swiftly called up his sidekick, Purnell, as planned.

Angie was relaxing in a hot bubble bath, thinking about how she could get out of work later when her phone rang. She dashed towards the bedroom, leaving puddles and suds behind with each step. As soon as she caught a glimpse of the caller I.D., a sly grin parted her lips. "Hello, Magic," she answered softly as she made her way back towards her awaiting bath. "No, he's not here," she added before he could even speak.

"Hey, Angie. How did you know it was me?"

"Caller I.D., Einstein."

"Oh," he replied dumbfoundedly. "Where's he at?"

"Home with his other bitch, I guess. I got the night shift," she said sourly.

Angie had made the bath for two but, Purnell didn't show up as promise, so she was upset with the world. "You know how you yellow niggaz are. Y'all play house with wifey in the daytime and call the ride-or-die bitches when you wanna get fucked real good."

"Haaa," he sighed. *Here we go*, Deshonne thought. "Well, what time do you think he'll be there, cause I need to holler at him."

"I don't know. Maybe he'll bring his trifling ass in here by the time I drop my daughter off at daycare."

"Ah-ight cool. Then bring him straight here after you get situated," Deshonne said, knowing that he was going to need all the help he could get bagging up everything in 5/8 baggies.

"Why do I gotta bring him?" Angie asked. Out of nowhere Angie began to caress her own breasts as she spoke to him, imagining that it was his touch. "I know my way there."

"Goodbye, Angie," he said, trying to cut her advances short. He could hear the water sloshing around in the background and wondered if she was alone.

"Magic, you know he doesn't care about me. He just likes the way I ride his dick and swallow his nasty-ass nut."

"Hey, I'm not gonna get into that. Sorry. What y'all do is on y'all."

Sitting on the edge of the tub, she spread her legs and leaned up against the nearby wall. "What me and you do can be between us," she suggested as she closed her eyes.

The way she talked turned him on. He was even more curious about her bedroom skills now that she certified herself a freak. "Angie, you not my type," he told her.

"Magic, my pussy's wet right now. Can you hear it dripping?" she said as she slipped in her two longest fingers.

He had to refrain from touching himself as she started to breathe harder. "Yo, did anybody ever tell you that you got a filthy mouth?"

"No. But they have told me that my fuck game is serious," she informed him.

"I'm just giving you a opportunity to fuck me from the back. I guarantee you that you'll come back for more once you've tried this pussy out."

"Are you gonna bring him over or what?" Deshonne asked, trying to ignore her enticing moans.

It sounded like static was jumping in on her line for a moment. "Did you hear it talking to you, Magic?" she asked after rubbing the receiver against her shaved bush of pubic hair. "She fits tight around all sizes. All you gotta do is say yes."

Click. He hung up the phone before he was too far gone and took her up on her offer. Glad that they weren't in the same room right now, he just sat at the kitchen table for a minute and laughed at what had just transpired.

Angie was also smiling at that same moment. She grabbed her nearby toy out of the medicine cabinet and finished what she had started alone, fantasizing about being fucked hard by Deshonne.

*****

As soon as his parents were on their way to work, Deshonne put the beginning phases of his plan into action. The screen door was locked, but the front door was wide open, as well as all of the first floor windows. The mini-blinds were tilted so that he could see out but no one could see in as he sat at the kitchen table and played chemist.

Knowing that there was only one way to build a block of loyal customers, he made the strongest uncut product he could without using a flame. He stirred up the entire big eighth (125gms.) in a glass jar half filled with (a hazardous cleaning agent), slowly stirred the jar until the unwanted cut clinged to its walls, and every rock was solid. As he stirred, his mind wandered, from his distribution plan to his overall profit margin once things got organized again.

Awaiting Purnell's arrival seemed endless, so he called up his trusted companion, Desiree, knowing that she would be there to help him before he hung up the phone.

*****

"Here they come," Deshonne said with glee as Angie's car approached.

Purnell and Angie came in dressed like twins, in white tees, Akademic jeans, and Air Ones. Deshonne glanced at them, but continued to bag up. "Lock the screen door and the front door," he commanded as they approached.

"Damn! It smells like straight drop-n-pop up in here. What time is your peoples getting off?" Purnell asked.

Angie covered her nose to the strong stench as she sat on the couch.

"Later," Deshonne answered dryly. Angie's gut was rumbling as she stared at Deshonne's unpleasant face. She wondered if her boldness was about to backfire on her.

"You should open up some more windows in this joint, cuz, because if mommy comes home early, you gonna get fucked up," Purnell suggested.

"Why you just now getting here to help me bag up Pee-Wee?"

"Because I was busy doing something for Angie."

Deshonne briefly glared over at Angie. Angie stared back slyly at him, prompting Desiree to stare her down.

"I'm sorry, Magic but I quit. My fingers are cramping up," Desiree said as she dropped the small, empty bag onto the rock-filled plate.

"Come on Dee, we're almost done."

"No, we're not, baby. I'm sorry. I think I did more than my part," Desiree stated as she walked upstairs.

"What you need me to do?" Angie asked, approaching the kitchen.

"You can grab up one of these safety pins and finish chipping up the rocks she left on that plate, please." Purnell stood beside him, watching, as if amazed. "So what we working with?"

"Trigg said it was four ounces, but the chemical probably ate up about 7 to 14 grams worth of cut, I think. So I made two piles. These are fat bags on this side, and those over there are skimpy," he said as he pointed.

Purnell wondered to himself why Deshonne didn't stretch their package to the max, but didn't question him. "Okay, I'ma open up the rest of these empties first, then I'ma start bagging up," Purnell informed his partner.

Desiree reappeared behind them after washing her hands. She was recklessly eyeballing Angie because she felt that something had happened between her and Deshonne.

"What you doing, Dee?" Purnell asked as soon as he noticed that she had returned.

"Nothing, I'm just gonna clean up when y'all get finished. That's it."

"Yo, it's no looking back from here, Magic," Purnell proclaimed.

Deshonne caught Desiree frowning as she gathered the cleaning products from under the kitchen sink. He knew that she wasn't fond of his decision, but said nothing to discourage him for fear of pushing him away again.

"We'll see what happens, Pee-Wee. I'm not looking ahead until I give these niggas their change first." "What we owe 'em, $3,825?" Purnell asked.

The question annoyed Deshonne. He hated discussing business, especially in front of other people. Deshonne stopped what he was doing to look at his inquisitive friend. "Can we talk about this later on? You came to help me, remember? So chill with the questions," Deshonne stated as he wiped beads of sweat from his forehead.

"I got you," Purnell said and then dug in to help.

Meanwhile, Angie was smiling at Deshonne flirtatiously from across the table, hoping to catch his attention.

I'ma have to hurt this little bitch! Desiree told herself as she alone caught her attention.

*****

Pine Street was the block off 23rd that was jumping after midnight, but it was cluttered with hand-to-handers. So Deshonne posted up a block up on the corner of Jessup, in hopes of catching the stragglers and short money.

Desiree sat a half a block up from him with her hand on the horn, slouching down in her seat, eyes fixed on the rearview mirror.

Deshonne walked up to the car on the passenger's side, which was closest to the sidewalk, and tapped on the window. She turned the ignition one notch to let the window down.

"You alright?" he asked as he dropped the money on the seat for her to collect.

"No. I'm not feeling you standing out on the corner by yourself. Where is Purnell at? I thought he was supposed to be out here, too." She straightened the crumpled 18 dollars he had just handed her.

"They're over on 17th Street, doing the same thing I'm doing."

"How much longer are you gonna push your luck with all these police riding back and forth, It's 1:30 in the morning, Magic. Wouldn't you rather be in bed with me right now?"

"Why? What, you ready to go home already?"

"I do work in the morning. And I can't afford to get sent home because I can't keep my eyes open."

"Ah-ight. Well, go head home, and I'll see you tomorrow. You can come and scoop me up on your way to work, so I can drop you off," he said as he stood up cautiously and looked both ways.

Upset because she felt like history was repeating itself, Desiree put the window up while he was still trying to talk to her and turned the radio back up. Golden Girl, the radio personality for Power 99FM instantly drowned him out.

"I should leave his ass right here, too," she muttered as she crossed her arms and watched him walk back to the abandoned barber shop steps.

I'm the shit! I wish she would leave me, he thought as he tossed his pack in stride.

CHAPTER 13

Seven thirty-six in the morning, and someone was already ringing the doorbell like a madman. Too tired to move because he had just gotten in an hour earlier, Deshonne lay in bed, wishing it would stop. But the unwanted chimes continued.

"Deshonne! Deshonne, I'm in the shower!" his mother screamed. "Answer the door!"

"Shit!" he mumbled as he attempted to pull himself together. The bell continued to ring until he reached the bottom of the steps. "Who is it?"

"Probation and Parole. Is Deshonne Robinson here?" a male voice barked with authority.

Deshonne's heart dropped at the sound of the unexpected guest's question. His bare feet and hands caught chills as he reached for the doorknob. *Fuck! What do they want? Did I miss a curfew call last night? Did somebody snitch on me already?* All sorts of thoughts quickly followed within seconds as he decided whether or not to open the door. *Oh, shit, I missed work this morning! They must've called my job this morning, he realized.* "Think, think, think," he told himself. Then he took a deep breath and partially opened the door with his foot behind it as a stopper, just in case they tried to storm in. "What's up, Mr. Howard? Is there something wrong?"

Bruce Howard was considered the worst probation officer in New Castle County. He disliked all criminals, no matter how light or extreme their charges were. But for some strange reason, he hated convicted drug dealers more than anyone, which made Deshonne public enemy #1 on his client chart.

"I don't know. You tell me. Have you done anything wrong between Tuesday's visit and now, Mr. Robinson, because you look real nervous."

"Me nervous? Nah, not me, sir. All I've been doing is working, eating and sleeping. But I know you don't usually make house calls this early in the morning. So what's up?"

To Howard everyone looked nervous and guilty. He thought that everyone had something to hide or was trying to get over on him, so he always tried to catch them off guard with unscheduled visits and surprise urines. The gray-haired, pudgy officer attempted to step in as he asked his questions, but was rejected by Deshonne's foot. The fiery look Howard flashed frightened Deshonne, so he stepped back and let the two officers in.

"It's a social call, son. Don't assume so much. It makes you look guilty," Howard said as he surveyed the front room for anything out of the ordinary.

The female officer walked over to the stairs and then peeped into the kitchen while Howard interrogated his client. "I just stopped by to check out your living quarters."

Deshonne kept his eye on the wandering woman as he spoke. "Okay, follow me, and I'll show you where I sleep at," he said and turned towards the steps.

Howard grabbed his shoulder firmly. "Wait a minute, Mr. Robinson. You just tell me where your room is, and I'll check it out for myself."

"Umm, the second room on the left," Deshonne said with a confused look.

Howard pointed to his partner to check out the room while they waited downstairs.

Deshonne stood there for a minute in a daze, praying that they only searched that one room in the house, or it was all over.

Luckily, the search only lasted ten minutes and then they were on their way to the next probationer's house. Deshonne was relieved to watch them drive away without him in the back seat of their car. His mother was another story. She sounded off from the moment she came face to face with Howard's partner.

"I'm tired of this shit already, Deshonne! I shouldn't have to come out of my bathroom and come face to face with a damn white woman," his mother yelled from her bedroom as she got dressed, not caring if the P.O.s heard her. "You gonna have to fly straight, or get your ass out of here soon and get your own spot. Me and your dad work too hard to go through this."

He closed the room door and picked up the telephone.

The name on her caller I.D. brought a smile to Angie's face.

"Good morning, Magic!"

"Hey, Angie," he responded skittishly.

"Before you even ask, no, asshole isn't here. And since you already knew he's never here before 12, I'm assuming that this call is for me, right? So are you ready to taste this pussy, huh?"

"Angie, not now, please. My morning is already fucked up enough, ah-ight."

Angie rolled over onto her elbows, facing the mirrored headboard, with a look of interest on her face. "Why, what's wrong, sexy?"

"Man, P&P just left my house all fucking early. That's why I'm calling your house for Pee-Wee. Because they're probably on their way to harass somebody else, so I wanted to give him the heads-up, about those clowns."

"He didn't find anything, did he?" she asked, only out of concern for herself.

"Hell nah! Do you think I would be talking to you if he did?" *Damn, this bitch is dumb!* he thought.

"Well, you don't have to worry about your stuff if that's what you wanted asshole for because it's all gone. And I have your money here," she informed him.

Deshonne's face lit up at the announcement. He slowly sat down on the bed, feeling as though a weight had been lifted off of his shoulders. "Word! That's what's up, Angie.

90

Good looking out," Deshonne gushed, as she imagined he would be after hearing the good news.

"No problem, Magic. You know that I got your back."

Oh, shit, they dumped a G-pack in one night. It's on! he quietly told himself. "Hey, that's definitely love, shorty. And I want you to know that I got yours, too," Deshonne added to proclaim his own loyalty.

"That's sweet, but I'm from the show-me state, and words can't keep me warm at night, boo."

"Angie, I already told you that I'm not on that type of time, so just cut it out cause you mess with my peoples."

"Correction, I'm just fucking your boy when it's convenient for him to sneak out. And just so you know, that's about to stop too, because I like dick when I want it, not when another bitch is tired of it."

"I don't see why we have to keep going through these conversations every time I call, Angie. You need to take up your problems with that brother cause I can't help you, in no way possible."

"Yes, you can, Magic. I've already done my homework on you, and I know how you get down after dark. So you might as well quit fronting and let me put it on you."

Man, this broad is really trifling, he thought at each passing minute.

"Angie, I'm sorry that I have to cut our conversation short, but I have to get dressed so I can pick D-e-e up for lunch in a little while," he said with strong emphasis.

"I keep secrets, if that's what you're worried about," she assured him. "As a matter a fact, I'm offering you every man's dream. You can keep Dee if you want to. Because I bet you that she can't suck your dick better than me," Angie challenged confidently.

Deshonne laughed her off as if she was joking and said goodbye without waiting for her to respond.

Angie just laid back down and fantasized until she dozed back off. "When I get a hold of that nigga, I'm gonna turn his yellow ass out, watch," she said to herself.

CHAPTER 14

The awning over the porch shielded Deshonne from the afternoon thunderstorm. He had been sitting there for a good while, thinking about Evelyn as he watched and listened to the rainfall. A part of him was still upset that she had burnt him for the quarter pound of marijuana, but he missed that shot so much that he was willing to forgive the costly setback and start fresh, in the bedroom. He decided that he had allowed her to avoid him long enough, so he picked up the phone.

Hello? Eve? Hello, is that you?" he asked and then paused once he noticed that it was her answering machine. At first he hung up, but then realizing that he had so much to say, he called back to leave a message. "How long is this gonna last, Eve? I'm not mad at you for what happened. As a matter of fact, it was my fault in the first place, for real. If I knew that giving you that pack would've damaged our relationship like this, I swear I would've never given it to you. I put you in a fucked up position, and I'm sorry." Then he paused for a moment, hoping that she was listening to his words. "When you get this message, call me, okay? I miss you."

*****

The windows were open just enough to allow the fresh smell of rain into the musky living room. B.E.T music videos were playing on the television in front of them, but no one was watching them because they were preoccupied.

Bent over the sofa, topless in her favorite, extra-short, plaid, catholic school skirt and knee-high stockings, Evelyn was too busy to answer her vibrating cell phone. Her small breasts bounced in rhythm to the sound of her own moans.

Crissy, dressed in an oversized police uniform shirt and riding boots, played good cop/bad girl by continually rearresting and illegally searching her handcuffed victim, so that she could torture her with her tongue.

Evelyn's skirt was flipped up, and her panties moved to the side, as Crissy began to probe her insides with a sex toy. Evelyn held open her own butt cheeks for easy access, at Crissy's request. Then Crissy grabbed a handful of her hair, thrusted forward, and yanked back. "I love you, boo," Crissy said with each thrust of the strap-on.

Evelyn took in every plastic inch on all fours, biting on a rubber bone while getting double-ended by her partner. "Mmm!" she moaned as Crissy gave rough pleasure to her pussy. Hearing the faint sound of her phone, Evelyn spit out the toy and reached for her phone on the coffee table. "Hold on, Crissy. Stop! Wait a minute," Evelyn commanded as she collapsed forward onto the carpet. "My phone's ringing. I have to see who it is."

Crissy grabbed a handful of her skirt and yanked her forcefully back onto the rod. "I know you're not trying to stop having sex with me so that you can answer that fucking phone because it's not happening."

"I've been waiting for an important call, Cris," she said. And then swiped her girlfriend's hand away and reached for the phone.

Crissy angrily pushed her forward, making her bump her head on the middle of the coffee table. "What the fuck, eve! What can possibly be more important than what's happening right now? I knew that I should have never told you how I felt about you because you're starting to take me for fucking granted."

Rubbing the sharp pain just above her eye, Evelyn tried to explain. "Girl, I don't know what you're talking about. You're taking this shit all out of context for nothing."

"Bitch, you know exactly what I'm talking about. I'm talking about that nigga you was letting stick you."

"No, it's not what you think," Evelyn objected. "That's exactly why I didn't want to go outside of our relationship in the first place because you're so possessive."

"Look, bitch. I'm not possessive. I just don't like no man ruining what's mine, that all. Besides, I told you that you could have any woman you wanted in that party, not a man."

"The last time I checked, I wasn't married," Evelyn pointed out as she removed the hanging restraints from her wrists. She reached for the phone again, so they struggled until Crissy knocked it onto the floor. Evelyn got up off of the floor, grabbing her belongings. "If I knew you was gonna start acting like this, I would've stayed at home."

"You're the one that's acting all stupid over a piece of lousy meat, eve not me. You act like a woman's touch isn't good enough for you anymore."

Not able to find her bra in the dark, Evelyn buttoned up every other button on her white blouse as fast as she could. "I don't see nothing wrong with Magic, because I like dick too," Evelyn confessed.

Crissy grabbed a handful of Evelyn's hair and yanked her back onto the couch. "I know you don't have feelings for that nigga. Especially since I'm the one that takes care of you."

"Cris, what me and you have, and what me and Magic have together are on two different levels. Now let me go," Evelyn demanded.

Tears began to flow down Crissy's face, causing Evelyn to feel guilty.

"Cris, you understand my needs and my pains, so you should know that Magic isn't anything serious. I will never share my heart with another man after what my daughter's father put me through. Magic just fills a void that plastic can't take the place of. Once you've enjoyed the real thing, that's it."

Crissy crossed her arms and stared down her lover for a long moment, contemplating her next move. "Okay, well, if it is what you say it is, then you won't have no problem with me fucking him too, then, right?"

"What?" Evelyn asked, startled by Crissy's odd request.

"You heard me. Share your little friend," Crissy said with a smile.

Evelyn laughed it off as she bent over to pick up her phone.

"I'm not joking, Eve."

"Cris, you've got to be fucking joking because you don't even know what dick feels like."

"I will, if you want to keep fucking that nigga and me, too. And I'm not playing."

She'll never go through with it, Evelyn thought. "Okay, fine. Have it your way," Evelyn agreed while checking her messages.

Crissy walked over to her and grabbed her wrist. "I love you. And I'm not going to play second to a man. Ever."

"It's your choice," Evelyn shot back as she pulled away.

*****

Sweat poured down Angie's chest as she rotated her size-four waistline feverishly in hopes of an orgasm before Purnell's premature fainting. Chest to chest, with his hands around her back, pulling her down by her shoulders into his lap as he gave her short, fast pumps of joy, Purnell wasted no time in reaching his own destination. She had his mouth filled with her warm tongue as he shot hot cum into her wet walls within minutes.

Angie rode his dick as if it was her only mission once she felt him emptying inside her, but it was too late for her to achieve the same gratification. So she rose up, frustrated, as soon as his penis became limp and ineffective.

"I guess this is it, huh?" she asked as she stood on the side of the bed with her shirt, wiping the running cum from down her inner thighs.

"Angie, I'm tired," he gasped as he tried to catch his breath. "Just give me a minute to catch my second wind, okay?" Purnell playfully slapped her on the ass.

"Stop it," she told him, pushing his hand away. "I wasn't referring to my lack of orgasms. I was talking about our future."

He sighed. "You get most of my time. What more do you want?" he asked.

"I don't know, Purnell, but this isn't enough for me or my baby."

He gently grabbed her by the hand. "Can't you just lay back down, and we can talk about this later? I'm ready for round two."

"I'm done. Get dressed and go home to your girl."

"I'm not going home. I'm staying with you tonight."

"Don't be here when I get out of the shower. Just lock the door behind you," she said out of disgust and then walked into the bathroom and closed the door.

Purnell rolled out of bed and headed towards the bathroom. "I guess I got to eat this bitch's pussy tonight to keep her happy," he said to himself.

But the door was locked for the first time, and she didn't let him in.

CHAPTER 15

Kenny's condominium was a poor man's dream of a bachelor's pad. It was furnished by an up-and-coming interior decorator, Tracy, one of his closest late-night female companions from Penn's Grove, New Jersey, who frequently did house calls.

As soon as Deshonne walked into the living room, his eyes lit up in admiration. *This is how I want my spot laid out in the next couple of months*, he thought.

Kenny led him back into the bedroom, where he was playing NBA Live on his Play Station II.

"So what's up, Magic?"

"Ah, nothing much, cuz. Same shit, different day," Deshonne said as he continued to look around the magnificent home. He dipped into his front pocket and pulled out a small envelope containing $4,100 in 7-11 money orders. "I just came by to straighten out my bill and put something on Pee-Wee's."

Kenny waved off the payout. "Why didn't Pee-Wee bring me the change?"

"Man, come on with that nut stuff, Kenny. Does it really matter who pays you your money as long as you get paid?"

"Not really. It's just the principle of the whole situation, Magic. Feel me?"

Kenny took the envelope for a moment, then handed it back. "I don't understand why you brought me that other change though, because I got nothing to do with that. That goes back to Trigg."

Deshonne looked at Kenny like he was trying to belittle his character by handing back the money and pushing him off on someone else. So he got upset and let his pride kick in. "Well, since this money isn't yours, I don't gotta worry about paying nobody back, then. So tell whoever gave it to me to get it like Tyson because they can chalk this change up as a loss."

Kenny shook his head and then paused the game for a moment to straighten Deshonne out. "Stop playing, Magic. Jerking niggas for a couple of dollars is petty to niggas like us. You know we don't get down like that."

"Oh, no? And what about you talking to me like I'm one of the flunkies you got working for you? We get down like that now?" Deshonne asked.

"Come on, man, I don't even know why you getting all caught up in your feelings like that. I told you what the deal was, up front. I'm not disrespecting you, so don't go there. I just don't want nothing to do with drugs no more if I can help it."

"Man, I'm your peoples though, Kenny. How you gonna push me off on them niggas?" Deshonne complained.

"I wasn't joking when I said that I was done with the game. Especially when I can make the same caliber money the way I'm doing things now. It's not worth the hassle," Kenny justified.

Kenny walked over to his dresser and picked a handful of party fliers out of a box for his upcoming party and tossed them to Deshonne.

Deshonne looked over one of the two-sided fliers. The invitation showcased some of Delaware's most enticing women partying in Club Utopia. The photos on the flier were from one of Kenny's recent parties.

"So why haven't you brought me in on this shit, yet? You already know what I'm capable of bringing to the table when it comes to business," Deshonne asked.

Kenny leaned up against the wall with his arms crossed as he spoke. "I will in time. But you just gotta be patient for a little while and give me some time to put things together first."

"Yeah, be patient, huh? And in the meantime where does that leave me, financially-broke?"

"Wouldn't you rather be broke now if it meant that you would be well off in the future?" Kenny asked theoretically.

"Kenny, you already know the answer to that question. But tomorrow's not promised to no one but the man above, cousin."

"You gotta stop thinking short term, Magic."

"Man, sometimes I feel like I'm still locked up," Deshonne said in reference to his parent's rules and his probation.

"So what if you have to do minor shit for your peoples here and there. You living rent-free, bill-free, and you eating up all your people's shit, for free. And besides, they brought you into this world, remember? They deserve to be catered to sometimes, don't you think?"

"Come on Kenny, you know what I'm talking about."

"No, I don't, and neither do you. You're just making up excuses to hustle, like you always do." each sentence that Kenny uttered cut Deshonne deeper and deeper. He started to become frustrated. "Whatever, Dr. Phil," Deshonne said sarcastically.

Kenny had to smile at his friend's remark. "See, you still think that life's a joke. I'm just trying to let you know that I see what's in your eyes, that's all."

"What you see in my eyes is starvation, cause I'm hungry."

"Well, if that's it, then I'm done preaching. Do you, baby." Kenny insisted, then he walked over to the bed and flopped back down to resume his game.

Deshonne could see that Kenny was disappointed, by the way his whole demeanor changed. "Yo, I'm just trying to maintain until you do make that big deal for both of us, feel me? Who knows, maybe I'll hit the Power Ball for us," Deshonne wished.

The openness Deshonne displayed was hard for Kenny to overlook. And Kenny knew him well enough to know that he wasn't going to change his mind without a real profitable alternative, so he decided to just let him make up his own mind.

"Here, Magic. You'll need this number to drop off the money," Kenny instructed as he handed him a McDonald's napkin.

"I already got Trigg's number. What you giving it to me again for?"

"Because it's not Trigg's number. It's my peoples, Wood, Kenny stated. "He's good peoples, too, so don't stick him, Magic. I already told him that you're a stand-up dude, so all you gotta do is call him and do what you do best, ah-ight."

"What happened to Shaheed?" Deshonne asked out of curiosity.

"It's election year. He's falling back for the summer. And I'm falling back forever, so that's your new connect."

Deshonne looked at his friend in disbelief for a moment, then stood up, shook his hand, and went into the envelope to retrieve Purnell's partial payment.

"That nigga owes me two stacks. What the fuck is this?" Kenny asked as he looked at the little money order.

"It's $500 towards Pee-Wee's bill, cousin. Don't worry. I got you every flip. My word," Deshonne said to calm his friend.

Kenny looked at Deshonne oddly for a minute, as if to read his thoughts. "Ah-ight. Make sure you hand Wood that change yourself, okay? No third person."

"Aw, shit!" Deshonne blurted out.

"What's up?"

"I left Dee outside in the car by herself," Deshonne explained as he rose up to leave.

"I got another party coming up in three weeks, y'all coming?" Kenny asked on their way to the door.

"I don't know about Dee, but I'll be there," Deshonne assured his friend before leaving.

As Deshonne approached the passenger's side door, he thought about what to say so she wouldn't cuss him out. But the murder-one grit that she gave him as he slid down into the seat beside her instantly threw off his thoughts. He put his hand on top of hers as she put the car into gear. She didn't snatch hers away, but the look she gave said enough. All he could do was smile and laugh inside as he thought about how bogus her look was before moving his hand.

"Where are we going at now?"

"Back out the way unless you got something to do first."

"No, I don't have nothing to do. And since you don't, either, I'm dropping you off and going home."

Deshonne rubbed her thigh as he spoke. "Why you acting like you got an attitude?"

Desiree stopped the car and removed his hand. "I don't have an attitude. I'm tired. So I'm going home early tonight if you don't mind."

"I gotta meet somebody later on tonight. You gonna come back and get me, right?"

"You better tell them to come get you because I'm not coming back out tonight," she said tartly.

I know she can't be as mad as she's acting, he thought. Then he tried to shift the blame. "Dee, I'm sorry for taking so long, but it wasn't my fault. You know how long-winded Kenny can be."

"You should've remembered how long-winded he is way before 45 minutes, Magic. So I'm not even trying to hear that dumb stuff because you know better." *You think shit's sweet*, she thought.

Her feisty attitude, mixed with her tight jeans, was turning him on. All he could think about at that point was how to get her to stay. "We could take a nap at my people's spot since you tired. I'll even massage you to sleep if you want me to."

I know that he don't think that I'm gonna give him some of this pussy after what he just did. Yeah right, she told herself. "I'm going home and getting into my own bed tonight, Magic."

"I guess it's a first time for everything, huh?"

Not responding to his last statement, she drove on in silence until she reached his house.

Bam! Deshonne slammed the door so hard that it rocked her car.

Desiree quickly put her window down before he reached the porch. "Boy, I know you don't got no attitude because I'm going home. So don't start acting all petty."

"I'll talk to you later, Dee. Keep it moving," he said loud enough for her to hear him without turning back.

The hard stance she took since leaving Kenny's flipped back to passive. "Come back and sit in the car so that we can talk, Magic."

"I'm tired, Dee," he said as he put the key into the bottom lock. Besides, the sun is already going down. I don't want you to be tired for work tomorrow."

"Is this the game you wanna start playing, Magic? Because you not the only one that knows how to play games."

"I don't know, is that what I'm doing? Because I'm not the one that's tired at five in the afternoon," he said and then walked inside and closed the door.

"See you later," she muttered, then pulled off.

*****

Not even an hour passed before he regretted not apologizing to Desiree. As he was putting together the Play Station II that he bought for himself, he realized that his sex life was contingent upon Desiree's happiness, especially now that Evelyn was out of the picture, limiting his choice of sexual partners to one. The phone rang as soon as he plugged in the last adapter.

"What, Dee?" he answered without checking the caller I.D. first.

"Sorry, babe, wrong chick," a soft voice answered back.

"Oh, my fault. Who's—who's calling?"

"It's Eve. And who's Dee?" she asked while walking to her car, sipping on a bottle of Belvedere.

So elated by the sound of her voice, he forgot all about the money she owed him. "Dee's one of my friends," he quickly informed her.

"Well, I just called to see what you were doing tonight since I haven't heard from you in a while."

"Nothing. I'm just sitting here, bored, as always," Deshonne replied.

"Ask him," Crissy whispered insistently as she repeatedly kissed Evelyn on her lips.

Please say that you're on your way over, he thought.

"Me and Crissy are on our way out New Castle to go to Blockbuster, and we were wondering if you wanted to hang out with us tonight. That's if you don't have any plans already."

"Say yes," Crissy said into Evelyn's ear as she licked it.

"We?" Deshonne repeated as if he heard her wrong.

"Yeah, us. Crissy's bored, too."

"So do you want us to pick you up, or what?" she asked as if it really didn't matter either way.

"Sure. Y'all can come and get me now if it don't involve me spending money because I'm broke."

"The movies and drinks are on us tonight, sweetie. All you have to bring is your body," Evelyn boldly stated and hung up.

I can't wait to see how she reacts once Magic sticks dick to her for the first time, Evelyn thought as she obeyed her girlfriend's request and spread her legs wide enough for fingers to enter her panty-less jean skirt.

She just don't know what I'll do to keep her happy, Crissy told herself. *I hope I can get drunk enough not to remember this shit*. She thought as she tilted the bottle hard, twice.

CHAPTER 16

Deshonne had a hard time going to sleep the next morning. As he sat at the kitchen table with his father, last night's events kept replaying in his mind. Gazing out of the open front door, he noticed Tonya's car pulling up to drop off Purnell.

Mr. Robinson took one last gulp of his favorite blend, grabbed his hardhat and goggles, then headed towards the door. Dressed in a snug-fitting white T-shirt, jeans spattered with cement specks, and dusty steel-toed Wolverines, Mr. Robinson always made his shadowy presence known. "You don't speak when you come into my house no more, Lil Pee-Wee?" Deshonne's father asked as he passed by Purnell on his way to work.

"I'm sorry, pops. Good morning," Purnell respectfully said.

Deshonne laughed at the way his father always put his friends in check.

Purnell waited until he heard the old pickup backing out of the driveway before speaking again. "Well. Did you see him yesterday? What did he say?" he inquired about Deshonne's visit to Kenny's.

In between bits of French toast Deshonne answered, "I talked to him for a minute."

"Well, is everything cool on the crack tip or what?"

"Shhh!" Deshonne pointed upstairs, where his mother was so that Purnell would watch what he was saying. Then they walked out onto the porch, closing the door behind them, to finish their conversation.

"Nah, we don't got the work, yet. I'm still waiting on a phone call as we speak."

"You already paid him, right?" Purnell inquired.

"No, I just gave him five from you." Deshonne checked his pockets first and then said, "I still got the other change, right here."

"Why, though?" Purnell asked, bewildered by the awkward transaction.

Even though the front door was closed, Deshonne continued to speak in an undertone, for fear of his mother overhearing their conversation. "He turned me onto another dude that's gonna start hitting us off. He said this dude's a heavy hitter."

"Who?"

"Some cat named Wood."

Being in the dark always made Purnell feel leery and expendable. *I've never heard of him.* Purnell thought. "Don't you mean that this new dude is gonna start hitting you off?" Purnell proclaimed jealously. "You making all the deals, and they giving you all the packs, right?"

What Deshonne was hearing made him realize that his friend was far from slow. So he wondered if the jealousy he was expressing now would come back and haunt them both later. "So what if I'm making the deals? We still splitting everything down the middle, right, Pee-Wee? Don't you got $1,500 more in your pocket now than you had last week?" Deshonne sermoned deceitfully.

"Yeah. You know what, Magic? You right. You have been looking out for us since day one. And I appreciate that, fam."

"I'm just doing for you what I know you would do for me," Deshonne stated modestly.

The front door crept open, and a headful of sponged rollers appeared at the screen. "I need you to go to the store for me, Deshonne," his mother told him.

"Hey, moms," Purnell said.

"Good morning, Pee-Wee."

"What you need, Mommy?" Deshonne asked.

"A gallon of milk and some eggs since you and your daddy ate up every damn thing."

She opened the screen door to hand Deshonne some money, but he waved her off. "I got it, Mom. Is that all you want?"

"Yeah, baby, thanks," she said and went back inside.

They both jogged to the Wawa on the next block, waiting to continue the serious part of their conversation until they came briskly back down the small hill.

"Is Dee taking you to work, or do you need me to call Angie?" Purnell asked, looking at his fugazzy Movato.

"Luckily I'm off today, cause Dee left me to fend for myself," Deshonne informed him.

Purnell knew Desiree wouldn't intentionally leave him home unless he did something to her. "What you do, Magic?"

"Nothing, really. But I'm glad she caught a attitude last night because I fulfilled one of your greatest fantasies."

That statement instantly caught Purnell's interest. "Word! Which one? And with who?" Purnell inquired excitedly.

"Eve. She put something so serious on me last night that I haven't been asleep, yet."

"Man, ain't that the high-maintenance broad you told me about, that stuck you for the Q.P.?"

Deshonne felt dumb for telling him that he got beat by a female. "Yeah, but her and Crissy gave me my money's worth last night. I-"

Purnell cut Deshonne's sentence off as he opened the gate for him. "You did just say her and Crissy, right?"

"Yep. Crissy, Eve's girlfriend," Deshonne said with a proud smile.

As they made their way to the front door, he could hear the phone ringing inside. "Mom! If it's for me, I'm here!" he yelled from the yard.

Purnell stopped at the porch steps and sat down. "Yo, hurry up and put that stuff up, so you can come back and tell me about the bitches." "Ah-ight."

After a few minutes on the phone, Deshonne came out and told Purnell that they had to take a walk to the barber shop, on New Castle Avenue.

"Why are we walking to the barber shop instead of calling a ride?" Purnell asked as they turned left at the top of the corner, onto Briarcliff Drive.

Deshonne's parent's resided in Overview Gardens, which is comprised of two-story, single -family homes in the suburbs of New Castle. The conveniently located home is nestled in between route 13, which travels through the majority of Delaware, and New Castle Avenue. Each home's price varies from 130, to 180 thousand dollars.

"Because the Ave. is too hot to for us to be transporting caine in a car, that's why," Deshonne answered.

"Well, since we gotta walk, you might as well finish telling me about the bitches. And don't leave nothing out, either," Purnell advised with a light backhand to Deshonne's chest.

"Play by play?" Deshonne asked.

"You damn right, play by play nigga! This ain't no short walk."

"Ah-ight, ah-ight. Okay, look, I'm on the couch sipping on a deuce-deuce Corona, staring at a blue television screen, waiting for some corny-ass love story that they picked out to come on, right…"

*****

As Deshonne stared at the 19-inch Magnavox, mesmerized by the sight of porn starlet Janet Jacme eating another woman's vagina while she's bent over the foot of the bed, his penis rose to flag pole attention. His heart began to flutter as he anticipated what the movie stars would do to each other next.

Evelyn and Crissy came parading into the living room seconds later wearing nothing more than lace thongs and socks.

She grabbed Crissy's hand and twirled her around to show off her prize. "What'cha think, Magic? Ain't my baby's body sexy?"

Deshonne's eye's had to answer her question for him because he was at a loss for words. *Oh, shit!* he thought, almost choking on a mouthful of beer as they strutted around the room in circles for his viewing pleasure.

The first thing that Deshonne noticed was that Crissy's breasts were enormous. Her plump, round, 40 DDs bounced around softly with each step. Evelyn's chest was just a mouthful, with perky, almost pinky-finger size pink nipples poking out. Nonetheless, they were both strikingly beautiful and sexy in their own right, with thick-country builds from the hips on down.

Evelyn bent over to a ninety-degree angle to assist her excited friend with his jeans.

The jitters were beginning to overcome Crissy, so she was far from her normally talkative mood. She reached under the couch and pulled out a filled cloth bag. Then, mimicking the leading star on the video, she lay on her back, closed her eyes, and parted her legs as far as she could, causing her vaginal lips to swallow and drench her panties. Then she began to erotically fondle herself, to knock the nervous edge off.

"We decided to give you a special treat, if that's okay with you," Evelyn told him.

"But you have to watch first," Crissy stated.

Then Evelyn pulled out his penis, squeezed it firmly, and kissed the tip. "Just watch, boo. It's your lucky night."

*****

"**Yo**, I'm telling you, that shit had me fucked up in the head. You hear me?"

"Man, stop interrupting the fucking story if you gonna tell it!" Purnell demanded.

"Ah-ight, ah-ight, my fault," Deshonne apologized.

*****

Crissy raised her legs high, in a V-shape, and moved her black thong to the side so that Evelyn would have easy access, with whatever instrument she chose to insert.

I can't believe this shit is happening! Deshonne thought as he watched two of the most beautiful women he'd ever known go at it, up close and personal.

"Mmm!" Crissy moaned as Evelyn rammed her tight pussy with a three-finger-thick cylinder. "Do me like I do you!" Crissy cried out.

Watching Crissy caress her own titties while Evelyn lubricated the dildo with her forbidden juices had Deshonne going crazy inside.

*****

"**Yo** Pee-Wee, I'm telling you, I couldn't take that shit no more. Between the noises Crissy was making, Eve's pussy lips curving around that little-ass thong right in front of me, and the DVD, I was about to skeet on myself if I didn't take matters into my own hands, you feel me?"

*****

Deshonne got up, dick swinging, and positioned himself directly behind Evelyn. Feeling his presence, she glanced over her shoulder just as he was slipping two fingers deep inside her wet pussy, sending chills throughout her body instantly.

"Ssss," Evelyn exhaled and stopped.

Crissy could sense the change in her partner's actions, so she looked up to see Evelyn wiggling out of her panties for Deshonne. Crissy grabbed Deshonne by his dick just as the head was piercing Evelyn's pussy lips.

"Not yet," Crissy told him, holding on to his throbbing penis…

*****

Deshonne and Purnell both laughed as they walked along the side of the Bowlerama, a bowling alley along New Castle Avenue.

"I would've smacked the shit out of that bitch, fam. You hear me?" Purnell said.

"Man, I'm telling you, I was hot because that bitch had a strong, manly ass grip on my shit. I'm like, what the fuck's up! But I still let her guide me back to the couch by my joint..."

*****

Crissy's legs locked around Evelyn's hands as she quietly quivered in satisfaction. When the orgasm subsided, so did her hold on Deshonne.

"Now it's your turn," Crissy said pleasingly.

"Do you wanna do him first?" Evelyn asked Crissy playfully, licking the length of the soiled dildo.

"Yeah. Let me show him why you love me," Crissy confessed proudly.

It's on! Deshonne screamed inside. *Please don't cum too fast*, he prayed as Evelyn climbed onto the couch and began to kiss him passionately.

Crissy opened the bag of goodies and pulled out a bottle of strawberry syrup. Squirting the sticky substance all over his dick to sweeten the taste...

*****

"That stuff felt so good as she rubbed it in, I almost nutted in her hand," Deshonne confessed.

"Man, if you don't stop fucking up the story!" Purnell complained.

"Who you wolfing at like that?"

"Nobody, clown. Just finish."

"Oh, that's what I thought," Deshonne said tauntingly before going back to the story....

*****

110

Evelyn held up Deshonne's dick as she kissed him, for Crissy to take in. Crissy just closed her eyes and made a slow descent. Her soft, sensuous, Angelina Jolie lips swept down his dick.

"Damn," he moaned as Evelyn pushed Crissy's head down to his balls. She sucked so masterfully that her jaws revealed never-before-seen dimples....

*****

"**Word**, she swallowed! Tell me that bitch swallowed," Purnell prompted anxiously.

"See. Now you interrupting the story, you lame. Just listen...."

*****

"**I'm** about to cum," Deshonne whispered, in between smothered kisses.

"Go ahead. She wants to experience everything for the first time tonight," Evelyn informed him.

And just like that, Deshonne's precum began to wet Crissy's
mouth, causing her to ease back and release her grasp.

You're not cumming in my mouth. I don't know what she's talking about. I'm done, Crissy thought.

But Evelyn held her girlfriend's head in place until he emptied himself inside her mouth. She gagged at first, but Evelyn made sure that she got every creamy drop.

Upset, Crissy got up with her mouthful of nut, sat on Evelyn's lap, and French kissed her, transferring the fluids.

Deshonne happily watched as they kissed, knowing that his cum was going from one sexy mouth to another...

*****

"**Crissy** was acting kind of funny with eve after that. So she takes me into the bedroom and we start play wrestling with each other. Just having fun, like always," he explained.

"Yo, you the nigga! I gotta give you points for that one," Purnell congratulated.

"I'm still not done, though."

*****

"**Mmm**, mmm!" Evelyn moaned loudly as he fucked her missionary-style on the bed. "I missed this dick," She confessed.

"How much?" he asked also attempting to make love to her mind.

"A—a lot," she stuttered.

Crissy stood in the doorway, upset by the pleasure that Deshonne was providing her soulmate. She ventured into the living room, vowing to outdo him as she retrieved her bag of tricks. Crissy sashayed into the room. "Can I join in on this game too?" she asked. "Eve, remember this?" she asked, presenting a double-headed dildo.

"Come on, ma," Evelyn said, inviting her girl into the bed with them.

"Move over, baby," Crissy said with a little arm nudge.Bending over the bed with her favorite toy, Crissy tried to disguise the vengeful look in her eyes.

Still on her back, Evelyn braced herself for the pain Crissy was known to inflict on her pussy. Deshonne lifted one of Crissy's titties to his lips and began to tease her nipple while Evelyn continued to play with his dick. "Oww!" she whined as Crissy stuck the dildo in, fast and hard.

"Fuck my girl, boo!" Evelyn cried out to Deshonne.

Not giving Crissy a chance to decline the gracious offer, Deshonne swiftly pulled her thong down. She stepped out of them without objecting and spread her legs as wide as she could, hoping that it would ease what pain was sure to come.

"Go slow," Crissy demanded just as the tip of his dick began to slide inside of her virgin pussy. She buckled onto the bed moments later, clenching the sheets as he showed her no mercy, destroying her pussy and her pride from the back. Drawing blood from her bottom lip as she bit down hard to contain her own screams, Crissy's eyes rolled around in her head as she became dizzy. "Mmm, yes, harder, Magic!" Crissy pleaded just as her pussy erupted like a broken water main....

*****

"**Pee-Wee**, I'm telling you. They both bent in positions I never dreamt possible last night. Every time my man squirted, one of them licked him off real good. And then they licked him back to attention, so I could take turns fucking them both until I came again. I was in heaven last night, you hear me?"

They both shook on his accomplishment as they crossed the last street to the barbershop. Avonbeula's is the hangout for go-getters in New Castle. Everyone passes through the multi-barber shop/ beauty salon/ and mini-store for one reason or another. Whether it was the occasional strippers night, crap games, or Play Station II tournaments after hours, the spot stayed jumping, and drug dealers flocked.

"I'm not going inside," Purnell said as soon as he noticed that Kenny's car was parked in the farthest space.

"Why not? I thought you said that you wanted to be in on the meeting," Deshonne questioned.

"Yeah, well, I changed my mind, ah-ight. I'ma just walk over to the Star Center to see if any touters are out that we know will redirect that traffic our way."

Deshonne noticed Kenny's car and realized why Purnell changed his mind. "Yo, Kenny ain't gonna do nothing to you in front of me. You're my peoples, just like he is. I ain't gonna let nothing go down," Deshonne reasoned.

"Man, I ain't worried about Kenny. It just ain't cool to be smiling in a nigga's face when you owe him change, that's all."

"Ah-ight. I'll call your cell phone from the pay phone when I'm done then," Deshonne said while reaching for the side door.

"No middleman means cheaper prices, Magic. So don't let them talk you into getting them for $900 again."

They didn't charge me $900 a ounce the first time. But as long as it's drop, I'll live with a little price hike, Deshonne thought as he walked in.

*****

Three of the four chairs were occupied with clients, as well as the single shampoo chair off in the corner. Music was playing low in the background, but all eyes were focused on the new 50 Cent documentary DVD, which was playing on the 60inch Zenith wide screen at the front of the barber shop when Deshonne walked in.

Deshonne stepped into the snug room, surveying every face. Except for a handful, he either knew the individuals in the room well enough to eat at their home, or he had at least met them before this day.

Kenny came out of the bathroom wiping his hands, with his ear to his shoulder, holding his cell phone in position. He quickly greeted his friend. "You're late," Kenny whispered into Deshonne's ear as he hugged him.

"My fault. I had to walk over here," Deshonne explained.

Kenny led Deshonne over to the first chair, directly in front of the storefront's window, where Smallwood was getting a line. "Wood, this is my cousin, Magic," Kenny said, making their introduction official.

Deshonne casually looked over the stranger. He was nothing like Deshonne had pictured the kingpin to be. As he stood up to show Deshonne the same respect that Kenny displayed, Deshonne sized him up with a firm shake and hug.

"What's up, Magic! I've heard nothing but good things about you since you've been home," Smallwood said.

"Word. Well I try my best to live up to my own expectations these days, feel me?"

"I heard that," Smallwood agreed. He then turned to pay the barber $20 for trimming the split ends off of his braids and the shape-up.

Kenny sat down while the two of them walked out front to talk in private.

114

"So, how did your clientele like the product?" Smallwood asked. "You didn't have any problems offing the work, did you?"

Deshonne reached into his pocket and handed over the money order envelope. "Nah, none. As a matter of fact, the only problem I had was turning down fiends money after I ran out."

Curious as to why an envelope containing a $3,150 payoff looked so thin, Smallwood calmly sat down on the curb between two cars and opened the envelope for a quick peep. *Money orders, hmm. I like this dude already,* he said to himself. "So, where do you want to go from here, Magic?"

"Wherever," Deshonne confidently replied. "Whatever you hit me with, I can dump."

"How much change did you bring with you?" Smallwood asked, even though he knew ahead of time what type of deal they were supposed to be making.

"I was under the impression that you and Kenny had already talked about my situation, so I didn't bring any money with me, fam. I'm sorry," Deshonne explained with a dumb look. "But I do got a little change at the spot to go towards whatever you decide to hit me with."

Smallwood then looked at Deshonne, wondering to himself, *Will I have to hunt this joker down for my change?* "Normally I don't front work to outsiders. But you did come correct with the work. Plus, you my man's relative, so I gotta give you a shot, right?" Smallwood explained.

"Word. I'm ready for whatever," Deshonne guaranteed as he rubbed his hands together.

"Okay. But there is one condition, though."

Here we go with the bullshit-ass price hike. Deshonne thought. *I'ma beat this clown if he gets outrageous with his numbers.* "What's that?" Deshonne reluctantly asked.

"Instead of $700 a onion, I have to charge you $750 this time because it's on consignment."

Deshonne didn't hesitate to think about the terms before agreeing because he already had his mind made up that, either way, he was leaving with the work in his hands.

115

Smallwood reached into his own pocket and pulled out a single key. He dangled it in front of Deshonne's face until he agreed. "You sure?"

"Yeah. I'm in, cuz," Deshonne agreed.

Then Smallwood dropped the BMW 745li key into Deshonne's awaiting hand and gave instructions. "Down the street and to the left. It's a black quarter-to-eight sitting at the dead end," he stated, pointing directly behind the barber shop at Rose Hill, one of the smaller New Castle developments. "It's nine soft onions duct taped together inside my glove box for you, Magic. Can you handle that in seven days?" he asked as he stepped back into the doorway.

"No problem," Deshonne assured him, but inside, he said to himself, *I hope I can.*

"That's all it is, then. Go ahead and grab that joint out of my car and bring my key back. And I'll see you in a week," he agreed, sealing the deal with a handshake.

It's on now! Deshonne thought.

Halfway down the block Smallwood yelled, "Yo, Magic! It's a bookbag in the trunk! Grab that, too!"

"Ah-ight, I'll get it!" Deshonne turned to yell back, and at that moment he noticed that art, Trigg's brother, was standing next to Smallwood, staring at him sneakily.

*****

Deshonne didn't realize it until the return trip to his house, but the noon sun was scorching for the first day of June. Beads of sweat blotted their t-shirts with each step.

"Are we gonna walk back in silence, or are you gonna tell me what happened?" Purnell questioned.

"I was just thinking about what Kasi mentioned as we were leaving."

"You act like I was in there with you. I can't read your damn mind, Magic. What did he say?"

"He said that the motels be jumping. And that there's some New York boys eatting," Deshonne stated, almost amazed.

"Aw, I could've told you that if you asked me. That's where Kasi and Tranz be pumping at late night. Trick City."

"Yo, we definitely have to look into that gold mine this week. You hear me?" Deshonne suggested.

"Ah-ight, that's all it is," Purnell agreed.

As soon as they came out of the old path, behind Dunleith Church, Purnell tapped the bottom of the bookbag Deshonne was carrying. "What's up with this? What we working with?" Purnell asked. "I know we got to be holding because that nigga gave you a bookbag to carry the shit with."

Deshonne looked around before stopping on the corner of Anderson Drive to partially enlighten his inquisitive partner. "He gave us six days to dump nine ounces, at $850 apiece," Deshonne stated, with a day shaved off for a cushion and the figures slightly elevated for his personal profits.

One of Deshonne's main rules was, never reveal your whole hand to friend or foe.

"That's what's up. We'll definitely be sitting on some funds after we bag everything up this time around, feel me?"

"I hear you, Pee-Wee, but I think the only way we're gonna pull this off and make the deadline is if we got at least two workers on our team going hard with us," Deshonne observed.

"Don't worry about that. I'll call my cousins after we get situated. They always come through for me. We'll have Jessup jumping 24/7 like Riverside's late-night shift, watch!" Purnell proclaimed.

They started to pick up their pace again.

"He put two hammers in the bookbag for us, too. So it's no way that we go backwards again. You hear me?"

And with a nod and a handshake, they continued their journey.

CHAPTER 17

Trying to get speedy, satisfactory service in any restaurant on route 202 during the lunch hour was like being stuck on the New Jersey turnpike during rush hour. And T.G.I. Friday's was no exception, but it was Desiree's favorite spot, so they made time to stop in at least twice a week for the cheapest thing on the menu: appetizers.

Like always, people were standing around, procrastinating, impatiently waiting for a table as Desiree and her usual company made their way to the far corner of the bar with their order already in mind.

Iyanna looked for familiar faces as they waited for their chicken fingers and fries, but none registered. "So when you gonna talk about it?" Iyanna asked as soon as the waitress placed their meals down.

"Talk about what, Yanni?"

"Talk about why Mr. Married Man has been buying us lunch for the past week. Why you're back to driving yourself to work every day. And what happened to your boy, Magic," Iyanna stated all in one breath.

Desiree pulled out the Platinum Visa Card that Alex gave her earlier and slowly waved it in the air as she spoke. "Alex offers to pay for our lunches, so I accepted. And as far as the other two questions are concerned, there's a first time for everything is all I can say."

The waitress returned with the leather binder containing the check and placed it on the edge of the table. Desiree placed the card inside and went back to picking over her meal.

Iyanna was a signifier who couldn't help herself, so she fed her addiction by jumping at the opportunity to pick her

118

friend's brain for juicy problems. "Don't tell me Magic got locked up again already?"

"Not that I know of, thank God."

"Girl, he didn't burn you or get you pregnant, did he?" Iyanna asked in a hostile but concerned manner.

Desiree noticed how animated Iyanna had become with the questions she was asking and had to laugh. "No, Yanni, the man didn't do any of those things to me. But, to be honest, I don't know who did what to who."

Iyanna's imagination began to roam, and then the obvious answer kicked in. "Oh, my, God! No, you ain't," Iyanna blurted out as she slid around the table, almost in Desiree's lap. "Bitch! You pregnant by him, ain't you?"

The accusation threw Desiree completely off guard. She dropped her fork onto an empty plate and felt strangers eyes glaring at her. Every word made the mood even more awkward, so she attempted to tone down the volume to avoid any further embarrassment. "No. I'm not pregnant, by anybody. So please stop saying that before you jinx me," she whispered from behind closed hands.

"Well, why don't you just tell me what's wrong because I'm tired of guessing."

"I will, as soon as you stop causing a scene." *Where is the waitress?* Desiree wondered.

Seconds later the waitress reappeared, so she quickly paid the bill and got up from the table without saying another word until they were in the car.

"Me and Magic got into a petty argument last week," Desiree confessed.

"Well, whose fault was it?" Iyanna asked.

"I don't know."

"Well, what happened?"

"Nothing really. He asked me to take him somewhere. I took him, and he took too long to come back out. And I blew the whole situation out of proportion. So I guess I'm to blame, if you want to get technical."

119

"Well, if you think it's your fault, why don't you call him up and apologize?" Iyanna suggested as she locked her seatbelt into place.

"I tried. But it didn't quite go like I planned," Desiree stated as if there was more to the story.

"Why not?"

"Because he had the nerve to ride past me in another bitch's car when I was on my way to his house to apologize."

"Girl, no, he didn't! You lying!" Iyanna yelled out in surprise.

As soon as Iyanna got ahead of the traffic, Desiree reached into the back seat and grabbed her dusty work shirt so she could change back.

"Did he see you pass him? Who was he with?"

"No. he was too busy leaning forward from the back seat, cheesing at that chicken to notice me," Desiree replied.

Iyanna twisted up her face in disgust and instantly became violent. "See, you better than me, girl. Because I would've ran his ass off the road and kept it moving." She swerved the car to show that she meant business.

Desiree giggled as she pulled off her polo shirt, exposing her snug-fitting wifebeater, which allowed her breasts to overflow momentarily before the swift change. "My car's not paid off, yet, so I can't afford to be denting her up for a man that ain't even mines."

"Fuck that! I would've at least followed them so that I could've found out where the bitch lived at," Iyanna said with a mischievous roll of the eyes.

"Magic's not my man, Yanni. We're friends, remember? He's free to do whatever he pleases, with whoever he pleases. And so am I," Desiree pointed out with a pat on her new Coach bag. That's exactly why I'm not turning down any more gifts or invitations from Alex. And I don't care who he's married too."

"So let me get this straight. You're giving up on the love of your life just because he rode past you in another bitch car. And now it's anything goes with the rich, married guy, despite your morals."

"Yep, that about sums it up," Desiree agreed proudly. "Oh, and I got Alex on a new sex diet this time around, too."

"Really?" Iyanna stated with a curious smile.

"Yes, girl. I haven't even let him tap the prize since he's started coming back over."

"Well, how do you keep the cash register rolling and his hormones tamed?"

"Easy. I sit on his face for at least an hour a visit. And that keeps us both happy," Desiree said with a laugh.

They gave each other a high-five as Desiree demonstrated her sexual movements on the seat. "Aroma therapy," they both said together, which was their personal saying.

A few traffic lights later Desiree was talking serious again."I'm tired of falling weak to my emotions just to turn around and be played like a fiddle, Yanni. If he wants to be a player this time around, then so be it."

"At least with Alex you won't want for nothing girl, because that man is rolling in money, foreal. And he don't got no problem sharing it with you."

"I know that's right? I'm not a bad-looking woman. And I didn't asked him for nothing he couldn't provide freely. Plus, I'm as sincere as they come. He should've been more than content with what I had to offer."

"Not to mention your fuck game is serious!" Iyanna shouted out jokingly to boost her friend's credentials.

"I know, right? He got it twisted, foreal," Desiree agreed.

They went back to staring out of the window in silence. Deep down she hoped that their relationship wouldn't end like this. After all, he was her only love.

*****

After years of hard work on Deshonne's parent's behalf, they had achieved every minority family's dream, which was to own a home. They not only got a home at a young age, they got a home with a basement and a yard. It was hard at first, but little by little they furnished their home, room by room. So it was only right that Mom Robinson would take extra special care of her home, cleaning every free chance she got.

Most of the time Deshonne chose to stay in the basement because it had all the commodities of the living room and bedrooms upstairs, with new furnishings, a 36-inch television, a wall-to-ceiling entertainment center, fully equipped with a pioneer stereo system, and a homemade bar for his pleasure, which he never used.

Deshonne lay on one of the couches while his mother vacuumed upstairs, talking on the phone, when his mother cut in from an upstairs line. She sat breathless for a minute, trying to see whom he was talking to.

"What's up, Mom? You know you can't be sneaky," he said, hoping that she would reveal herself without him getting up. "I know you on this phone, listening to my conversation, Mom. What do you want?"

"Deshonne, come up here for a minute, please?" she finally asked.

"Hey, Mom!" Purnell said.

She ignored his greetings. "Deshonne, now," she demanded.

"Mom, you ain't hear Pee-Wee just speak to you? He said hi."

"Deshonne, I want you to get your narrow ass up these steps, right now," she stated in the most cynical tone she could muster.

"What's wrong with you?"

"Come and see," she said, and then hung up.

"Yo, Mommy seems mad at you cuz-o. You better go and see what she wants before she snaps," Purnell teased.

Deshonne quietly asked himself, *What could have her so riled up?* Then the obvious hit him so hard, his heart dropped to his feet with fear. "Oh, shit!" he said.

"What? What's wrong with you?" Purnell asked.

"Yo, Pee-Wee, I need you to come over here as soon as possible."

"For what? I ain't trying to have mom dukes riffing at me, too. I ain't do nothing."

"Yo, I think she just found the dirty dishes I left in the bedroom," Deshonne said in code. "I need you to come and run interference for me."

Purnell dropped his head onto the back of his couch in disbelief. "What the fuck, Magic! Why you just ain't eat all the food as soon as you cooked it? You know she hates dirty dishes. Especially lying around her house."

Deshonne didn't have time to be lectured on his most recent slip up, he had to think fast. So, using his free ear, he listened for his mother's footsteps. The phone line picked back up.

"Don't be down there whispering, nigga. And don't make me wait for you either, because you know what I want," she told him. "Now come and get this shit before I flush it down the toilet."

"Mom, I'm coming right now. Please, just hang up the phone," he pleaded.

"Boy, you better be in front of me by the time I get finished reaching under this bed. Because if you not, I'ma flush you down after that damn plate," she promised. Then she sat the phone down for a second, put the plate on his dresser, and sat on the side of the bed to tie her Reeboks. "You know what? You ain't gotta come up here," she said. "Pee-Wee, I'm about to put his sorry ass out on the street. So come and help him get his shit out of my house, please, before I call the Salvation Army."

Deshonne and Purnell were both afraid to speak up, so they tried to wait until she hung up the phone.

"I'll be damned. In my motherfucking house that I busted my ass to pay for," she said to no one in particular before hanging up.

"Pee-Wee. Yo, Pee-Wee!" Deshonne whispered.

"What, man? See what you got me into?" Purnell snapped.

"Man, just hurry up and get here," Deshonne said. And then went to plead for his mother's forgiveness.

*****

Mom Robinson watched Purnell pull up to the house from the living room window. Deshonne was already on the porch, waiting on him to come, hoping that she would cool off before he had arrived because his plea for forgiveness had been in vain. Or so he thought.

"So, I see all the criminals have come together to help you move your stuff," Mom Robinson stated, coming out of the house to load up her things for work.

Thinking that this was his last shot at making a plea for forgiveness, Deshonne quickly begged for a minute to explain. "Mom, would you please come back into the house, so I can talk to you for a minute?"

"Nope. For what?"

Deshonne gave Purnell and Tonya a look that directed them to disappear. They walked back to the car, where they stood on standby in case they had to help him move his things.

"What do you want, boy? I gotta get ready to leave for work in a minute," she barked.

"Mom, you really gonna put me out on the street? I told you that that stuff was from the last time I was home. I found it the other day in the attic, and I was trying to get rid of it, but you found it first."

She knew that he was lying his ass off, but she never really had any intention of putting her son out on the street. She just wanted to make him sweat for a minute, to think about what he was doing. Pointing up the street, she said, "Take that shit somewhere else, Deshonne. You hear me? Because if I find that shit in my house again, we won't have nothing else to talk about." She then walked to her car in the driveway.

Deshonne took that speech as a second chance and swiftly waved his friends back over with his things. "Have a nice day at work, Mom."

She looked back. "Don't rush me boy. I don't have to be to work until two o'clock." And then she came back onto the porch and stood next to them. "And you never know when I might come back home either," she said slyly.

"Mom, can I talk to my friends for a minute?"

"If you don't want me to listen to what you're saying, then take your slick ass up the street somewhere. I pay the bills around here, nigga."

"Come on y'all. We gonna leave Mrs. Evil here to be grouchy by herself," Deshonne said and stepped off of the porch.

His friends looked at him as if to say, don't put us in the middle of this. She's mad at you, not us.

"You ain't gone yet?" she sarcastically asked.

They all walked over and got into the car. She followed them, keeping her eyes on Deshonne's paper bag to make sure that it didn't make its way back into her home.

"Whose car is this you're driving without a license, Purnell?"

"Pull off, pull off," Deshonne whispered.

Tonya looked over at Purnell as if to say, You better not!

"It's mines, Mrs. Robinson," Tonya said.

Mom Robinson leaned over into the car. "You ain't trying to get your car taken, are you?"

"No, ma'am."

"Well, if I was you, I would make these two crooked-ass niggas walk that bag around the corner. It's full of nothing but trouble."

"Bye, mom. Pull off, Pee-Wee," Deshonne repeated loud enough for his mother to hear this time.

"You better not," Mom Robinson challenged.

Purnell cut the car's engine off.

Damn, Deshonne thought.

"Get out of that girl's car and walk, Deshonne. Don't use her like that. I raised you better."

Deshonne opened the car door and stuck one leg out. "If I'm walking, you're walking too, Pee-Wee. So get out," Deshonne instructed.

"She can stay here with me until y'all get back," his mother suggested.

Purnell kissed Tonya, then started walking towards the corner with Deshonne, headed for Arbor Place, the next development over.

"Deshonne!" his mother called out as he reached the corner.

Deshonne stopped to see what his mother wanted.

"I can sense when something's wrong in my house. So don't think about bringing that stuff back while I'm gone," she warned. "You hear me?"

He just waved her off and continued walking.

CHAPTER 18

Deshonne made arrangements with his probation officer to meet every Tuesday morning at 7:30. Since the office unofficially opened at seven and Deshonne was normally on the corner, anyway, he made sure that he was on time. To throw his probation officer off and make him seem like a law-abiding citizen, Deshonne came to the visit dressed in his navy-blue work shirt and some old jeans even though he didn't go to work until five in the afternoon.

"How are you doing this morning, Mr. Howard?" Deshonne always asked as his opening icebreaker.

"I don't know, yet. The day hasn't really started for me yet, Mr. Robinson. My day depends on how many people I have to violate."

That shut down Deshonne's common courtesy.

While waiting for his Dell computer to boot up, Howard came from behind his desk to lock the door. It was a habit of his, as well as a scare tactic.

Deshonne could somehow feel Howard's eyes slowly scanning him from behind. He wanted to look back just to confirm his suspicious feeling, but fear of guilt wouldn't let him. Howard took his time sitting back down. Just as he was about to, he leaned over and snatched Deshonne's left arm.

Shit! Deshonne said to himself as soon as he realized what was going on.

"Are those diamonds authentic?" Howard asked, twisting and turning his arm as if he was examining a deadly rash. Kenny's diamond-encrusted, platinum Jacob & Co. watch was flooded with yellow diamonds.

Deshonne knew his probation officer was far from a fool, but he lied, anyway. "No, sir. I bought this watch at the Farmer's Market over the weekend."

"It looks real nice for an imitation, Mr. Robinson. I might have to stop over there on Friday and get me one," Howard said sarcastically.

"I bought it from one of them merchants outside, so you might have to look around until you find his booth. It was a old Amish dude with a beat-down pick up."

"I'll be sure and remember that description. But until I do find that booth, I would appreciate it if the next time you came in here, you didn't come with that watch on. Because it doesn't look like a janitor's watch. You're a convicted drug dealer, Mr. Robinson. That watch makes me wonder whether or not you've been completely reformed."

"Don't worry, sir. I'll make sure to leave it at home from now on," Deshonne passively agreed.

"Good. Now, have you had any police contact in the past week?"

You fucking fagot! he thought. "No, sir."

"Do you still live at the same address stated on this paper?" he asked with the paper turned in Deshonne's direction.

Deshonne looked at the paper as if he was really checking the location to verify it before answering. "Yes, sir."

"Are you still employed?"

What does my shirt say dumb ass? he thought as he pulled out his most recent paystub for verification. "Yes, sir."

After examining the pay periods, he returned the stub to his client. "Is there anything else you would like to tell me?" Howard asked as if he knew something more.

Yeah, I hate your fucking guts, you bitch! his conscience screamed. "No, sir, nothing that I can think of. Everything's the same."

Howard paused for a minute to look at Deshonne. As he stared at him, he wondered if the anonymous phone call on his answering machine, from a so-called concerned citizen, had any merit. But he decided to hand him the sign-in sheet anyway without tipping his hand, which meant the visit was over. "Make sure you have that $50 fine payment next Tuesday," he reminded Deshonne before he unlocked the door. "And call me if you run into any problems."

"Okay," Deshonne said, but in his mind he was saying, *Fuck you*!

Purnell was next. But he knew that his urine was still hot from the Dro session he and his little cousins had a week ago, so he kissed Tonya as if it was his last and then passed Deshonne slowly, with Tonya's microwaved urine in a condom taped to his inner thigh just in case, asking the only question that mattered. "Did he piss you?"

Deshonne smiled. "Nah, you cool."

*****

Zenda stomped into Marie and Kelia's room visibly upset and half naked. Her hard, flat breasts went from waving in the air to flapping against her belly with each step. Her white cotton panties were saturated with the semen of her latest sexual partners. She looked around for the person she wanted to address, but that person seemed to be long gone, so she decided to redirect her anger.

Kelia was awakened by Zenda's familiar after-sex stench.

Towering over the couch bed, Zenda asked, "Where did your mother go?"

Knowing that Zenda was looking for an argument, Kelia didn't acknowledge Zenda at first. She looked over at the clock to see what time it was. Then picked up the book next to her that she had been reading before she dozed off. It was "A Thirst After Dark" by the best-selling author, Antjuan Sierra.

"I don't know," Kelia uttered indirectly, with her face in the book. She told me that she was leaving early in the morning to get our cousin's car, so we could go shopping for my summer clothes. So that's probably where she is now."

"Did she take y'alls phone with her?"

Kelia looked over at the phone's charger. "Nope. It's right there."

"Well, did she at least leave you the $50 that she borrowed from me on check day?" Zenda asked.

That question got Kelia's attention out of the fantasy novel. She nonchalantly raised her head, feeling queasy as soon as she focused in on Zenda's degrading attire. *This bitch is trif*! Kelia thought.

"Zenda, don't take this the wrong way because I'm not trying to be smart. But you asking the wrong person questions. My mom doesn't tell me anything. And to be honest, I don't think she has your money. Because if she did, we wouldn't have to go shopping."

Zenda put one hand on her hip and the other on the doorknob. "Well, is y'all taking my kids with y'all? Because I need a break from them two little motherfuckers."

"I don't think so because my mom called for baby Wali last night."

That statement triggered Zenda's short fuse. She pushed the plywood door back as hard as she could into the wall, indenting the brass knob, and began ranting. "Y'all gotta go! All y'all do is run in and out of my house, eating up my kids shit, and make shit harder on me."

I don't know what you talking about because we always look out for you and them kids, you slutty-ass whore! Kelia said to herself.

"Zenda, what you telling me for? I don't really want to be here, no way!" Kelia snapped back. Kelia threw the paperback book down onto the floor, and sprang up in Zenda's face to let her know that she wasn't afraid of her. "I'd rather be down my grandparents' house, anyway," she told her.

"I'm tired of this shit!" Zenda yelled, waving her hands in the air wildly as she backed up a bit. "I'm telling you, just like I'ma tell her cute ass when she comes back here. She can take you and these stolen-ass clothes to wherever she's been laid up at because I ain't no fucking babysitter. And my house ain't no damn storage box, either."

Too riled up to realize how much she feared this woman, Kelia wouldn't back down. She balled up her fists and stepped a little closer. "Don't say nothing else to me," she threatened through clenched teeth. "Tell my mother to her face when she comes back."

Zenda could see the fury in Kelia's eyes. So without saying another word, she backed out and slammed the door behind her.

Upset by the whole situation, Kelia burst into soft sobs as soon as the door closed. She swiped the radio, her mother's perfume, and all of their cosmetics off of the nearby stand.

Hearing the commotion, Zenda yelled from the other room, "If you throw something else, you can leave now!"

"I don't care!" Kelia yelled as she picked up the cell phone.

*****

Dressed in an oily, ripped t-shirt, cut-off jeans, and some raggedy canvass Converse sneakers, Shane sat outside on his steps, plotting over any man, woman, or child who could possibly provide him with his next free hit. He looked every bit the part of a low-down fiend to the normal eye.

Marie came rushing out of the house without saying a word. Her hip-hugging Calvin Klein jeans, pink blouse and prada sandals inspired infatuation, catching the attention of every male and a few straight women.

Shane's stalking turned away from bystanders to his beautiful cousin in a flash. Nasty thoughts had him looking at her as if she were a stranger. He lustfully gawked over her every step, in picture-perfect slow motion, admiring every inch of her curvaceous figure until she reached the corner. "What's wrong, cuz?" he asked as soon as she got halfway back to the house.

"I gotta find a ride back across town to my child because this bitch got it fucked up."

"Who?"

"That fat bitch, Zenda, that's who. Kelia just called me crying, Shane. She said that bitch is over there talking about some money that I owe her. But I don't owe that bitch shit! She got it fucked up. All the shit I do for that bitch and her bad-ass babies. I put food in the house when my stamps come. I steal clothes for this bitch and don't even charge her. And Kelia is always babysitting for free while she's out somewhere with her legs gapped in the air. This is bullshit!" she screamed, leaning on the wooden porch railing.

"Marie, you need to just calm down. You know Zenda ain't right upstairs," Shane said. "You said it yourself not even a week ago. That broad gets a S.S.I. check even though nothing's physically wrong with her. That's enough right there to tell you that the broad is bipolar."

"I hope she's still got all that mouth when I get there, so I can bust her right in her fucking face! Because I don't give a fuck!" Marie shrieked. "I'm sick of this bitch and her temper tantrums. And I hate living with that retarded smut. I can't wait until I get my own shit."

As soon as tears of anger overcame her, he saw his opportunity to benefit from the moment. So he stepped in close to comfort her with a gentle embrace. *Damn, cuz titties feel soft*. He pervertedly thought as he held her even tighter. "Do you want me to get you something to drink? I got a case of Steel Reserve in the fridge," Shane offered.

"No, thanks. With the way I feel right now, I'd probably be calling y'all from W.C.I. [Women's Correctional Institute] if she gets it twisted. You can let me go, though," she stated. *Because you stink*. She thought as she stepped back.

Out of the corner of his eye, Shane saw a city patrol car drifting down the street a block away. He slowly backed into the doorway for cover, reaching into his pockets for the beat-bags of drywall he had prepared for a quick sting on an unsuspecting white boy. "I gotta go, cuz. But your cousin," which was his oldest daughter, "should be home from work in a few minutes."

"Okay, I'll be here on the steps if my baby calls back." She started to say, "and don't lock me out, either," but he was upstairs before she could finish, watching the cops ride by.

*****

About 20 minutes later, Purnell, Tonya, and Deshonne came creeping down Shane's block trying to catch him off guard. Purnell spotted a female the moment he turned the corner, from a block away. So he decided to park halfway down the block in case she was worth hollering at.

Damn! Who's that? Purnell asked himself as he approached on foot.

He looked back twice to see if Tonya could see him clearly from the car. Realizing that she could, he manufactured a quick pick-up line to catch the female with. "Ooh, shit!" he mumbled just loud enough for Marie to hear once he realized just who she was.

Marie looked up just as his shadow eclipsed her.

"Hey, Marie!" Purnell said as friendly as possible. "Is your peoples home?"

She looked at him with a mixture of flirtation and confusion to throw him off because she already knew whom he was there for and why. So she prepared to lie for her family without hesitation even if he was in the wrong.

"It depends on who you came to see, because I think just my aunt's in there."

"I came for Shane. Do you know when he'll be back, so I can stop back?" he asked, not knowing that Shane was peeping out of the window at him.

"I couldn't tell you. He wasn't here when I got here. But I'll let him know that you stopped by."

Marie got up and wiped the dirt off of her butt, leaving Purnell speechless as he watched it shake like Jell-O.

"You—you know what?" he stuttered. "Just tell him that I stopped by and that I know that he's ducking me. So I'll catch up with him later."

You stupid for giving a crackhead a pack in the first place, she said to herself. "Pee-Wee, it's none of my business, but if he messed up something of yours, it's nobody's fault but your own for giving it to him because you already knew that he had a habit," she said on her cousins behalf.

Not accepting Marie's excuse, he changed the subject. "You know what? I got somebody in the car that's been asking about you for a minute now. Do you want me to go and get him real fast for you?"

"No, thank you," Marie said, as disinterested as possible. "I don't need any new friends right now. I'm trying to get rid of the old ones."

"Marie, ain't nothing new about Magic."

"Magic? Little Magic from out O.V.G.?" she replied. "I thought that he was locked up out of state somewhere."

"He was, but he's out now. He's been home for a minute. Shane ain't tell you that he was asking for you?"

"No, but you can tell him I said hi. And stay out of trouble."

"I will." *Damn! She's blazing!* Purnell thought as he made his way back to the car.

"I gotta tell Magic it's her. But if he don't go on her, then I'm dropping them off and coming back myself," he swore.

As soon as Deshonne heard whom the body he had admired from afar belonged to, he sprang out of the car into action. She watched him coming down the street, and thought about going inside, but changed her mind. Once he got close enough for her to notice his muscular frame, she was glad that she didn't.

"What's up, Marie? Long time, no see," Deshonne said as he sat down on the steps beside her.

"Yeah. Long time, no see, stranger!" she replied with a smile. Her smile revealed the prettiest white teeth, as she looked up and asked shyly, "how have you been?"

"I can't complain. And yourself?"

"Me either. Same shit, different day."

"I was asking your peoples about you not too long ago. Did he tell you?" Deshonne inquired.

"No, that sorry-ass man ain't tell me nothing. But I'm here now, so what's up?" she asked with an discomforting stare.

134

Deshonne wondered what she was looking so hard at. "Do I got a boogie on my face or something? Because you really looking at me like it's something wrong."

I don't remember you being this cute when you were younger, she thought. "No. I'm not used to you wearing glasses, that's all."

Deshonne took them off and looked at them oddly, as if they were missing something. "What's wrong? Are they ugly or something?"

"No. You just look different with them on. But in a good way, though."

"Oh, really? So if that's the case, why didn't you want me to come and holler at you? I thought that we were better than that."

"It wasn't that, Magic. We're still cool," she said, using her knees for support to get up. "I just wasn't trying to meet any new people today. I'm not in the mood. Plus, Pee-Wee didn't say who it was at first," she lied. "You know I'm always happy to see my people from back in the day."

Marie stepped to the side so that the cousin she had been waiting patiently for could go inside.

"He's cute," Marie's cousin said in passing, without acknowledging him personally.

Marie just smiled at the comment, but inside she said, *I know.* "I'll be up in a minute to talk to you, Quessa."

"Okay," Quessa said as she started up the steps.

"Like I was saying, Magic, if I knew it was you, I would've came over to speak."

"Really? Because I was kind of hoping that I was worth more than a simple hello," he said.

"I don't know about that. Are you?" she shot back.

"Hell yeah! I know I'm worth at least a deep conversation or two. All you gotta do is name a date and time that your schedule isn't filled, and I'll make magic happen," he stated, rising to his feet.

"I thought that we were talking now," she said.

Purnell blew the horn as he came through the stop sign, bringing their conversation to a halt.

"Damn!" Deshonne blurted out.

"I think that's for you," she said once she spotted Purnell driving.

"Yeah, unfortunately. I forgot that they were up the street waiting for me. I gotta go to work," he said, eyeing his watch.

Marie looked him over curiously. Deshonne seemed dressed too clean for work, in a crisp, white $5 t-shirt, some Roc-A-Wear jeans, and a new pair of white and red Bo Jacksons. But Kenny's platinum chain and Jacob watch told her something different. "You don't look like you're going to nobody's job to me."

Deshonne looked himself over. "Oh, my work clothes are in the car."

"Oh, okay," she said.

The horn blew impatiently.

Marie smiled and said, "Well, it was nice to see you again, Magic."

"You trying to get rid of me already? I must be bad company or something," he playfully suggested.

"No. But I know how it is when I go somewhere on somebody else's time."

Deshonne looked back at his ride with his hands up.

"Boy, you better come on if you want to make it to work on time!" Purnell hollered.

"Well, I guess I am kind of pressed for time. Sorry."

"It's okay. It was nice to see you again," Marie said.

"Can I come back and finish this conversation after I get off?" Deshonne hinted.

"I don't know. It depends on how late you come back because I don't live here."

"I get off at nine. Is that too late?"

"Tonight it is, sorry. I have to be somewhere in a little while."

Shit! Deshonne thought.

"It's quarter to five, Magic. This car can't fly," Purnell hollered, reminding Deshonne that he had to be to work at five.

Deshonne waved him off. "Well, can I call you and take you out later? Or maybe stop by your spot so that we can continue this? I promise I won't bore you," he said, as charming and persistent as he could without seeming desperate.

"Do you got a pen?" she asked.

Deshonne looked back and hollered, "pen?"

"Yeah, hurry up!" Purnell said.

He walked over to the car and came back. He knew that he was cutting it close when he stepped in close to hand her the pen and napkin, but he wanted to see if she smelled as good as she looked. She in turn stepped in even closer, her lips a foot from his, then wrote her number on the front of his t-shirt.

"I know you won't loose this," she said with a confident smile.

Deshonne looked down at his t-shirt. "I'll call you later."

"Okay, I'll be there," she agreed and then walked into the house.

"What did they say to you, cuz?" Shane asked as soon as she reached the threshold to the living room, where he was still staring out of the window.

"What's up with Lil-Magic?" she asked, ignoring his question.

"I owe him money. That's what's up with him. Why, what did he say?" Shane repeated.

"Why was Pee-Wee the one talking about the money instead of Magic?"

"I don't know why, because its Magic's money. At least that's the way it seemed to me because everytime he gave me a couple bags, he had to clear it with Magic first."

"So, Magic is doing ah-ight then, huh?"

"You damn right. He got that beige Blazer!"

In hearing that, the wheels in her head began to turn. "I can't wait until he does call me," she said on her way to the basement to see her aunt. As soon as she opened the door, a strong stench of burning crack cocaine filled her nostrils. She caught an instant contact. *Damn, Auntie, what is you doing down here?* She asked herself with each step.

CHAPTER 19

A little past midnight Deshonne came strolling out of Wawa dressed in all black, concealing a police-issue Glock 9mm and 100 dime bags of crack. He scanned the gas pumps for a potential ride to his next destination.

"My, my, my. Look who's out of the house past curfew," Angie said as she came from around the side of the building. Angie was dressed in her night clothing, a faded Playboy bunny t-shirt, a pair of sky-blue sweat pants that sagged low enough to reveal the color of her thong, and some yellow furry Tweety Bird slippers.

"What's up, Angie!" Deshonne sat the bag of goodies he had just purchased on top of one of the pay-phones and gave her a friendly hug. "Girl, am I happy to see you," he said as he hugged her.

Angie slid her hands from his back to his butt cheeks, and pulled him in as close as she could. "Really? Cause the feelings are mutual."

Her character was not only enticing, but also amusing, to him. He just wouldn't cross that line with her. So he stepped back with an uncomfortable look on his face that he was sure she would notice.

"I need a ride down to the motels, Angie. I'm supposed to be meeting Pee-Wee and some other cat at the 6, in about a half-hour."

"I'm sorry, Magic, but the only way I'm going near a motel tonight is if it leads to you putting me on my back," she boldly proposed. Standing there waiting on a response had her stomach turning.

She can't be serious. This has to be a test, he thought to himself. "What you need a couple dollars for, gas or something?" he asked, to avoid the last question. He then reached into his pocket and pulled out the remaining $11 he had from the $20 he brought out and handed it to her for compensation. "It's only down the street."

She handed his money back. "I already told you what type of time I'm on. You don't have to worry because I'm not a gossiper. But I am dead serious. So unless you are willing to show me what you're working with, I suggest that you start jogging or walking."

"Yo, that's crazy. Why you acting funny towards me?" Deshonne asked.

"I'm not acting funny I'm just not catering to men I'm not fucking no more, that's all. Because I'm tired of being used and abused, and that goes for your boy Pee-Wee, too, with his shriveled-up dick," she said, sticking out her pinky finger to imitate Purnell's penis size. "So as soon as you finish jogging to him and catch your breath, you can tell him to lose my number cause I'm done."

"Why you acting all weak for nothing? I thought that we were cool," he challenged.

She looked back first to see who was behind her and then beckoned him to follow her around the corner with her finger. The side parking lot was well lit around her car, but empty. So she went around to the driver's side of her car. "Come here," she said flirtatiously.

As soon as Deshonne was within five feet of her, she dropped her sweatpants and her thong down to her ankles. She grasped her ankles, looked back at him from between her legs, and said, "It's your choice, Magic." Angie held the picture-perfect back-shot pose long enough for every inch of her to be etched into his mind forever. Her breasts even fell out as her shirt covered her face. "I'm not only flexible boo, but I'm open to new things too," she informed him.

Angie's open pussy lips were bald and betrayed her inner pinkness.

Damn! This bitch pussy is phat! he thought. "You've got to be joking," Deshonne said as soon as he found his vocabulary.

Angie turned, stepped up close, and grabbed his dick.

"No, I'm dead serious."

He didn't stop her, he continued to let her hold and massage him because she had his hormones going.

She could feel him swelling underneath his jeans. "See, he likes me already, and I haven't even sucked him, yet," she said.

"It's not gonna happen, Angie. Pee-Wee's my peoples," he told her. But his body was saying, *You damn fool! You better let her suck me off. You know she swallows.*

After a second, she realized that he wasn't going to take her up on her offer, so she pulled up her pants and got back into her car. Feeling offended, she put her window down as soon as she started her car and voiced her opinion. "Fuck you, Magic."

"Look, it won't take you no longer than three minutes to drop me off. I just need a ride down Memorial Drive. That's all."

"Well, if you jog nonstop, you should reach your suckerass friend in about 15 minutes," she replied. "And don't forget to tell him what I just did and said. That way he'll know that I'm serious when you tell him that I'm done."

"Man, fuck you, you dirty-ass bitch!"

"That's all you had to do, and you could've been riding to the moon if you wanted to. You clown," she said as she backed up.

"Clown?" Deshonne repeated as he walked back to his bag. Then he quickly opened up the quart of orange juice he had brought and threw it at her car. Before she could react, the carton was already inside her car. It smashed on her dashboard, wetting everything, especially her.

She stopped the car and was about to get out. That's when Deshonne raised his hands as if to say, What? and that's when the butt of his gun flashed at her.

"Fucking faggot!" she yelled and then pulled off.

"Shit," he mumbled. "I should've just fucked that phat pussy bitch. I know the pussy is good. It's gotta be. Damn!" he cursed himself again for not laying pipe to her as he began to walk.

*****

As always, Kenny's Friday night party was overflowing with the city's hottest partygoers. Bone Crusher's Outside the Club was banging inside Club Utopia.

"*I ain't never scared...*" the crowd chanted in unison.

Kenny, the female magnet, was the life of the party. he had three beautiful women, dressed in different-colored Baby phat sweatsuits, posing for the camera while he held up two bottles of Grey Goose vodka, and all eyes were on him.

"Kenny, come here!" a female yelled as she made her way through the crowd.

Recognizing her as Kasi's wife, Lilly, he pointed his finger to the room behind the DJ's booth, the V.I.P. room and made his way to her.

"Heyyy! I'm glad you could make it to the party. What's up?" Kenny yelled over the music as he hugged her.

Lilly's physical features were average compared to a lot of the other women Kenny knew. So he had designated her to be his sister years back. And they developed a brother-sister bond.

"Have you seen your boy today at all?" Lilly asked.

"Nah, but I was hoping that he stopped through tonight so I could cuss his ass out for missing another meeting yesterday," Kenny informed her as they sat down in the corner love seat. "The distributors won't let me sign his name on any of the contracts. And his absences are making us look really irresponsible and unprofessional lately."

"Oh yeah, well, I hope that he gets it together for your sake because I know how much you have invested in him. But as far as I'm concerned, wherever he's been the last couple of nights, he can call that home from now on because I'm done. I've already packed up his stuff and sat it by the door," she said and stood up to leave.

"Hold up, Lilly, slow down. Why don't you start from the beginning and tell me what's wrong because I'm confused here. I don't understand how things got to this point so quickly. What happened?"

"Kenny, don't play stupid. You know what's going on. He's gone for two and three days at a time, and he has our bill money with him."

Aw, shit, that nigga really is back at it again, he thought as he listened to her. "Why did you let him leave with y'alls bill money?" Kenny asked, while beckoning a bartender to bring her a drink.

"Because we were short $500 and he said that he didn't want to ask you because you were already helping us enough. So he said that he would handle everything. And like a fool I believed him.

I'm scrapping now because of him. But he still could've borrowed $500. Kenny thought, not paying attention to the rest of her narration.

A female boldly came over to them while Lilly was still talking and handed him a napkin with her measurements and phone number on it. Kenny pocketed the number and caught the tail end of what Lilly was saying.

Lilly rolled her eyes at the slut that interrupted her conversation before continuing. "All we have financially is in his pockets, Kenny. And all of our bills are past due."

"If you don't mind me asking, how much are y'all behind?" he asked, expecting to hear thousands.

"Just everything for this month."

Okay. I can handle that if he did fuck everything up, Kenny calculated.

"Ah-ight, listen, Lilly. I'ma shoot down to the projects as soon as this party ends and see if I can find him. Don't worry about nothing because everything is gonna be okay."

"Are you sure?"

"Have I ever let you down before?" he asked with a confident smile. "You're at a party, so just relax and enjoy yourself, okay." Kenny took off his V.I.P. pass and hung it around her neck. "I'll call you later on. I promise," he said. And then he looked at the measurements on the napkin.

*****

A state of the art, wall-mounted, 36inch plasma was playing HBO's "Naked States" in surround sound throughout the living room of the expensive Delaware Avenue, Rockford Park home. The only movement were smoke rings being puffed into the air by a mysterious curly-haired Caucasian man known only as Big Al while he relaxed on the couch. His cell phone rang. As usual, he reached over to the coffee table to check the caller ID screen before answering. Annoyed by the caller's interruption, he answered the call from his employee with an attitude.

"Why are you calling me ahead of schedule?" he asked in a stern, low voice.

"Yo, son. The block is jumping tonight, but my crew ain't eating," the caller informed him.

The caller was a New York native, a drug dealer named simply the God. Like most out-of-towners who come to Delaware after hearing about the perfect gold mine, he thought he owned the block he set up shop on, which was infested with drugs.

Big Al killed the sound of the TV and turned up the lighting with the touch of a remote. He then stood up and walked over to the winding stairwell to check for eavesdroppers. "Who's taking food out of my mouth, tonight?" he asked in his usually cocky tone.

"It's them same two crumb snatchers that came through here last month."

"We only come out for big fish, God. You of all people should know better than to bother me with this. My time is money, and it's never to be wasted."

The God knew that he wouldn't have to get his hands dirty if he could persuade Big Al to come out, so he attempted to dramatize the situation by adding money as an incentive. "I know, son. And normally I wouldn't bother you, but they holding heavy. And they must got that fire, cause even our loyal smokers is passing us by."

"Where are they at now?" Big Al inquired.

"In the back of the Gulf gas station parking lot, cutting off all of the whore's trap money."

Not pleased, he decided to act. Big Al put out his cigar and looked at his watch. "This better be worth it."

"Yo, son, the longer them niggas stay outside, the longer it's gonna take me to pay you, bee," the God reasoned.

"Tell your crew to close down and take the rest of the night off. I'll take care of your problem."

"Okay, no problem."

"And boy, you better have my payment in full, in 48 hours," Big Al demanded, then he hung up.

"Yo, son! Yo!" the God hollered into the receiver, confused.

"Who the fuck does that white boy think he is?" the God asked himself as he hung up his throwaway cell phone. "Yo, Quan! Go and tell everyone to close up shop," the God ordered his right-hand man. Then went into the bathroom to recount their day's earnings.

*****

The #1 prostitution strip in Delaware is route 13. Up until three years ago, two motels, the Delawarr and the Red Rose Inn, were leading the state in soliciting, but have since been demolished to be turned into Wawa stations, scattering the working women and men throughout the city.

New Castle Avenue is the second-largest hoe strip in the suburbs, which earned the street names "Trick City" or "The Triangle." Not only are the Days Inn, Super Lodge, and Motel 6 homes to the night-life, located conveniently yards away from each other, but the Gulf station is located in between the three motels, with a little alley of bushes running behind it called "Pick-Up Strip." It's where the low-level dealers catch the whores before they can cop from the rooms.

On any given day you can buy anything, from heroin down at the north end of the avenue to the South Bridge projects, to pills, marijuana, or crack cocaine in between, along the avenue called Rose Gate, Oakmont, Dunleith, or Arbor Place. But by far the motels are the most lucrative spots on the avenue, because the freaks truly do come out at night. And what only women possess, all men need.

"Psst!" Kasi called out from the bushes to his runner as soon as he saw a potential customer.

"Yo! We got that drop over here!" Tranz called out.

A suspicious-looking white man came staggering out of the Super Lodge entrance, tilting a brown paper bag to his lips.

Kasi's touter dashed over to see if the man wanted to spend.

Tranz could hear the two men negotiating as they approached, so he darted over to his Chevy Malibu, parked in the nearby McDonald's parking lot. Looking around the lot for anything out of order before he went into the stash spot, Tranz asked himself, "Where did all the bitches go?"

"What you working with?" Kasi asked the dusty-looking man after he removed the bottle from his lips.

"An eight ball," he responded groggily.

"An eight ball? Why'd you just ask me for a forty then?" the touter asked.

Kasi gave the touter his shut up look without saying anything.

"Man, I better be getting more than one from this cracker, because I made this deal happen," the fiend demanded.

"What's taking Tranz so long?" the fiend asked.

"I don't know?" Kasi said, and then looked back over his shoulder to see for himself.

Pop! Pop! Pop! Gunshots rang out within seconds, destroying the overhead street lamps in the parking lot.

Deafened by the loud blasts, Kasi turned back around to see what had happened. That's when he saw that the shooter had him at gunpoint.

"That was your warning shot," the perpetrator announced as he shook off the paper bag that concealed his weapon. "Now lay down on the ground, or you'll never move again."

Kasi looked over in Tranz's direction for help, but three masked gunmen were manhandling him.

"Help! Help!" Tranz screamed after each punishing blow to the head.

Realizing that no help was coming, the touter began to plea for his life. "Please, don't shoot me!"

"Where's your stash at? this can't be everything!" one of the masked men asked Tranz after grabbing a zip lock bag containing $1,100 in cash and 131 dimes from the armrest.

Just as the man was about to smack Tranz with the butt of the gun again, a familiar sound came from a nearby bush. Clack-clack. a shell was being loaded into a shotgun.

"Wait. Did you hear that?" one of the men asked.

At that moment two of the three men called out to the man holding Kasi at gun-point and then turned towards the bushes.

"On three, run," Kasi whispered to the whimpering fiend beside him.

"I'll check it out, boss," one of them called out as they made their way over to the other men.

The lead man gave the go-ahead nod. Once the man got close enough to see through the shadows, sparks lit up the bushes, sending pellets everywhere. In all the confusion Kasi and his touter got up and started to run in opposite directions. And just as quickly as the gun battle started, it ended with bloodshed.

CHAPTER 20

Desiree came out of Club Utopia wiping the sweat off of her face with a hand towel that Kenny had just given her. She was exhausted from work, but still came out to dance in hopes of running into Deshonne at the party. But the party was ending, and there was no sign of him, so she decided to beat the party traffic and leave a couple of minutes early.

"Damn, Dee, you looking good as shit tonight," Art complimented her from across the street.

Desiree could smell every drink he had consumed as he opened his arms to hug her.

"I'm sorry that I didn't get a chance to dance with you tonight," he told her as he tried to pull her in close.

"It's okay, Art, but I think that you've had a little bit too much to drink," she said while prying his wandering hands away.

Art went from a meaningless hug to aggressive groping. "It's my nigga's party. I'm just trying to have a little fun," he said, still attempting to touch her cushion.

She finally grabbed both of his hands and then raised her voice to attract attention. "I'd appreciate it if you'd go somewhere else with your drunk self. You've grabbed my ass one too many times already."

"This is a party, Dee. Chill. We just having fun with each other."

"The party's over if you hadn't already noticed, you clown," Desiree said. She then intertwined her left leg with his and pushed his chest with all her might, causing art to drop like a rock.

The parting crowd stopped to spectate and laugh at the well-known man.

That's gonna hurt, Desiree said to herself as she backed up.

Still on his back, Art began to reach into his pockets in search of his keys. "Shit! Where's my keys at?"

"I don't know," Desiree answered. "But you might want to leave your truck and find a ride before you kill somebody, asshole."

"I'm going home with you, so I can help you take off those jeans," Art said as he stumbled back to his feet. He reached out and grabbed her arm before she could get out of range. "Dee, tell me, is there any more room for me in those jeans?" he sang to her.

Everyone, including Desiree, had to laugh at his imitation of Ginuwine's song.

"Boy, now I know you really smashed," she informed him as she snatched away her hand.

"No I'm not. I'm just trying to wake up in a strange place, with a familiar face. And I already know you with it, so you might as well stop fronting."

Desiree turned to walk away without responding. He swiftly smacked her soft ass so hard that his hand stung. "Come on, Dee, you've been rubbing that phat ass on niggas all night. So I know you ready to fuck."

Desiree got up in his face. "Look, I don't know who told you that you could touch me, but you better keep your motherfucking hands to yourself."

"Aw, bitch, I don't know who told you that you was top notch, but they lied."

Tired of talking, Desiree pulled out her key chain and snatched out the small safety pin on the can of mace. "Why don't you take your drunk ass somewhere, boy? I'm tired of playing with you."

Art got face to face with her and began to huff and puff as if he was hyping himself up to strike her.

Desiree held onto her only protection, ready to spray, hoping that someone would break up the argument before someone got hurt.

"They told me that you was a tease."

"No, I'm not. And whoever told you that can kiss my ass!" *Cutting her eyes both ways, she said to herself, Why ya'll just watching him? Somebody come and get this clown.*

"I don't know why you so hung up on that nigga Magic. He ain't about shit. He's a worker."

"Magic ain't my man," she said, once more setting the record straight. Please, just leave me alone because you fake."

Someone cool with Art finally came over and tried to pull him away from her. But Art wasn't finished disrespecting Desiree. "Fake?" he shot back. "Ain't nothing about me fake, bitch!" he said while waving his platinum necklace in the air by its diamond-clustered charm. "What's fake about me, huh, you dirty bitch?"

And before anybody knew what had happened, Desiree had slapped the spit out of art's mouth with a strong right hand. After finding his bearings Art tried to lunged forward, but his friend held him back. "Like I was saying, bitch, whatever you see in Magic we gave him because he works for us. So what's his is ours."

Art pulled the drawstring on his linen pants, and then whipped out his dick in front of everybody. "Ain't no need in sucking his dick for free when you can suck on this tree right here and get paid for it," he said with his dick in his hand…

*****

"**And** that's when I sprayed half a can of mace in your boy's face, Kenny. I was more than happy to watch him choke in front of everybody," Desiree told him as she finished her account of the night's events. "Gonna tell me to suck his dick," she repeated.

Kenny laughed on the other end of the phone as he envisioned art choking and gagging for water. "I'm sorry about what happened tonight, Dee. You know how niggas get when they can't hold their liquor."

150

"He was lucky that Magic didn't answer his phone when I called him."

"Well, it's over now, Dee, so don't worry about it. And you don't have to tell Magic, either, because I'ma handle it from here, okay?"

"I think you'd better tell Magic then because he be hanging with that faggot. And, drunk or not, I know he meant that shit he was saying."

Kenny quickly changed the subject. "Speaking of Magic, Dee, what happened to him last night, anyway?"

"I don't know. I'm not a part of his circle anymore. He has a new best friend now."

"Somebody sounds jealous," Kenny joked.

"You must got bad hearing because it ain't me."

"Okay," he said with a small chuckle. "Look, I gotta go Dee. So I'll talk to you later on, okay?

"Ah-ight," she agreed.

"Oh, and I should see Magic later on, so I'll make sure that he calls you, okay?"

"Kenny, I'm not gonna hold my breath. Bye," she said before she hung up.

*****

Kenny was coasting through the hottest neighborhood in the city after midnight, riverside projects, looking for Kasi, along Bower Street, at that very moment, giving head nods and waving to everyone that acknowledged him along the way. The riverside projects are the only remaining projects in the inner city of Wilmington. It looks like a virtual ghost town in the daytime and the Okay Corral at night. Even with 50 percent of the housing project boarded up, it still supplied thousands of dollars in heroin a day to dealers and addicts alike.

"Kasi," Kenny said into his cell phone, waiting for the line to connect.

In a panic-stricken voice Lilly answered the phone on the first ring. "Hello, Kasi?"

"Nah, Lilly, it's me, Kenny. Are you okay?"

"Have you found him, yet?" she asked as she stubbed out another half-smoked Newport.

"Nah, I'm in the projects right now, but I don't see him or his cousin out here pumping."

"Well, where could he be at, Kenny, because he hasn't even called home in the past 24 hours."

"I don't know, but I'm about to ride through Market to see if he's out there and then check a couple other spots." *I hope he's not in one of these base houses*, Kenny thought as he stopped at the light by the liquor store.

"If he don't call soon, I'ma call the police and all the hospitals, Kenny," she warned.

At that moment, his other cell phone began to vibrate in his pocket. As soon as he saw the name on the display his worries vanished. "You can calm down now, Lilly. I just found him."

"Where? Put him on the phone," she demanded.

"He's on my other phone. So let me answer it real quick. Hold on."

*****

Project Safe Streets is comprised of the state police and probation and parole, working together. They help each other watch over convicted felons. But in most cases they just become badgers to the felons and their innocent families.

The ringing doorbell awoke Mom Robinson at a little past one. She could see the flashing lights shining across her porch through the stained glass front door as soon as she reached the bottom of the steps.

Oh, GOD, let my baby be okay, she thought as she reached the door. "Who is it?" Mom Robinson asked from behind the door.

"Project Safe Streets, ma'am. Does Deshonne Robinson live here?"

"Yes."

"We need you to open your door, please."

"Open my door, for what?" she asked as she peeped out from the curtain.

Each probation officer had a bulletproof vest with Police painted across it in bright lettering. There were two probation officers on the porch, accompanied by one state trooper whom she could see. Flashlights moved around the back of the house, shining light into all the windows. She figured that they were guarding the back door, which made her nervous.

"Ma'am, Deshonne Robinson is on Level 3 probation, so we need a facial verification to verify that he's in the house for his 10-to-6 curfew, or else we'll have to violate him," he threatened.

She switched on the porch lamp to see if it was his personal officer speaking. Not recognizing any of the faces she said, "my son's upstairs, asleep, and I'm not waking him up this late because he has to be to work in the morning."

"Ma'am, we're allowed to conduct curfew checks at this hour," the officer informed her as he skimmed through the picture book.

"Well, I'm not on probation, and this is my house that you're disrespecting with this nonsense. I said that I'm not getting him up, so I'd appreciate it if y'all would get away from my door and get off of my porch."

"Ma'am, if he doesn't show his face, we have to assume that he isn't inside. He will be violated and sent back to prison."

"Put your warrant up against the window so I can see it, and I'll go and wake him up," she advised him, knowing that he couldn't produce one.

"Ma'am, we don't need a warrant."

"Well, I don't need to open up my door or wake up my son. So get off of my porch and outta my yard."

Frustrated by her lack of cooperation, they did the only thing they could do.

"Ma'am, since you're unwilling to cooperate, tell Mr. Robinson to report to his assigned officer in the morning," he informed her, meaning that Deshonne had violated.

"Don't you worry. He'll be there, bright and early, and so will my lawyer. Now get off of my porch and close my fence!" she ordered.

Before they could turn to walk away, she cut the porch light off and retreated to her cozy bedding, upset, jittery and scared for her son.

Dirty Living

CHAPTER 21

Tranz sobbed uncontrollably as the masked robber applied stern pressure to the back of his neck with the sole of his rubber cleat. Both Kasi and the touter had been shot during the exchange of gunplay, along with one of the robbers. As he quietly prayed for his own life to be spared, he could hear the dying gunman twisted up beside him gurgling his own blood.

"Stay down. You hear me?" the lead man ordered. "Count down from 100 loud enough for me to hear you," the robber said while tapping the barrel of his 40-caliber against his lacerated scalp.

"Please don't kill me," Tranz begged.

His captor, still standing over him, hog spit on the side of his face.

"Boss, come on, we gotta get outta here fast," one of the robbers reasoned while the other two dragged their accomplice back to their stolen getaway van.

"Number three is bleeding real bad, boss. Finish this and let's go, now."

"Please. I gave y'all everything," Tranz pleaded. "Please don't kill me."

The man eased his foot off of Tranz's neck and mashed his gun against his temple. "Shut up and start counting like I told you."

Tranz began to cry. Warm urine soiled his jeans as he slowly mumbled out the numbers.

The man laughed at Tranz. "I hope you believe in hell, boy." Then he pulled the trigger.

Click-Click-Click….

*****

"And that's how it all went down, Kenny, I swear," Tranz stated. "It's only by the grace of God that his clip was empty."

"What are the doctors saying?" Kenny asked, pertaining to Kasi.

"They said that it doesn't look good for him because the bullet is lodged in his spine. But they won't know for sure until he comes out of the operating room."

The information hit Kenny like a ton of bricks. He didn't know what to do next. *How am I supposed to explain this to Lilly?* He wondered. "Tranz, you hustle down there all the time. You were supposed to be watching your cousin's back. What happened?" He asked blaming his friend.

"I don't know. I just don't know!"

Tranz started to whisper after a New Castle County police officer came out of the hospital for a smoke break and stood beside him. Traumatized by the whole ordeal, the sight of an approaching ambulance made Tranz almost hysterical. "One minute I was going in my car to get a ballgame. And the next, I was in a fucking crossfire. My blood's on a fucking operating table, Kenny. We have to get even."

"How, Tranz?" Kenny barked. "You just said that you didn't know the white boy. And you didn't see the rest of them, or who was in the bushes. So all we know for sure is that the fiend is dead. That's it."

"I think I know who sent that white boy. We can get at him," Tranz suggested.

"You just said—"

Tranz cut Kenny off in mid-sentence. "I know what I just said. And now I'm telling you that I think I know who did it. So are you gonna help me or what?"

Headlights blinded Tranz, but they did not stop the tears from rolling down Tranz's face as he spoke.

"You better be right," Kenny warned.

Kenny's Lincoln detoured back towards Governor Printz. He needed a drink before he broke the news to Lilly.

So he headed towards the Highway Inn, a late night liquor store, in hopes of drowning his problems.

*****

After a long night on the block all Deshonne wanted to do was sleep. He crept in about 5:00, looked in on his parents, and went straight to bed. At 9:30 sharp, a dose of ice water killed his peaceful slumber, awakening him into shock.

"Aah!" he screamed as he tumbled out of bed onto the floor.

His mother was standing over him with the pitcher in her hand and a look of destruction on her face. "Where have you been for the past day and a half, Deshonne?" she demanded.

"Around the corner in arbor place at some broad's house. Why?" he replied as he tried to dry off with the t-shirt he had taken off not too long ago.

His mother tossed the plastic pitcher onto the bed in disgust. "Was it worth it?"

Please don't say my P.O. stopped by here, he thought. "What are you talking about, Mom?"

"Was that tail worth your freedom?"

Deshonne got up and sat on the drenched bed, speechless. He knew she wouldn't have woken him up like this unless it was serious.

"They surrounded my damn house for you last night, boy."

"Did you let 'em in?"

"Let 'em in for what, so they could ransack my house, looking for you? Unh-uh. I learned my lesson last time when they came for your brother."

"What did you tell'em?" he asked with his face in his lap.

"I told them that your ass didn't live here, so it wasn't no need in them coming back."

Deshonne looked over at his mother for a second. *I know you ain't sell me out like that*, he thought.

She just stared back with disappointment until reality kicked in.

"Either way, I'm violated, so I might as well go on the run," he tried to rationalize. Deshonne's cell phone began to ring. He reached into his jeans pocket to answer it.

"You'd better not, nigga. I ain't done talking to you, yet."

"What, Mom, huh? What else is there to talk about now? Any shot I had at talking my way out of this situation is gone now because you told them that I didn't live here." His voice began to shake. So he paused for a moment before continuing."So, you tell me what else is there to talk about, huh? He challenged. I don't know why you even answered the door in the first place."

"Because it's my damn door," she said. "You in my house, Deshonne! I'm your mother. You ain't mines."

She kicked his pile of dirty clothes over towards the dresser.

Deshonne just sat there with a blank look on his face because he knew that he couldn't black out on his mother.

"Mom, can you please just get out of my room and close my door so I can get dressed," he asked as passively as he could.

She turned her back and grinned a little. "You need to hurry up too, because the lawyer, a news crew and Pastor Tahlia are all going to meet us at the probation office at 11."

"For what? That ain't gonna stop them from locking me up on a curfew violation. You already killed my shot when you told them that I didn't live here."

"Get dressed dummy," she said as she closed the door. "And bring them dirty clothes down when you come!"

*****

The aroma of a good home-cooked meal made Purnell's mouth water in his dreams. His children running around the house brought him back to reality. "Tonya, go and tell them kids I said get ready for day camp," Purnell mumbled.

158

When she didn't respond, he patted her side of the bed to see if she was still next to him. Realizing that she was not there, he rolled over to check the alarm clock. One of the children fell so hard that he felt it in bed. And then the crying and whispering started among them.

"Sit y'alls asses down!" Purnell yelled. "Tonya!"

"What?! I'm trying to cook!" she screamed back from the kitchen.

His stomach growled as the scent led him into the kitchen. "Good morning, boo," Purnell said as he kissed the pit of her neck. "What smells so good?"

With both hands full she used her rear end to back him away. "It's what I always make, Purnell, steak and eggs," she said with a tone of voice that set off a caution alarm.

"What you mean, it's what you always make? You don't never cook me no steak and eggs for breakfast," he said as he slipped his hands around her waist.

"Why should I cook you anything when you're never here, anyway?"

Purnell tried to untie her robe, but was shoved away by a sharp elbow. "Stop!" she demanded.

Getting the hint, he stepped back and held his distance. "Tonya, I'm always here. I live here, remember?"

Tonya turned the flame down low, flipped over the steak, and turned to chop up an onion and some cheese for her eggs. With her eyes focused on what she was doing, she continued to talk. "Purnell, these last two nights have been the first you've come home early in months. And, knowing you, you've only been coming in because the police were outside."

If you could hear yourself and understood the shit you put me through, you probably wouldn't come home either, he thought as he sat down at the dining room table. "Why don't you stop exaggerating, girl? I'm always here."

She cut her eyes in his direction. "Crawling into bed at five and six in the morning isn't what I call being here!" Then she stuck the butcher knife deep into the block of cheese and leaned over the counter, with her head lowered.

A minute passed before Purnell noticed her sniffling. He then noticed tears running down the side of her face. So he got up to comfort her even though he was lost to the reason why.

She kept him at arm's length and wiped her own face off with her sleeve.

"Come on now, Tonya. It's not like you don't know where I be at, and who I be with," he reasoned.

"Where do you really go every afternoon when you leave out of here, Purnell?"

"Why you asking me stupid questions? You know I'm either on the block or over Magic's. The same fucking places every day," he said, and then he turned to walk away.

Unwilling to except his lies anymore, Tonya just let out what had been on her mind since last night. "She said that she wants you to come and pick up your clothes before she burns them."

That statement stopped him dead in his tracks.

"Don't stand there looking stupid," she said without looking in his direction. "Why don't you come back in the kitchen and finish lying to my face?" She turned around to face him.

"Man, I don't know what you talking about," he said as he turned to face her.

"Your bitch called my house, Purnell," Tonya confessed. "So don't say that you don't know what I'm talking about."

"I don't know what the fuck you talking about! If anybody called here, it was probably your jealous-ass girls, hating like always. You know they keep trying to break us up because they don't like me," he said in his defense.

Tonya put on a hot glove and grabbed the hot frying pan off of the stove. "You got one more time to lie to my face like I'm stupid, and I'ma pour this hot shit on you."

"I wish the fuck you would! We'll both die in this bitch," he warned as he edged a little closer.

Tonya stood there with the cast iron pan extended, keeping him at bay for a minute. Then she just dropped the pan back on the stove and cut it off.

Purnell always unconsciously repeated a question when he was lying, and she knew it. So she questioned him. "Where's your Dr. J throw-back at?"

"What you mean, where's it at? I been told you that I was gonna let Magic wear it to Kenny's party."

Tonya walked past him and picked up the living room phone.

"Who you calling?"

"I'm calling Magic so I can get your jersey back and take it to the cleaners so I can wear it," she bluffed.

Purnell walked over, snatched the phone out of her hand, and hung it back up.

"Don't be snatching nothing away from me, you liar."

"Magic ain't home," he said flatly.

"I bet he ain't," she said sarcastically.

Purnell turned serious in a flash to throw her off. "Tonya, I've been coming in early the last couple of days because somebody got killed down the motels the other night, and I was right there. I watched the whole thing go down from the second floor of the 6."

Tonya looked at him as if it was just another lie. "Who was it?" she asked.

"I don't know, I wasn't that close. But I did see the get-away van the shooters pulled off in," he enthusiastically added.

"Did you tell the police what you saw?"

"Hell no! I came straight home and took my ass to bed. I'm on probation, remember? They would've locked my dumb ass up."

Tonya picked up the phone and threw it at him, shattering the mirror. "You lie so fucking much. I hate you!"

"Girl, what are you doing? I'm not lying!" he said as he rushed over and grabbed her before she could throw something else. "Ask me anything, and I'll tell you the truth. I'm not lying," he pleaded.

Tonya looked him straight in the eyes. "What's her name?"

161

He pushed her away. "What you mean, what's her name? I don't even know what you talking about. I didn't hear no phone ring last night. And I damn sure didn't give no bitch our number."

"Ah-ight, well, go get dressed then, since you don't know what I'm talking about, Purnell. Because the bitch gave me her address to pick up your stuff."

Purnell continued to deny everything to the end. "What is you talking about? All my stuff is here. I'm not fucking nobody else but you. And I don't got my shit nowhere else but here."

"Either you go with me to get your shit from Angie's house, or you can get your shit outta my house!"

Damn, this bitch done fucked my shit up! Purnell realized as soon as she said her name. "Tonya, listen to me." He tried to reach for her, but she pulled away.

"I swear, if you touch me again, you gonna need plastic surgery to fix what I'ma do to you."

"Look, I can explain. I'm telling you, whoever it is, is lying," he implied.

Tonya looked at him until her eyes began to water. Sizing him up as best she could, she flung a glass cup at his head.

He dodged the glass, and it too shattered on the broken mirror behind him. "What the fuck is you doing! I'm trying to tell you that I ain't do shit."

"You cheated, on me Purnell!" she screamed and then ran into the bedroom.

All three children stood mute behind their bedroom door as their mother ran past.

"You cheated on the wrong bitch!" she repeated as she locked the door behind her.

Purnell couldn't believe what had just happened. He slowly slid down the living room wall in disbelief.

CHAPTER 22

From the street you could see that all the windows were squeaky clean. And the vacuum cleaner was humming.

Things never change. Kenny thought as he came up the Robinson's walkway. He watched his second mother happily clean through the screen door for a minute before he knocked.

Mom Robinson cut off the vacuum cleaner and wiped her eyebrows before checking to see who her Saturday-morning visitor was. "Come on in, Lil Kenny. The screen door isn't locked," she said with an inviting wave.

Kenny came in and gave her the usual kiss on the cheek. Then they both sat on opposite couches.

"Good morning, Mom Paulette. How you feeling?"

"Oh, baby, I'm okay. And yourself?"

"I'm good," he said.

"Well, I guess I'd be a little better if knucklehead knew how to stay out of trouble."

Kenny immediately knew whom she was talking about. "What did he do now?"

"What doesn't he do is a better question," she answered.

"Is it that bad?"

"Not to him, it isn't."

Kenny looked upstairs towards the bedrooms. "Is he here?"

"Yeah, I think his hardhead ass is up there unless he snuck out this morning. It's time for him to get up anyway, so you can go and get him."

Kenny got halfway up the steps before she spoke again.

"Do you want me to cook you something to eat, too, Lil-Kenny? I'm about to make breakfast for everybody," she offered.

"Yeah Mom thanks. I'm hungrier than a hostage," he said.

The vacuum came roaring back to life as soon as he entered Deshonne's room.

Kenny looked at Deshonne for a minute and laughed. Deshonne slept like a dead man, flat on his back, with the covers over his face. He walked straight over, sat down on the bed beside Deshonne, and shook his leg. "What's up, fam?"

Deshonne didn't move at first, he just spoke. "I guess me, since you woke my ass up," he mumbled.

Slowly sitting up, he asked, "What time is it?"

"Nine-forty-five."

"Damn, I overslept again!"

"A long night, huh? You must've done the graveyard shift," Kenny commented.

"Yeah, you know I like to hug the block from twelve to six."

"Is that why mommy's mad at you?"

"Probably, but that ain't the only reason."

"Oh, yeah. What is, then?" Kenny asked as he walked over to his boy's closet to admire the new wardrobe.

Deshonne leaned over and picked up the pair of sweatpants he had on yesterday. He explained his mother's reason for having an attitude as he got dressed. "Safe Streets came through Thursday night, and I wasn't here. I was around the corner, smutting some broad. So she's mad at me."

"So, basically, you got violated over a bitch?"

"Almost. Until the female Johnny Cochrane downstairs stepped up and represented me. She flipped out in the probation office yesterday."

"Say word!" Kenny said as he turned around with a curious look on his face.

"Word. She had the News Journal, our pastor, and her lawyer in the probation office with us. And she did all the talking, cuz. She had my P.O. shook up in that spot. He was so fucked up, I walked out scot-free," Deshonne said, still amazed by his mother's performance.

"Yo, I can imagine her doing that shit, too!" Kenny stated proudly. "Cause I can still remember a lot of days when we did something wrong, an she used to just look at us and break us down."

They both laughed at some of those unforgettable memories.

Deshonne tried to tidy up a bit. Kenny went back to taking inventory of the room's new items.

"Yo, I'm sorry I missed your party. But you know how it is when you get a hold of something strange," Deshonne said apologetically.

"It's cool."

"So why you outside so early?" Deshonne asked.

"Actually, I came out for a couple of reasons."

"Oh yeah? And what might they be?" Deshonne asked, as if he already knew.

"Well, Wood called me about that work he gave you last week. He wanted to know how you was coming along. Are you finished yet?"

Offended by the question, Deshonne stop cleaning. "Is that the only reason you came and woke me up, to check on your boy's money?"

"No. I told you that I stopped by for a couple of reasons. I already had to run some errands this morning, plus stop by my mom's house. Wood just told me that you missed the deadline, and asked me why you hadn't gotten back at him, yet. But I didn't have an answer for him, so I just told him that you would get at him soon. No problem. I decided to come by on my own to check in on you while I was up the street. It really didn't have nothing to do with that stuff."

Kenny opened up a couple of sneaker boxes as he spoke. Deshonne just stared at him curiously. "Tell that lame I'll give him his money tomorrow. I gotta make sure I'm done first."

"What you mean you gotta make sure? Either you're done or you aren't, Magic. There's no in-between."

165

Deshonne decided to show Kenny exactly what he was talking about. He picked up a pair of balled-up socks and hit him in the back of his head with them to get his attention. "Hand me that sneaker box you was just looking in."

Kenny laughed. "You got jokes this morning, huh?"

There were 13 boxes of new sneakers stacked up in two piles. One stack was an assortment of Nike Air Ones, and the other 574 New Balances.

"Which box, clown boy?"

"Oh, my fault," Deshonne said with a smirk. "The third Nike box from the bottom."

Kenny pulled out the box and opened it before he handed it to Deshonne. He could see rolls of money sticking out of both sneakers. $5,000 in fifties and twenties.

"Damn, you nosy," Deshonne said as he snatched away the box.

"That doesn't look like $6,750 to me Magic."

"That's because it ain't. It's two short. Pee-Wee owes me a stack, and so do Kasi. So it'll be straight by tomorrow."

"Oh, brother, here goes the bullshit," Kenny mumbled, assuming that Deshonne already knew about the shooting that took place.

"Man, ain't no bullshit. I told you that I got everything under control," Deshonne said confidently.

"Since when you start fucking with Kasi?"

"What you mean? He peoples? He told me that he was gonna have a problem paying his bills this month, so I looked out. What's wrong with that?" Deshonne replied.

Kenny flopped down in the chair beside the bed and looked over at Deshonne for any sign that he was gaming him. "Magic, Kasi's laid up in Christiana hospital with tubes coming outta every end of him."

Deshonne sat down on the bed slowly, shocked by the news. "What happened to him?"

"Somebody robbed him down the motels. And when he tried to run, they used his back for target practice. The doctors got one of the bullets out, but they had to leave one in because it's in his spine."

166

"Is he gonna live?"

"Yeah, I think so. But he probably won't never walk again."

Deshonne shook his head in disbelief. "Do you know who did it?"

"No. all I heard was that it was four dudes. And at least one of them was a white boy. Tranz claims that he knows who had something to do with it. But I'm waiting for Kasi to wake up first before we get down and dirty."

"You know, if it was somebody from Delaware, the streets will definitely be talking in no time. So I'ma keep my ears glued for Kasi, too, and definitely keep him in my prayers."

"That's what's up," Kenny agreed.

Silence overcame the room for a minute. Deshonne picked up the sneaker box next to him again as if he was reading Kenny's mind. Kenny said something first. "So what you gonna do about that stack you're short? You know how it goes. It's your bill, not Kasi's."

Deshonne looked at Kenny as if he himself was being robbed. "What I'm supposed to do? I'm short a grand, and it ain't my fault."

"Come on, Magic, you know how the game goes. You wanna play, sometimes you gotta pay."

"Man, that's bullshit, Kenny, and you know it!"

Kenny just threw his hands into the air and hunched his shoulders.

Deshonne looked over at Kenny. "Man, hand me them jeans you sitting on."

"You really should organize your room better," Kenny suggested as he tossed him the jeans. "I never could understand why you and your brother always left y'alls clothes lying around for your peoples to pick up."

Deshonne reached in all four of his pockets, pulling large sums of money out of each one. He counted out $1,750 and handed Kenny the whole bill.

"This isn't all you got, is it?"

167

"You see all this stuff I bought, don't you?" Deshonne shot back rudely.

Deshonne never told the truth when it came to money, to anyone. He always tried to save a little something extra for a rainy day. But for some reason this time he got a little carried away without even noticing how much he was spending.

As Kenny looked around the room, he realized that Deshonne was trying to play catch-up. he had a brand new platinum chain and bracelet, plus a new Oris-975 Swiss-made watch, all draped around the teddy bear that Desiree bought him five Valentine's Days ago. Not to mention the new clothes, sneakers, and throwback jerseys.

Kenny lifted the chain from around the bear's neck, and held it in the air. "I know you ain't gonna sit here and tell me that you wasted a quarter of a brick on this stuff."

Deshonne looked at him, dumbfounded. "Okay, I won't tell you, then."

What Kenny saw in Deshonne upset him because he thought that he was all grown up and ready for the world. "You stupid, yo. You risking your neck for nothing, like you still a little kid that has nothing to loose." Kenny tossed the chain onto the bed next to him.

Deshonne just sat and listened to his best friend chastising him.

"You can't start your own business with this shit," Kenny stated with a wave around the room. "Name one bill you can pay with that necklace."

Deshonne picked up the $2,700 dollar chain and hung it back around the bear's neck without answering.

"What? Am I talking a different language here or something?" Kenny asked. Then paused for a proper response. "Tell me you can't see the stupidity in hustling for material things?"

"Breakfast is ready!" Mom Robinson yelled upstairs, halting the one-sided conversation.

Kenny walked down to eat without waiting for an answer from Deshonne.

Deshonne came and sat down at the table, wondering if he even had one.

*****

Desiree felt bored and alone as she window shopped, her weekly treat, as Alex called it.

"Hey! Dee!" Iyanna shouted as she hopped up and down with one hand in the air, so she could be seen over top the crowd.

Desiree stopped in front of The Limited and sat down on one of the benches until her friend reached her.

"Hey, Dee."

Iyanna was dressed down in Banana Republic because it was not only sophisticated attire, it was tight-fitting and sexy.

"Hey, girl! Don't you look cute today," Desiree complimented.

"Thanks, girl," Iyanna said with a quick spin. "I'm trying to catch a lawyer or a doctor this weekend."

Desiree just laughed because she knew how serious Iyanna was about finding a man.

"Girl, where did you get them Yves Saint Laurent Jeans at?"

Desiree wore $400 dollar jeans lately like they were going out of style. Today she wore them with a white tube-top shirt and some white Air Ones. Her micros were freshly done as well.

"Don't ask me, Yanni. Dumb ass bought me four pair of these jeans back from New York last week after I told him that he was starting to get on my nerves and I needed a break."

I knew I should've slept with that man when I had a chance, Iyanna thought. "Girl, you gotta keep that man. His taste in clothes is not only cute, but expensive too."

"I know, right? I've got him wrapped around my finger tighter than this thong I'm wearing," Desiree said, flipping down the waistband of her blue jeans to expose the white string to her friend, then wrapped the string around her finger one time and giggled. "I'm still single and independent, though."

They both began to stroll through the mall together.

"Dee, you know you're full of shit, right?"

"No, I'm not. I don't ask for the stuff that he gives me. And I don't need a man by my side to sleep at night just to validate my femininity, either."

"Girl, now you in denial," Iyanna said. "Every woman wants a nice slab of meat next to them at night," using both hands to show her fantasy-size penis.

"You's a nasty slut," Desiree said with a grin.

"Girl, where I come from these cravings is normal. We eat, sleep, shit, and swallow dicks in all varieties of shapes, sizes, and colors," Iyanna told her with a straight face.

They walked into the food court and got into the shortest line they could find, which was Arby's.

"Men these days are headaches, Yanni. That's why sometimes I think that I would be better off with just my fingers as friends."

"Let me guess. Your feelings towards men have changed since that day with Magic, huh?"

"No. I could care less about him right now. He's just a figment of your imagination," Desiree said as if she had truly moved on. "I haven't heard from him, and don't really care to at this point." *That punk ain't never home to answer his phone no way. He's probably laid up with some bitch*, Desiree thought.

"Dee, you know you ain't really happy without him. So I don't know why you trying to play stubborn."

"I'm not playing anything, cause I couldn't really care less," she said as she reached the front of the line.

After ordering their meals, they sat down to eat. Iyanna tried to test her friend by sliding her a cell phone. She had already thought of the perfect advice to help Desiree.

"What's this for?" Desiree asked. "I got my own phone, remember?

"It's written all over your face, Dee. So I was thinking that you should just call the man one last time, invite him over to your house for dinner and a long talk, and then fuck his brains out. That way you can either get back together or get him out of your system forever."

Desiree wiped the side of her mouth and then slid the phone back across the table to her. "Sorry, but I think I'll pass because that would only complicate the situation even more. Even though I could use the exercise. You know a good sweat never hurt nobody, right?" she said with a lustful smile. A quick flash of their last encounter gave her a hot flash. She got up and gathered her things.

Iyanna happened to look over and catch a glimpse of the front page of the News Journal. The sight of the Motel 6 made her remember something she had heard earlier in the week. "Hey, girl. Did you know that one of them New Castle boys got shot the other night down at the motel? They said that somebody robbed him and then shot him in the back because he didn't have enough money."

"Who?" Desiree asked.

"Somebody named Kasi."

"The one that raps?"

"Yeah, that's him," Iyanna said, then she continued to tell the juicy gossip that she had heard as they continued their stroll.

Desiree listened, but thought only of Deshonne.

CHAPTER 23

Deshonne and his partner in crime, Purnell, decided that it would be best to wait until well after midnight to moonlight down in Trick City as drug dealers, after their last probation visit, just to be safe. On their first night they squatted in an empty field adjacent to all three motels and the gas station for a couple of hours straight so Deshonne could make a mental note of all the stopping cars and faces.

Purnell had grown weary of sitting while the street life passed him by, so to stay occupied every 30 seconds or so, he would click the safety of his gun from locked to the unlocked. Then he would check his cell phone, just in case he missed a call. "I don't understand why we keep walking down here with crack on us if we not trying to catch none of the money coming through. This is whack."

"Chill, cuz," Deshonne stated with a disapproving wave. "You said it yourself. We don't know none of the fiends or hustlers down this end. So let me do this my way for one last night, okay?"

"Doing it your way, I'll never finish this pack," Purnell mumbled, still playing with the loaded handgun as if it was a toy.

"You should've been done that one ounce by now, anyway. I dumped five by myself this week alone."

"Hell, we lucky that I still got this shit, because Tonya started to flush it down the toilet after she beat Angie the fuck up yesterday."

"Say word, she beat that ass!" Deshonne said with a smile.

172

"Word. She did. Me and Tonya was home arguing one minute, and the next…"

*****

Trying to avoid Tonya because she wanted to go and confront his other woman, Purnell stayed out of her way for most of the day. He was taking a hot shower and preparing to go to bed when all of the sudden, all hell broke loose. He swiftly turned off the water and grabbed a towel once the screams pierced the thin walls.

"Help! Bitch, get off of me! Stop!" a female voice screamed at the top of her lungs from the living room.

Purnell didn't recognize the voice at first, but realizing that it had to be something serious, he dashed out of the bathroom, wrapping his towel as he moved….

*****

"**Magic**, it was like "WrestleMania" in my motherfucking spot. You hear me!" Purnell stated as he relived the whole fiasco.

"Who won?"

"Man, you know who won," he stated as if Deshonne's question was completely ridiculous. "It was like watching the Tyson-Spinks fight all over again, but with sexual benefits. Angie had to go home with one of our towels wrapped around her…"

*****

The living room looked as if it had been hit by a hurricane by the time Purnell finally reached the ultimate fighting match. The floor was littered with knick-knacks from off of the Cherry Oak coffee table, a recliner was leaning onto another sofa, and there was a trash bag of clothes ripped wide open and wedged in the doorway, which he assumed was from his second home.

173

"Kids, get y'alls asses back in the room!" he yelled once he realized what was taking place. "Tonya, let her go!" he demanded while trying to pry them apart.

Angie was spitting and gasping for air as Tonya sat on her small, exposed chest, trying desperately to choke the life out of her.

"I'ma kill this bitch! Get off my arm, Purnell!"

"Oww!" he screamed as soon as his fiancé bit down on his thumb.

Her prey was beginning to see stars and now wished that she had not called and come over out of spite...

*****

"**Yo**, I told you that your girl was the truth!" Deshonne said as they both gave each other a firm shake. "She should be the one out here pumping with me, instead of your whining ass."

"Yo, I swear I didn't know that she had it in her. I couldn't believe it when I saw Angie all choked up in the mickey, turning blue on the floor. You know she's already a chocolate joint."

Deshonne laughed at his friend's irresponsible stupidity.

"I'm glad that someone finds humor in my situation. Because I had to use some of our money to pay for my room last night at the Courtyard Marriott."

The Courtyard Marriott was located in downtown Wilmington, right off of 11th and King Street, directly across the street from a branch of Wilmington Trust Bank, where Deshonne worked.

"Nigga, is you crazy? Them rooms cost a buck and some change apiece," Deshonne reprimanded.

"Hey, what did you expect me to do? You know that P&P stay running in and outta these motels and the ones on 13, and I damn sure wasn't sleeping out on the street."

"Man, if you wouldn't of gotten yourself caught up like that in the first place, you wouldn't of had to worry about where you was gonna sleep at."

Deshonne was obviously upset by his friend's mismanagement of their money. He became quiet while continuing to case the strip for potential customers or problems.

"Don't worry, Magic. I'll take the $250 outta my end. Everything will be straight," Purnell assured him as he stood to stretch.

"I hope so cause I need that stack for something," Deshonne said as he turned in the opposite direction to piss.

"For what?"

"Because I had to kick out the whole payment already yesterday. So I'm broke."

"Why you ain't duck them until everything was finished?"

"Because I thought that everything was done. And besides we was outta work."

Purnell just looked at him. "Yo, you better than me because they definitely would've been a stack short."

"Come on, Pee-Wee, you know the game don't work like that for real niggas like us," Deshonne repeated from the lecture Kenny had given him. "That's exactly why they keep hitting us off. Because we good money, no matter what," he stated as he returned to his friend's side.

"Man, fuck them niggas! They hitting you off anyway, not me. They lucky I'm not coming at them my own way, because I'm about this work, too," Purnell stated with a wave of the gun.

That would be fucked up. To get robbed with the same guns you passed off to protect your cheddar, Deshonne thought. "Alright, alright. You can calm down, now. Remember, we're next to somebody's house, and you all loud," he advised.

"Man, fuck this house, too! If they know what I know, they'll stay in it and keep their mouths shut."

Deshonne's prepaid was vibrating in his pocket. He hit a button and sent the caller straight to voice mail.

"Who's that?"

Deshonne didn't answer his question. Instead, he reached into his pocket and pulled out some money. "Here, take this $60 and go get a room at the 6. I'ma get us one at the Days Inn, too." Then he looked at his watch to confirm the time. "It's after four o' clock, so we should be straight for a whole day."

"Why we getting two separate rooms?" Purnell asked while tucking his pack and gun by the nearby house's fence.

"I'll explain it to you later. Just go ahead and handle that."

Deshonne sent another caller straight to voice mail after checking the number.

"Why don't you answer your phone? That might be them freak bitches calling."

Deshonne looked at him. "You of all people should've had enough of freak bitches like Angie to last you a lifetime. Now, go and get the room and call Tonya or something until I call you."

Magic must be trying to hog all the pussy for himself again. That's one sucker-for-love-ass nigga, Purnell thought as he started his walk.

A third call. This time he answered the phone as he began to cross over Memorial Drive to reach his destination. "What's up? Ain't it a little bit too late to be calling me?" he asked, already knowing who it was.

Purnell looked back and happened to see Deshonne on the phone, so he yelled back across the street. "Yo! Who dat!"

"Hold on," Deshonne said to his caller and then covered the receiver. "It's Angie! Why? You wanna talk to her?" he yelled jokingly.

"Aw, fuck you and that slimy bitch!" Purnell yelled while slowly jogging across New Castle Avenue backwards.

"So, what's been up with you, stranger?" Deshonne asked as soon as he returned to his call.

*****

Deshonne could hear the car horn beeping as he made his way down the three flights of winding steps. With each turn, he noticed two stationary cameras on each floor, directly down the center of the narrow walkway from opposite ends. All foot traffic had ceased, and only five cars and an 18-wheeler remained in the parking lot.

The sun had risen significantly during the two-hour conversation he had carried on. And only now had he realized that the night was lost, and he hadn't made one dollar at this location.

"Long time, no see, stranger," she said as soon as he sat in the car and got comfortable.

"It hasn't been that long, Dee. Only a couple of weeks."

Deshonne went straight for the open CD case in her lap and began to flip through the assortment of music. They were both trying not to be the first to say that they missed each other. Deshonne knew that his eyes would give him away, so he tried to occupy himself for the moment.

"So, what made you call me?" he asked without looking over.

"No reason, really. I heard about Kasi from my friend, and I wanted to know how he was doing."

I wonder if he has someone up there? she thought to herself. If he does, I bet you she can't work it like I can. Desiree was inhaling deeply, trying to see if she could smell the scent of another woman on him without being too obvious.

"Did you hear me?" he asked for the second time.

"Oh. No, I'm sorry. What did you just say?" she asked as if she was really interested.

"I said, why you ain't go over to the hospital and check on him yourself?"

"The same reason that you ain't just tell me on the phone yourself, smart ass."

"I didn't tell you on the phone because I wanted to see you. What's your excuse?" *and maybe ball your thick ass up on that bed upstairs if you let me,*" he hoped.

"If you wanted to see me so bad, then why didn't you just call me, because my number hasn't changed, you liar," she said as she waved her cell phone inches from his face. Picking up one of his hands. "It doesn't look like your fingers are broke to me." Then she grabbed his chin and turned his face until their eyes met.

"I've been busy," he claimed with the most serious expression he could muster.

Desiree, in turn, leaned over and gave him a soft peck on the lips before letting his chin go. "Sorry, but you're never that busy. I know you, Magic. Every inch of you. And you don't fuck that long, brotha."

"You crazy! I put in work!" he said with conceited spunk. "And I don't remember you ever complaining. In fact, I can recall days when I brought tears of joy to this cute face too. Sexy."

Deshonne returned the kiss with a little nibble on her bottom lip.

"I never said it wasn't good, Magic. I'm just saying that it's not cute to hype yourself up to be something you're not, especially when babies come outta here, sweetie," she stated while patting her prize.

Deshonne twisted up his face and repeated himself, "Like I said, I puts in work."

"I guess," she said as if to dismiss his last statement. "Was she good?"

"Who? Who you talking about?" he asked as if he had completely missed something.

"Whoever you invited to the room before me, Mr. Womanizer." Desiree manipulated him into bragging about himself, only so she could have an excuse to go upstairs. She even went so far as to play like she was jealous.

"I didn't have nobody upstairs. I got that room for Pee-Wee because he got put outta his own spot."

"Did you at least change the sheets in case I decided to come up?"

Deshonne took out the card key and rubbed it up and down her inner thigh. "Go and see for yourself."

"You would like that, wouldn't you?" she flirtatiously asked.

"And you wouldn't?" he shot back.

"Nope. Because I know you fuck every female that you come in contact with. And me and mines, don't get down like that," she said, lustfully rubbing his hand up and down her pussy. She then picked up his hand as if it was contaminated and dropped it back on his own lap.

"Well, it ain't my fault that you keep acting funny. So I gotta do what I gotta do, right."

Desiree flipped on him at the drop of a dime. "Yep. Cause I'ma keep acting funny with my pussy. Especially when you don't deserve it."

"Huh?"

"Magic, I gotta go and pick up my friend. I'll see you later."

And just that fast, he forgot whom he was talking to. "Oh, well, you can bounce. It ain't like I haven't fucked you already, anyway," he said while opening the car door.

Shocked by his obnoxiousness, her jaw dropped in disbelief. "I guess this is the type of time we on now, huh. You just talk to me any kind of way now, like I'm some type of bum bitch, huh?"

Deshonne looked at her as if he wanted to take back what he had just said, but his pride kept his mouth closed. He just played it all the way out. "Oh, well. This is how you made it, Dee, not me."

"You mean that?" she asked, hoping that he would be man enough to put his pride aside.

At that moment his phone began to vibrate. "Yeah, I guess I do," he said as he checked the number. "We on two different levels right now. And I don't think that I wanna get in your way." *Perfect timing, my nigga*, he thought to himself. Then he answered the phone. "Yo, what's up?"

She looked at him and then started her car.

"Hold on, Pee-Wee," he said and then covered the receiver. "What you doing? We ain't done talking."

"I told you. I have to go and pick up my friend."

"Man. Your friend *who*?"

"None of your business who. Do you want me to drop you off home, or you staying here?"

He looked at her again to see if she was serious, and then just got out of the car without saying another word.

Once he closed the door, he said, "I'll walk."

"Whatever, then. See you," she said and pulled off.

Deshonne went back to his phone. "Where you at?"

"I'm on my way," Purnell answered.

*****

Around seven a.m, the working class people came back to life on the Avenue. Traffic was already moving at a crawl by the time Deshonne walked around to the front of the motel. He crossed over the four-lane road to reach the McDonald's, where his partner was already conducting a breakfast meeting. Purnell waved him down from the back of the fast food restaurant, where he held down the corner table.

"Yo, what, she made you walk?" Purnell asked with a friendly grin.

"Nah, I felt like getting some fresh air this morning," he stated as he sat down in front of his pre-ordered breakfast.

Purnell looked at him. "You made her mad again, didn't you?"

"Stop asking me so many questions all the time. I'm hungry. Can I just eat this nasty-ass breakfast you bought me?"

"Sure, go ahead."

An older brown-skinned brother with a scarred bald head came limping in from the side door. Purnell quietly waved him over to their table. He quickly pulled up a chair in between them.

Deshonne glanced over at the grimy, skinny, tongue-biting gentlemen and quickly realized what type of person Purnell had been having breakfast with. So he just decided to listen and play everything by ear.

Purnell did the introduction. "This my old head, Fast-P."

Fast-P stuck out his hand for Deshonne to shake, but instead he gave a casual head nod and continued to eat his hot cakes.

"He just finished telling me how all the money down this end flows through his hands at one point or another throughout the day," Purnell stated.

"Oh, yeah? And how is that?" Deshonne asked.

"All, and I do mean all, the tricks on the Ave. come to cop rocks, from me." Fast-P said, with his hands spread wide, as he leaned forward so that only those at the table could hear his claim to fame. "They call me Daddy pimp and pops because I can smell drop-n-pop a mile away."

Purnell patted Deshonne on the back as if he had found gold.

Deshonne cut his eyes at his friend as if to say, *So what! You found a slick-talking fiend.* Then he turned his focus back to Fast-P. "So why are you here with us? Because if you're good as you say you are, I know you gotta be working with somebody else."

"You right, I am. But right now the rocks I'm buying ain't hard enough. And me and my girls are tired of buying the same old bullshit that doesn't get them high. So we decided to look for a new supplier. And young buck over here said that y'all crack is John Blaze, so we're open for negotiating if you want some steady, straight-money business."

"Did you try our product yet?"

"Nah, not yet," Fast-P admitted.

We was waiting on you to come first," Purnell added.

"Yeah, like I was telling young buck. I got $14 dollars over at my room, but one of my girls is on a date right now. So when she gets finished, I'm gonna bring him the change back."

Deshonne laughed and said, "Oh, now I get it." then he thought, *Now I see why they call you Fast-P.* "Come on, pops, don't try and game us all early in the morning. I know it's breakfast time, but I ain't just wake up," he told him.

"Ain't no games. I got the money in my room. I just ain't trying to share my wake-up bump with everybody. The bathrooms right there, right? And, uh—you can just walk me back to my room as soon as I'm done. As a matter of fact, you can even hang out in my room and make a couple of dollars, or buy some pussy if you want to. I'm telling you I got the cleanest bitches on the Avenue."

I do need me a good shot of dome, Purnell told himself, with a sly test-touch under the table.

Deshonne thought, *What can I lose?* It's only a dime.

At the same time, Fast-P was plotting. *I hope Apple's woke so that we can sting these niggas.*

Deshonne scanned the customers and the parking lot before agreeing to pass off.

"Go ahead, Pee-Wee, give him a dime."

Purnell then reached into his pocket, pulled out a fat bag, and passed it to Fast-P.

Deshonne grabbed Fast-P by the arm before he could move away from the table and gave him a quick lesson on the rules of the game. "You owe us five sells for that bag if you don't got my money in that room of yours."

Fast-P just gave him his normal devilish smirk. "We can renegotiate later after you see the pretty pussy in my castle."

CHAPTER 24

As he made his way over to the bed, Desiree's exposed breasts began to perk up with anticipation of his touch. Seeing his professionally-trained body and chiseled six pack glisten from the hot shower that she always made him take before sex stimulated her. She sat on top of the sheets, butt naked, with her thick thighs spread wide open, waiting for his skilled tongue lashing.

Alex's lengthy manhood hung as he used the towel to dry off his curly hair.

Desiree looked intoxicating as she patted the bed spot between her legs.

He dropped the towel to put on a condom. "I must admit I was a little curious as to which way our future was going when I got your message this morning to meet here before work."

"Why, Alex? Don't we always meet here when you want some sort of sexual favor from me?"

Alex crawled onto the bed, spread her legs even wider, and leaned over to kiss her bush. "It's usually me calling you," he told her before going downtown. His slippery tongue darted in and out of her pussy with ease. She scooted down some on the bed, and tried to enjoy what he had to offer.

"I—I have to be satisfied on a regular basis, too," she explained between deep breaths. "Mmm!" she moaned as she tried to play the role of a pleased woman. But deep down, she thought, *I wonder if Magic got somebody in that room*?

"Aren't you glad you called?" he asked. "You know that pleasing you is my favorite task, right?"

She arched her back and pulled her hair down as she began to overheat.

Alex was double-fucking Desiree. Working his middle finger gently inside her ass-hole, while equally thumbing her pussy, he delicately sucked on her clit.

"Mmmm!" she moaned even louder as she began to milk his mouth until it flowed down his chin.

Continuing to suck on her pussy lips as she quivered, Alex held her body down with one arm, mastering his technique until she went completely limp.

"You can stop now," she said after a few minutes.

Alex then climbed on top of her and kissed her once before she turned her head. Positioning himself just right, he slid up inside her wetness without any assistance and began to move about slowly.

"Alex, get outta me and get dressed."

"What? What's wrong?" he asked, still stroking. "Talk to me."

"Nothing," she said and just lay there until he finished. *Your fuck game is corny. That's what's wrong,* she thought, but refused to say it out-loud.

It took him about five minutes to cum. As soon as he pulled out to replace the condom, she wrapped a towel around herself and rudely repeated her last order. "Alex, get dressed. I need some time alone."

"What's wrong? Talk to me."

"I don't feel like talking. I can't talk to you or anybody else right now. Now, you've had your fun, and it was nice. But now I need you to go because I wanna be alone if you don't mind."

Desiree walked over to the mini-refrigerator and pulled out a bottle of Pinot Nior.

"Desiree, I'm here for your every need. You know that you come first," he pleaded while redressing.

"No, I don't. You're married, Alex. And I don't think that your wife knows how you feel. So until she does, that's where you need to be."

He stopped buttoning up his Brioni shirt midway to address her statement. "So what are you saying?"

She tucked her braids into a bun, dropping the towel as she entered the extravagant five-piece bathroom. "I'm saying that I don't want any company right now, so I'd appreciate it if you weren't here when I come out of the bathtub." She then walked inside to turn on the bath water.

"I could always stay and wash your back, oil you down, or massage your feet," he proposed.

"I don't need your help, Alex. I need some time alone. Can you please do me this favor?" *Oh, just get the hell out!* she screamed inside.

Alex walked over to the door and leaned in. Desiree was sitting on the side of the tub with her head down. He admired every fully-stacked inch of his mistress. "If it means that much to you, I'll let myself out, okay?"

"Thank you."

"I hope during your time alone, you think about us and not that Magic character."

Desiree jumped up, startled. "What did you say?"

"I said, I know everything there is to know about you and your high-school fling. And I hope that he's out of the picture now because he doesn't deserve your time or your beauty."

Desiree turned away and got into the steaming bubble bath.

"Alex, he never was in the picture. And to be honest, neither are you. We just satisfy each others needs from time to time."

"I'm the one that loves you, Desiree."

Hating that four-letter word to describe them she yelled, "Get out, Alex!"

"Kiss me first," he proposed as he eased a little closer.

Desiree stood up and reached for the last white monogrammed Hotel Dupont cloth robe. "You know what? Just stay here, Alex. I'll leave!"

"No, no, I'm going. I'm going right now. Just call me later," he urged while backing away.

She just stood there until the door was closed, and she was sure that he was gone.

Five minutes later the hotel phone rang. She left a trail of suds and water as she made her way into the other room.

"Hello, hello?" Desiree could hear Alex's voice as she sat the receiver down onto the nightstand. She straightened up her back in front of the mirror, and watched the suds run down her full-figured curves as she posed. Satisfied with her look, she put on the secondary door lock so she couldn't be disturbed and then proudly strutted back to her awaiting bubble bath. *Damn, I must be good!* she thought with a smile.

*****

Kenny patiently stood by the office window, waiting for Art to return from the bathroom. He must've counted at least five of the brother's runners, make two sales a piece within a couple of minutes, not to mention at least four patrol cars either circle the block or pass through. Just as Kenny was about to leave, Art came out of the back with a green bottle of Remy, tilted. Kenny looked over his shoulder, but remained in the window, watching the movie.

Art walked over to his new Staples office supplies desk and kicked up his untied wheat Timberlands. "So, what's up with your peoples, Kenny? I heard he had a problem paying that bill on time last week."

"So what. He ah-ight," Kenny shot back arrogantly.

"So you know we stop fronting lames work when they can't produce on time, no matter who they're cool with," Art stated harshly.

"Yeah, well, we both know that that's none of your concern, now don't we?" Kenny told him as he turned around to face him. Looking into his bloodshot eyes, he instantly started thinking, *I knew I should've brought my hammer with me.* "You ever heard the saying, you just a worker, and your boss is my man's?"

186

Art stared him down for a second. "Fuck you!" he jumped to his feet. "I'll shut you down like I'm about to do your boy."

"What the fuck is you talking about? You ain't gonna do shit to Magic."

"You'll see. Just let him keep eating off of my block, cutting my flow."

"Your block?" Kenny challenged. "Magic don't hustle on Market Street. He's down on Jessup. And if I'm not mistaken, he built that block back up on his own."

"Man, he stole some of my customers. So if I was you, I'd let him know that he's biting the hand that feeds him. And if he wants to keep eating, then he should shut down the midnight shift."

Kenny laughed as if Art's threats were completely empty. "Okay, what's this really about? You still mad because Dee maced you at the party?"

Art slammed his fist down on the desk. "Man, fuck that bitch! Kenny you know that from Market down to Parkside is ours. And if you ain't with that, then you're against us." he tossed the empty bottle at Kenny's feet.

"I know you ain't sitting here, trying to start a beef outta jealousy. You know you can't get money and beef because the two don't mix," Kenny reasoned.

All amped up on the double-stack Xanax pill he had mixed in the green bottle, Art became very rowdy. "If you not feeling what I'm saying, then it's whatever, Kenny! Tell your boy I said bring it!"

Now knowing where the situation was going, Kenny focused his eyes on Art's hand because he was known to be trigger happy. "Art, you really don't want to take it there. Things might not turn out the way you want' em to."

I wonder what type of hole this 45 will put in this nigga's stomach? Art started asking himself before he blacked out. "We can see how it's gonna turn out right now, pussy!" he bellowed as he held up his gun.

*****

187

Deshonne didn't make too much more on his second night down Trick City than he did on the first, so in hopes of catching an early start right after work, instead of taking the bus that would've taken him home down route 13 to the intersection of Memorial Drive, he took the #17 Dart bus, which rode him down the parallel street, New Castle Avenue.

Seeing the street already alive as the bus made each stop encouraged him to take a look at the scene for himself.

Deshonne wandered over to the Motel 6, where Fast-P, his only contact in the vicinity, was shacked up, hoping that he hadn't already checked out.

As soon as he reached the second floor, a state trooper pulled onto the motel's grounds, and paranoia overcame him.

"Please be here. I don't feel like running from the police today," he prayed as he knocked on door 245. "Hurry up and open the door," he whispered to himself. He tapped on the door a little harder once he realized that the car was circling around the parking lot again.

"Who is it?" a female shouted from inside.

Confused, Deshonne looked at the door number again to make sure he was at the right room. "Um--I'mmm looking for a friend of mines. He brought me by here yesterday." *Damn, what's dude name again*? he asked himself.

"Can you hang on for a minute?"

Bitch! I got this crack on me. Hurry up! Deshonne screamed inside as beads of sweat formed on his face. He saw the curtain move, which told him that he was being looked over. But when the door didn't open quickly he thought about the circling car, and the chance of being seen by the law. Because he didn't want to become a familiar face to the law, he decided to turn and walk in the opposite direction, which would take him inside the three-sided structure, out of the officer's line of sight.

Maybe he switched rooms. He thought as he made an abrupt about-face. Then the door flung wide open.

"You're an impatient one, aren't you?" the female said.

Deshonne turned back around at the sound of her voice, but what he saw in the doorway caught him completely off guard. His pulse increased spontaneously while the rest of his paralyzed body just melted at the beautiful sight. Instantly, he inherited two unfamiliar traits, a speech impediment and a never before case of shyness.

"Ohh, shit!" was all he could come up with. "It—It looks like you're busy. So I think I'll just come back la—later," he managed to stutter out.

The female before him was every bit five foot nine, and totally naked. The first thing that he noticed was the goddess's perfect 140-pound frame.

"Boy, if you don't stop stuttering and come in," she demanded as she grabbed him by the hand. "I'm not busy. I just got outta the shower, that's all," she informed him.

Her words brought him back from his momentary erotic fantasy. He then tried to be respectful and focus only on her face for a second.

She had the cutest little baby face, peppered with a light shade of freckles, and fire-engine red hair, cut into a 'Bob style', with curly layers down the back.

"You sure?"

She smiled and then waved her free hand up and down her perfected frame. "Don't I look sure to you?"

He just smiled back and stepped in. But in the back of his mind, he said to himself, h-e-l-l yeah, as he stepped in. *How lucky can I be? It has to be something wrong with this snow bunny,* he wondered.

While he double-locked the door at her request, she went back to grooming herself. As she stood in front of the wide mirror, lotioning up, all he could think about was what type of noises she could make while he plunged in and out of her stringy red bush.

"You must be one of Fast-P's nephews, huh?" she asked, bending over in an enticing, ninety-degree angle to oil up one of her long legs.

Oh, yeah, that's old heads name, he now remembered. "Yeah, I'm Magic," he said, introducing himself as he respectfully turned the only chair in the room towards the wall so she could get dressed without his lustful eyes drooling over every inch of her.

She slyly watched him through the mirror, lotioning even slower, just for his viewing pleasure. "What's wrong? Don't tell me you don't like what you see," she stated.

"Nah I—I definitely enjoy the view. Actually, probably a little more than I should. I thought the respectful thing to do would be to refrain from staring at you and turn this way," he explained over his shoulder.

"Believe me. I don't mind you staring, sexy. So you can turn back around because I love the attention."

Too embarrassed to turn around because he knew that she would notice the erection bulging in his sweatpants, he stayed facing the wall. *Damn, I wanna fuck you so bad. And the crazy part is, I know you know it, too. So just give me some type of signal, anything. Just say the words, please*! he begged inside.

"Do you think my butt's big enough to be in one of those Black Tail magazines?" she asked.

"Huh?" Deshonne thought he heard the question incorrectly, so he figured that that was the perfect time to turn around and get another unforgettable eyeful of her beautiful body. "Excuse me?"

"You heard me. I said, do you think I got a project ass?"

Bent over, with her elbows leaning on the dresser for support, she did her best interpretation of a B.E.T Uncut video vixen, each ass cheek bouncing at her command.

When he turned around to answer her question, her titties were hanging so that her nipples lay in the palm of her hands, her ass was shaking, and her prize-winning pussy was staring right at him. "Woo, most definitely!" he agreed at first. Then he thought to himself seconds later, *Man, I'm corny as hell! Why I ain't just say yeah or something? Now she probably thinks that I'm a freakball or something.*

But little did he know she was thinking, I got one! She then turned around and sat solicitously on the dresser. Her left arm held up one knee, gapping her legs wide open, innocently disclosing her Apple-size joy. Lustfully, she sucked her thumb, demonstrating the techniques of her learned profession as she spoke.

I know I'm getting ready to smash now! he thought.

"Does your dick always get hard when you watch females lotion themselves?" she asked.

Deshonne bashfully looked down." I'm sorry, but it has a mind of its own at times. I generally try not to get too excited when I'm around beautiful woman like yourself, but you know how things just happen sometimes. No disrespect intended, though."

"None taken. Umm, Magic, right?"

"Yeah, you got it right," he agreed as he returned her inviting smile.

"Good, cause I'm usually bad with names, Magic."

She then walked over to the unmade full-size bed, sat right in front of Deshonne, and lifted one leg over his head slowly until the chair was between her legs.

Deshonne, in turn, followed her lead and scooted in as close as he possibly could to her.

"Listen, sexy, I'ma cut straight to the point, okay?" she said while simultaneously pulling the string on his sweatpants loose.

"Ah-ight what's up?"

"What's up is I don't fuck for free. That's first. You can stare for free. Nothing besides dildos and fingers go inside me," she stated as she began to lay down the ground rules.

"Now, I'll suck your dick for $250, or I'll jerk you off for $100. And just in case you don't have a condom, I got them, too, for $5."

The speech she gave fucked Deshonne up completely. He stood straight up with a look of confusion on his face. *Damn, I knew it had to be too good to be true. Something just had to be wrong with this bitch, huh,* he said to himself. "Hold up, shorty. No disrespect, but I think it's time for me to roll."

She swiftly slid her hand down his pants. "Why, what's wrong? Don't you like what you see?"

"Yeah, but—"

"No buts, sweetie. Fast won't be back for at least another hour. And Baby Girl promised to stay in the bathtub with her sugar daddy until I knock on the door and give them the okay. So you can just lay back and enjoy yourself."

Politely, Deshonne pulled her hand out of his pants and stepped to the side. "Sorry, but I didn't come here to spend money I came to make money, shorty. So please don't get offended, but I think I have to pass this time unfortunately."

Seeing that her plan was getting nowhere, she walked over to the dresser and opened up the top drawer. It was filled with value packs of condoms, sleazy lingerie, and erotic toys. "You can play with it if you want to," she offered with a flirtatious wave of the huge dildo. Then, slowly, she rotated the tip of the pleasure toy along the crack of her vaginal lips, causing her dormant volcano to moisten instantly, soiling the aluminum rod as she slid it deep inside. "You should try this. It's already wet for you," she seductively whispered.

Deshonne could hear the slurps grow stronger. *Don't do this to me*, his mind mumbled.

"You said you came to off some rocks, right?"

"Yeah, me and Uncle P worked out something yesterday."

"Okay, then. Just give me five rocks and lose the pants, sexy. I'll take care of the rest later, I promise."

Aw, man. She's a fiend, too. I don't believe this shit! he cried out inside. "Hold up. You get high?" he asked to clarify her previous statement.

"As long as it ain't garbage, I do," she boldly answered.

"Stop playing. You look younger than me. How old are you, shorty?" he asked, still in denial.

"If you must know, I'm 21. And you can stop calling me shorty if you not spending because my name is Apple."

"Damn, you look good as shit for a smoker."

"Yeah, well, you look too educated to be a petty drug dealer. But you don't see me complaining, do you?"

Opening her mouth wide enough to insert the dildo, she deep-throated the toy slowly. Then, as if she were licking a lollipop, she slipped out her tongue to taste her own juices as

192

she twirled the toy around. "Do you want me to suck your dick or what?" she bravely repeated.

"Nah, I'm not here for that type of business. We on two totally different types of time right now."

"I don't know about you, but I always find time to mix business with pleasure," she said while stimulating her dime-size pink nipples with the same toy. "I'll even make a deal with you, Magic. I bet I can make you cum in under five minutes, or the blow job is free of charge."

Her movements and words were so heavenly that it hurt him to say no, but he held his ground. "I'll pass," he declined with a grimace. "But I must say, I love your persistence. It reminds me of myself a little."

Apple reached for the bottom drawer and pulled out her cracked-up glass stem, a couple of Bic lighters, a bent half hanger, and a burnt spoon. "Well, good. Since you turned my persistent ass down, can I at least get a tester so I know what you're working with? Because? Tranz is stingy."

"Who?" Deshonne asked as if he misheard the name.

"Oh, nobody important. Just some dude in the bathroom with Baby Girl. He thinks he's more than just her sugar daddy because she fucks him real good. So he don't share with nobody else but her because he's always got his raggedy little dick stuck up in her somewhere."

Deshonne started to walk towards the bathroom door. "Did you just say that Tranz is in the bathroom?"

She put her hands around his neck, gently pressing her favorite assets up against his chest. Ignoring his question, she asked "So what about my tester? Because I know that Fast had to already had to tell you that you would be in good hands with me. As long as I'm here, you're in the right place at the right time to get money, sweetie."

"Man, I don't know about that," he said as if he had to think about it first.

"I'm telling you. No bitch, white or black, walking the Ave., can get you more money than I can."

"Word! So how you gonna act, then?" he asked.

Apple stepped back and, held out her hand. "You keep me high, and I'll make sure that your pockets always stay as fat as that dick of yours. Deal?"

"Deal."

CHAPTER 25

After a week's worth of conversation Marie finally agreed to a first date with Deshonne, but no specific date was set. So he figured that since he had already gotten her permission, he would stop by early enroute to work, that way he would have enough time to talk to her, but not enough time to bore her. He sat at the bottom of the steps and called inside to announce his presence as soon as he had followed the directions that her daughter had given him to the corner house.

"Why you ain't call me first so I could've been ready?" Marie asked with a surprised smile. While standing at the top of the steps, she put her long pretty hair into a scrunchy, letting it hang in the back like a ponytail.

Deshonne turned around to greet her, but instead wound up watching her descend, step by step down the walkway. to him, her beauty was breathtaking, which made her his new and only challenge. "I did," he answered as he stood up to meet her face to face. "Your daughter told me that you had gone to the store for a minute, but you were coming right back. and since I already had to come this way to go to work anyway, I decided to stop by and see what you were up to."

Once she reached the bottom of the steps, she pointed in both directions to see which way he wanted to go. he pointed to her left, which meant that they were headed up 7th Street towards Broom, which was one of the quiet streets on the west side of Wilmington.

"You can't always listen to my daughter because she doesn't know everything. She only knows what I tell her, and I don't tell her too much because she's nosy," she informed him as they walked aimlessly up the hill.

"Oh, well, I guess I'll have to remember that for the next time then, huh?"

Marie looked over at him. "Who told you that there would be a next time? You only asked me for one conversation, remember?"

"Yeah, I remember what I said. That's why I'ma give you the opportunity to schedule our next encounter because I'm confident that you'll want to see me again."

"I like your confidence, Magic, but I'm not into making short-term relationships with drug dealers. Because people like you don't last too long."

"Who said that I was a drug dealer?"

"Does it really matter who said it?"

At that moment, the answer to her question hit him. *That punk ass nigga Shane must've told her that shit*! "No, it doesn't matter who told you what about me because I know what I'm about. But I'll tell you this. If you want me to change something that you don't like on the outside, then all you have to do is agree to give me a chance to change you inside," he said. Then he demonstrated by touching his own heart.

"And what would you change inside me, Magic?"

"Your heart, of course. Don't act like you don't know why I'm here."

"Boy, you is crazy!" she said while laughing at his remark.

"No, I'm not, I'm listening to my heart already."

"Oh, really. And what is your heart telling you right now?"

"It's telling me not to let you go now that I got you."

All she could do was blush because even though his game was kind of corny, to her it was also sweet.

"Is that beautiful smile coming from something I said? Because if so, I got more of that. This is only the beginning," he told her.

"Yeah, you made me smile once. But I'm still wondering when I fell into your arms because I don't remember being there."

"Oh, so what you saying to me? Now you don't remember our special moment?"

"Nope, sorry, I don't remember off-hand. But this is as good of a time as any to refresh my memory if you want to," she softly hinted.

Okay, baby, you on a roll. Don't stop now. Just keep her laughing, and you got her, he kept telling himself. "Ah-ight Marie, I'ma take you back down memory lane and refresh your memory. But you gotta listen close because I'm about to relive that special moment when I stole your heart from the world."

"The whole world, huh?" she repeated.

"Yep!"

Oh, brother. I can't believe that he's coming at me with this corny game. He lucky that he's cute and he getting a couple of dollars, or I would just cut this circus short and add him to my waiting list, she told herself.

"Ah-ight it was a nice, sunny afternoon, not too hot because you could feel the breeze blowing. We were both walking together, like now. You were wearing—" Deshonne paused the story briefly to check the front of her outfit again.

She had to smile because he was becoming more and more amusing to her.

"Sorry, just checking," he said, and then he continued. "You were wearing a cute gray Guess sweatsuit with some matching New Balances and a beautiful smile to make everything else about you complete."

Deshonne then leaned over and picked a weed out of someone's yard and handed it to her as if it were a precious flower. "And I remember giving you the most beautiful flower."

"Boy, you need to stop," she told him, still laughing.

Unable to hold in his own giggles any longer, they both stood still and laughed for a minute.

"So this is our special moment, huh?" she asked.

"Hopefully, this will be the first of many more to come," he suggested as they stood face to face on the corner of 8th and Broom.

Looking across the street, she said, "I guess you brought me up to the park for our first date. That's cute."

"Ever since I was little, I wanted to holler at you, but I was afraid of being rejected back then, Marie. So now that I'm a man, the opportunity has presented itself again. And I'm figuring that I just can't let you walk past me without at least trying to talk to you this time. So hopefully we can start with the basics and go from there."

"That's sweet, Magic, but I never thought of you in that way before. You was always little Magic to me."

"Its cool. I never thought that I would get this far, either. So if this is as far as my fantasy goes, then I achieved something," he reasoned.

She looked into his soft brown eyes. "So, where do we go from here? Because I know that our special moment doesn't stop at a corner."

"To the park, I guess, since it's right there."

"And if I decide to give you a chance to make more out of this than one afternoon, what do you have in mind?" she asked.

"Whatever you can think of, I'll make it happen." he held out his hand as they crossed the street.

*****

Big Al rolled over to glance at his alarm clock as soon as his cell phone began to ring. Too tired to pick up the phone, he just reached over and pushed the speaker button.

"Yes?"

"Yo, you busy, son? It's me," the God stated in a whisper as if he knew that there were others in the room, sound asleep.

"Hold on!" he grumbled. Then he looked over at his wife, got up, and took a walk downstairs. "You've been calling my home at all hours of the night lately, God, as if I don't have a family. How disrespectful must you be before I put you in your proper place?"

"I'm sorry, Al. But it seems as if we got another problem," the God passively stated.

The mysterious man sat down on his Italian leather couch and quietly raised his voice into the receiver. "I said, no more problems! Didn't you hear me the last time? No fucking problems. I told you then, and I'm telling you now, don't call me with that bullshit. All I want to hear from you is how much money you've made me. Nothing else."

The God held the receiver away from his ear until the screaming ceased. "Look, I'm sorry. But this is a problem that can't wait, son. Feel me?"

"No, I don't feel you. So you listen to me, you motherfucker, for the last time. Your last problem cost me a close friend. And I have yet to tell his wife that she's now a widow. So from now on, you stick to the fucking plan and handle your own problems. You hear me?"

"Yeah, I hear you."

"Good. Now get off my phone. And when you go to sleep tonight, you make sure that you thank GOD that I'm not sending my friends widow your heart for his."

Click. The phone went dead.

The God slowly closed his phone up and continued to stand by the window of his dark room, stalking his new problem across the street.

*****

Purnell knocked on the door of room 245 the following afternoon with a bagful of Chinese food which he had just picked up from over in the Crossroads Shopping Center. Deshonne knew who the visitor was, so he childishly disguised his voice as he answered the door.

"Who is it?"

"Yo, its big daddy! Let me in," Purnell said while wiping his face with the towel around his neck.

Deshonne peeped out of the curtain as he spoke while Apple squinted through the door's peephole.

"Sorry, you must have the wrong room because we don't know no big daddy in here," Deshonne answered.

Purnell started to turn away and call Deshonne's cell phone, but he heard laughter inside. "Man, why you playing, Magic? It's hot as shit out here. Open up the door."

The door came open at that second. Deshonne was already sitting at a small round table in the corner, immediately to his right. It was obvious that the female voice he heard was behind the door because it stayed open as he stepped in.

"Man, I'm out there sweating my ass off and you sitting here, chilling in the A/C," Purnell stated. As soon as he sat the food down on the table, Apple closed the door, dressed in just a see-thru thong and a pair of matching leather pumps. Purnell instantly realized that her first impression was her best impression. "Oh, shit! No wonder you ain't wanna open up the door. You got a stripper up in this joint," he said ecstatically.

Even though he felt uncomfortable, Deshonne allowed her to flop down on his lap. Without delay, she got the reaction that she desired.

"Fall back for a minute, Pee-Wee," Deshonne informed him as she went through the bags.

"Shit, I don't know what you talking about, Magic, but I got a few ones for you, shorty. All you gotta do is come over here and shake that thing for me one time," he said with a handful of her firm left breast.

Apple kindly removed his hand from her breast, raised his hand to her lips, and erotically licked his thumb from bottom to top. "Sorry, but no thank you. I'm all right where I am, sweetie. My passion costs more than ones."

At that moment the comforter on the bed slowly came up and an arm came stretching out. Apple looked over at her awaking co-worker. "What about you, Tasty? You need some ones?"

"What?" Tasty asked, still half asleep.

Tasty looked over at the new face to figure out what her partner was talking about. At the same time, Purnell was looking at her, sizing up her face and body. He figured that they were about the same age and that her chest had to be huge. Tasty adjusted her wig first, then showcased her only assets by cuffing the blanket under her arms so that her saggy 44DDs sat alluringly over her arms, for clear visibility.

"Do you want Magic's cousin's ones?" Apple asked again.

Tasty then pulled the sheets back over her chest, covering herself to the neck. "I thought you said that they were ballers, girl. He can't even stare at my Double Ds for singles. Wake me back up when some real money comes in," the caramel-complexioned prostitute stated firmly before rolling back over.

Apple and Deshonne just laughed at the look of confusion in Purnell's face.

"Damn, Magic. What type of strippers you got up in this joint that don't like money?"

Apple answered for him. "Excuse me, but we're not smuts, boo." Then she broke the thing down for him. "See, the smuts who suck and fuck for a couple of ones are beneath us because we're whores. High price whores." she clarified as she fixed Deshonne a healthy plate.

Deshonne just hunched his shoulders. "Hey cuz, don't look at me. What you see is what you get. It just has a price tag on it. They just like us, baby. About they work," he added.

"Tasty, you want something to eat?" she asked and read off the items.

Tasty climbed out of bed on the far side and walked around the room in just a pair of socks. After taking a long look at the food, she tongued down her friend and walked back towards the bathroom. Purnell swiftly reached out and grabbed a hold of one of her heavy breasts as she passed back by, giving it a firm squeeze.

"Next time, pay me first," she said and then walked over to the bathroom door and began to bang hard enough to vibrate the door.

They heard moaning from the time the door opened until it closed.

Apple strutted over to the compact refrigerator and pulled out a flat, two liter grape soda.

"The snow bunny with the donkey on her back is Apple," Deshonne said, finally making the introduction.

"Hey!" she said over her shoulder.

"And the conceited one with the watermelons is Tasty."

Purnell smacked Apple's ass as she walked past causing her to skip once. "Word! I can see why they call you Apple," he happily agreed.

Apple didn't snap at his cousin's violation. She just sat back on Deshonne's lap and shamelessly gave him a lap dance until the stinging subsided.

Deshonne just shook his head at Purnell's uncontrollable conduct.

"Man, fuck that. What's up with a orgy!" Purnell suggested.

"Pee-Wee, did you hear what she said to you earlier?" Deshonne asked.

"Man, I don't give a fuck about that. I'll just smash the big titty bitch when she comes back out. And we can switch later cause I know you sharing."

"Man, you and Tranz can do whatever," he stated with a smirk on his face that said, Good luck. "I'm about to leave in a few minutes, anyway."

"I'm sorry, sweetie, but I don't fuck, I suck. And believe me, you're not gonna wanna pay my price, so you might wanna stick with one of the other girls," Apple informed him before his ideas got out of hand.

"Whatever. What about your girl? Because I ain't that pressed for you, no way."

Apple rolled her eyes at him. "I don't know. Whatever she does is on her, because what she eats don't make me shit." Then she got up and turned around so that her legs were lying on the arm of the chair, and her ass cheeks were sitting directly on his swollen dick. "Where are you going, sexy?"

she asked as she put her arms around his neck and looked into his eyes. "I thought that we were gonna get some more money together again today. It's still early, you know."

"Yeah Magic, where are you going at?" Purnell asked.

"You know that I gotta go and get ready for work. I'll be back afterwards, though."

"Well, where's Tranz at? I thought that he was coming out with us, too," Purnell said.

"Who do you think is fucking in the bathroom?" Deshonne asked.

"Word. he got some more pussy in there, huh? What's she look like?"

Apple just held her breath and waited for Deshonne to respond.

Deshonne glanced at Apple. "She's ah-ight."

I'ma get you as long as you don't fuck none of these other bitches," she thought.

Everyone heard the toilet flush. Then Tasty came squeezing her way back out sideways.

Purnell caught a short glimpse of the third girl, through the mirror. She was kneeling down in front of the toilet, where Tranz was sitting with his legs spread.

"You can at least wait until she closes the door back before you start sucking my dick," they heard Tranz tell her.

Deshonne looked over at his drooling friend. "Yo, let me talk to you for a minute, outside."

"Why? All the pussy's in here," Purnell told him as he watched Tasty crawl back into the bed from behind.

Her worn-out vagina had long, hanging lips that drooped, like her breasts, but he enjoyed every minute of the show.

"Get your money up first, baby. We ain't going nowhere." Tasty told Purnell. *So we can empty out your pockets,* both females thought, as if they shared the same brain.

*****

As he stared at the prostitute's room from across the street at the Super Lodge, Infinite wondered about their next move. Out of all the soldiers the God brought down from the city with him, Infinite was known as the God's right-hand man, his lieutenant.

"Yo, God, why your sons ain't come through and dead them country niggas over there, yet? It's been a couple of days, right?" Infinite asked. His face was sunken in to the bone from all the purple haze smoking sessions he had participated in every day. His size-32 slim Evisu jeans sagged way below his waistline even though he wore a belt, and the X-large wife beater he wore just showed off his bony chest even more.

Even though he heard the question, the God didn't answer him at first. Instead of answering he walked outside and sat on the hood of his new Lexus LS 430, directly facing room 245 from the parking lot across the street. Everytime the door opened or the curtain moved, he knew it.

"They said that it's time for us to get our own hands dirty," the God said to all who were listening.

"What? And what do they call all them pies we dumping out here, white-collar crime?" Infinite asked.

"I don't know, but we on our own as far as beef is concerned," he answered.

Infinite came over and went into the passenger's side of the car to retrieve his marijuana. "So lets just go and work them niggas right now."

A bald-headed, muscular man limped over to join them. His name was Quan, the God's enforcer. "What the fuck is you niggas talking about?" Quan asked.

"We about to go over there and handle them crabs, son," Infinite answered after a pull on the leaf.

"No we not, Quan. Don't listen to Inf. I wanna see what type of time them niggas is on first before I make a move," the God ordered.

"Yo, you cupcaking again, God!" Infinite snapped. "I say we dead them niggas!"

"It doesn't matter what you say, now does it, Inf? Cause I'm still not moving on them unless they come outta that room and violate us by peddling on our turf."

"Yo, them niggas don't even gotta come outta that room to cut our cheddar off, son, as long as they got them bitches on their team," Quan pointed out.

"Yeah, yo. Them cunts done already flipped the script on us. So I say that we peel one of their wigs back to the white meat, just to show the rest of them whores that we won't tolerate being crossed," Infinite stated, again suggesting murder as their only alternative.

"Nah, Inf, I disagree. Them whores in that room are the heart of this strip, feel me? So if we go and knock one of them off, we might as well pack up and relocate because the others is either gonna starve our pockets or put the feds onto us. And, either way, we lose," the God explained.

God's scenario made sense to his crew, but they still wanted to make an example out of somebody. "I say that we cut the flow on that side completely. And if them niggas don't leave, then we pluck one of them ducks off," Quan suggested.

"Okay. But in the meantime, we can still squeeze that fiend Fast-P since he brought them down here in the first place," Infinite said. "I never liked that nigga, no way."

God just shook his head in disagreement, knowing that it was a bad move for business. But the other two out-of-towners gave themselves dap in agreement.

"Yo, you with us or what, God?" Quan asked while Infinite was walking back into the room.

These niggas don't wanna do nothing but beef with niggas all the time. They're forgetting what comes along with it, God thought as he turned to walk away. "Yeah," he agreed.

CHAPTER 26

Paulette Robinson was just getting into a deep sleep when the moaning began.

"Aah!" Deshonne whined out as he shot past her bedroom door like a missile.

She just laid there until the bathroom light illuminated her entire room. Thinking that it was the television causing the noise and that her son was just using the bathroom, she sat up for a second to tell him to turn down the noise as he passed by. But the noise grew louder by the second, and after a minute she knew exactly where the disturbance was coming from.

"Mom, Mom! Get up, Mom, I need you!"

"Oh my God, there's something wrong with my baby!" she said to herself as she jumped clean out of bed in her nightgown and dashed towards the bathroom. "Here I come, baby!"

"Mommy, I'm dying! Please come here!"

Fearing the worst for her son, the 15 seconds it took to reach the bathroom seemed like an eternity.

Deshonne was curled up next to the toilet once his mother finally arrived. The pain he felt inside was so excruciating that he wasn't even aware that she was standing right over him asking, what was wrong.

"Deshonne, what wrong baby?" she asked, almost in tears herself as she kneeled down to help her son.

"Mom, look, it's something wrong."

She didn't know what he was referring to because he didn't raise his hands from his knees as he spoke. So she lifted up his chin to get his attention, and repeated the question.

Streams of tears rolled down his face as he answered. "Look in the toilet."

She looked in the toilet, expecting to find blood, but there was none. "Baby, just tell me what's wrong with you, so I can help. And stop crying," she said as she wiped away his tears.

Deshonne slowly leaned over the toilet and pointed to the cause of his tears. "It's puss, mom. I just peed it out."

Once she put two and two together her fears turned to anger. "Deshonne, nigga, you ain't dying! And I know you ain't just wake me up for this, and you know that I gotta work a double tomorrow."

"Mom, how I make the burning stop?" he pleaded. "It hurts so bad."

She looked at him first, then smacked him hard on the back of the head for scaring her half to death. "Take your burning ass to the hospital," she informed him. "You know, that's what happens when you stick you little dick in every piece of ass that comes your way. Now maybe you'll slow your hot ass down," she stated in her favorite, I told you so tone of voice.

"Please call me a ambulance. My thing is swollen up real bad, and I feel like I'ma die."

Mom Robinson just stood up and crossed her arms. "Boy, I ain't calling nobody's ambulance. You ain't gonna die. You got a bad batch of ass, that's all."

"Mommy, please, I need a doctor."

"And who's gonna pay $500 for your behind to ride around like you really sick? I hope you don't think I am," she said with a smirk on her face.

"Why you laughing at me like it's a game. I'm sick."

"I'm not, baby. But you just so damn hardheaded that can't nobody tell you nothing. And it's a shame because I always tell you to put a hat on when you out there messing with them nasty little girls. You never know who else is dabbling in it. But I don't know nothing, so you don't listen to ya dumb old mother."

"I do listen."

"No, you don't because if you did, you wouldn't be laying on the bathroom floor at four in the morning, crying like a damn newborn baby."

While Deshonne swabbed the snot and tears away with his t-shirt, all that came to mind was, *I don't feel like hearing this shit!*

"Mom, can you please go and wake Dad up for me?"

Mom Robinson made a complete mockery of the whole situation to teach her son a serious lesson about safe sex. "For what? He ain't no damn doctor. He can't help you, neither. Ain't nobody tell you to jump into that pool just because your thing was hot."

Deshonne looked intently at his mother because he knew what she was trying to do, but all he wanted was to alleviate the pain. "Can't you see that I'm hurting? Why you keep playing?"

"I can't tell if you hurting or not because I ain't no damn doctor."

"Mom, can I please borrow your car since you won't call me a ambulance? Because I need to go to the hospital, bad."

"Why can't you just call whoever burnt you? Wake her nasty ass up out of bed and tell her that y'all need to go to the hospital together because her shit is hot," she said, then walked out on him.

As he continued to lie there, waiting to see if she would bring him back the keys, the pain deep within flared again. He reached inside his pants and squeezed his dripping penis as hard as he could around the head in hopes that it would stop the dripping and the pain long enough for him to get help. "Please don't pee again before I have to go to the hospital," he prayed out loud.

He heard his mother's keys slide up towards him. "Have your ass back here before I have to go work, too, stupid," she instructed him before turning away.

"Thank you," he said as he struggled to his feet.

"Don't thank me," she said over her shoulder. "Thank whoever gave you that gift."

*****

The first thing that Deshonne noticed as he walked into the gloomy hospital room was four semi-deflated get-well-soon balloons hovering in the far corner, by the window, and a small, round table cluttered with cards and stuffed animals. But a closer view unveiled the worst of his visit. Kasi lay eerily still, with tubes entering him from every angle from three machines that beeped non-stop, on the side of his elevated bed.

Deshonne tried his best not to show the small pain he felt from the horse-size tranquilizer needle he had just received 20 minutes earlier as he came in to show his support. "So, how have you been feeling, fam?" Deshonne sympathetically asked as soon as Kasi opened his eyes.

Kasi felt around until he found the remote to elevate his head a little higher. "Like a fucking sucker," he bitterly whispered. "It's still a bullet in my back somewhere."

"I know. But I spoke to one of the nurses before I came in, and she said that you should be walking in no time," Deshonne said as he swung his thumb backwards towards the open door.

"Yeah that's what they say, but I still can't move my legs, yet. I just started moving my toes the other day."

Deshonne walked around the room in circles, trying to keep his numbing leg from stiffing up on him, as if he were searching for something. "Where's Lilly?"

"She keeps crying all the time for nothing, so I sent her home," Kasi replied. "Plus, I hate that she keeps talking to me as if I'm a fucking baby."

"She's just thankful that you're here, cuz. You should really try not to be so hard on her. Keep in mind that she's a woman, remember?"

Kasi waved off his suggestion as if her feelings were not a serious issue. Then, out of the blue he said, "thanks, Magic."

Deshonne looked at him oddly. "For what?"

"You know, for paying all of our bills for the next two months. She told me how you and Kenny stepped up to help without her even asking."

Deshonne waved off the charitable deed as if it were nothing. "Don't worry about it," he said. "We peoples remember. I'll continue to do whatever I can to help her out until you get right again, cuz. I know you woulda done the same for me, right?" Deshonne added to uplift his friend's spirits, even though he wasn't sure that the same would have happened if the roles were reversed.

Kasi tried to smile, but his pain was evident, no matter how minimal the movement.

Deshonne walked over to the window and tried to count the cars below to keep his mind off of the painful dripping inside his jeans.

Kasi began to shed quiet tears when he couldn't position his upper body right. Drowning in self-pity, Kasi asked Deshonne, "Did you know that it was some bitch-ass white boys that done this to me?"

Deshonne could hear the frustration in his friend's voice, so he continued to look out of the window as he spoke. "Yeah, I heard a little about it. We've been keeping our eyes and ears glued to the streets for you."

"Did you know that they already had everything, and they still shot me in my fucking back?"

Deshonne just lowered his head in disgust. "Tranz told me that he never really saw the white boy's face, because he had a hat on. Did you get a good look at him?"

"Not really, but I'll never forget his voice, though. I hear it in my sleep every night like a nightmare Magic. The same nightmare over and over again."

Bang!

Deshonne flinched first before swinging around to locate the loud banging sound. Kasi had slammed his fist down on the attached wooden tray in front of him.

"Did the police have anything to say when they questioned you?"

"Nah. and I ain't tell them jakes shit either, because I wanna catch up with them dudes and get even on my own, feel me?" Kasi said with nothing but rage in his voice.

210

"Yeah, I feel you. And I'ma try and make it happen, too," Deshonne promised.

Two nurses came in, interrupting their conversation, with a bedpan, some bandages, and a fresh I.V. "Mr. Jones, we're sorry to interrupt you, but visiting hours are over for now," one of the nurses informed them, while the other nurse pulled the curtain halfway closed.

"Come back later. I'm talking to my boy," Kasi said sternly.

The nurses both looked over at Deshonne for support.

"It's okay, fam. Don't worry, I'll be back. I gotta go and take my mother her car, anyway."

"Man, fuck them nurses, Magic. We're still talking."

As Deshonne backed out of the door, he said, "Don't worry. If the opportunity presents itself, I'll straighten that problem for you, baby! You hear me?"

Kasi agreed, then he waited for Deshonne to disappear before he openly began to whine over his new handicap. as soon as Deshonne reached the elevator, he began to shed tears, too, for the same reason.

*****

The overweight, six-foot-four state trooper stooped low in front of room 245, with his right hand on his holster and his left ear cupped to the door. He knew that there were at least two occupants inside who he assumed were engaging in some sort of illegal activity. So after gathering the necessary information he needed from those unaware occupants, the officer sprang into action.

Bam! bam! bam! He smashed the butt of his heavy, metal flashlight against the scratched plexiglas window, then he announced himself. "Police, open up the door!"

Bam! bam! bam! "I know you're in here, so you might as well open the door before I use this key that I got from the front desk."

The door quickly opened a crack, with the chains lock intact. "Yes, Officer Adams. Is there a problem?"

Officer Adams was the head of the Drug Task Force Unit for the New Castle area, which mainly focused on the triangle. He made it his business to know every prostitute, addict, and dealer in his sector on a first-name basis. Everyone knew his schedule, so those who were smart stayed asleep from eight to four. But the prostitutes always tried to get over by slipping a date or two in before he made his usual rounds, and he always made time to lock them up before his shift ended.

"Take the chain off the door, Baby Girl," he demanded. "We need to talk."

"About what this time?" she asked as if she were awakened out of a good sleep.

Her date was hiding behind the door beside her, trying to get himself together before the officer decided to bust down the door. he tried to help her back into her panties as she spoke, but she kept reaching back, smacking his hand away.

"We're gonna talk about your freedom if you don't open this door right now," he threatened.

"Okay, well, let me put something on first because I was just asleep, and I don't sleep in clothing," she told him.

As soon as she closed the door, she wrapped up in the same towel that her date used to wipe away the evidence, and then she looked around the room for any visible drug paraphernalia, which would warrant a legal search of the room.

"Sit down baby, I got this," she told the frightened banker confidently.

Then she walked over, unhooked the chain, and stepped back so that the officer could enter. Adams came strolling in, locking the door behind him. he then canvassed the room while those inside sat side by side on the messy bed.

By the time he was finished his search, he had a hot crack cocaine stem from the bottom dresser drawer, residue-covered baggies from the wastebasket, and a condom wrapper from the side of the bed as evidence.

"Both of you," he instructed as he pointed towards the floor, "get on your knees and put your hands behind your head."

Baby Girl swiftly did as she was told, but her customer objected without first being explained the proper reasons why.

"For what!" he barked back. "I haven't broken any laws here. I'm just visiting my friend."

While attempting to pull the troublemaking man down by his belt, Baby Girl's towel came undone, unveiling every petite inch of her. She didn't bother to cover back up once she locked eyes with the officer.

Adams wrestled with the 50 year-old, gray haired bank president for less than a minute before he came to his senses and surrendered. Then, instead of asking the adolescent girl to put some clothes on so that he could restrain her, he just stared at her unblemished frame with lust.

"Sir, do you know how many felonies you've committed in this room today?" Adams asked.

And just that fast, all the resistance diminished.

"I—I—I just stopped by to see how she was doing," he stuttered. "And I was just leaving when you came to the door, officer."

Baby Girl turned to face the man. "No, you weren't, Daddy. You were about to pay me for my services."

"Officer, I don't know what she's talking about. She's a liar!" he frantically blurted. "The last time I checked, conversations were free."

Baby Girl rolled her eyes at the man, stood up, and then walked back over to the other side of the bed. She whipped back the sheets and picked up the used condom that she watched the man tuck just before the door opened. "Your juices don't fill up a rubber for free if you're alone with me," she stated while dangling the condom in front of the man's face as proof of her deeds. She then placed the slimy rubber on the man's shoulder and picked up another towel to cover herself. "So unless you want me to tell the officer how you were raping me before he came to my rescue, I suggest that you cough up my money."

213

Adams stood there, snickering, until the theatrics were over. Then he uncuffed the man and instructed him to remain in the same position.

"Obviously, you know that this is just a ploy on her behalf to get money out of me, which I refuse to give her because I haven't done anything. So I would like to be released," he passively reasoned as he swiped off his shoulder and stood.

"Sure, you can, now. But only after you pay the lady for her time," Adams answered.

The man was outraged. He snapped at Adams as if he were a civilian. "Pay her for what? We were just talking, I said."

"You better pay me for the two minutes it took you to cum or I'm pressing charges," she insisted with her hand out.

The banker backed up towards the door as if he was looking to make a run for it. Adams, in turn, unsnapped his holster to show that he meant business.

"Wait, wait!" the banker man shouted with his hands in front of himself to keep the officer at bay. "There's no need for that. I'm sure we can work something out, right?" he stated as he slowly reached back to pulled out his wallet. Realizing that his wallet wasn't there, he began to look around the room.

"Oops, my fault," Baby Girl said as she pulled the wallet out from behind the dresser.

He stretched for his wallet, but she swiftly opened it and snatched out the contents, then threw it in his direction.

Adams stepped between them before things got ugly.

"Officer, I know you're not gonna let her just steal $700 from me," he complained.

Adams kindly opened the door up for the man and stepped aside. "Sir, that's the risk you take when you pay whores for sex. You never know when you're gonna get robbed blind, right before your eyes."

With that said, the banker realized that the pair was scamming him. But with no defense all he could do was leave. So he peacefully walked out to his Audi A6, and pulled away.

She couldn't wait to land her five-foot, 110-pound frame on Adams, locking her slender legs around his waist. "Thank you, Daddy!" she said excitedly.

Adams just stood there without saying a word for a minute, holding her up, inhaling her strong perfume.

"What's wrong?" she asked when he didn't respond.

"Nothing. I'm just here for my usual," he stated, still without any sign of emotion.

"Today is only Friday," she objected.

While still holding her up, Adams unstrapped his belt and dropped his trousers down to his ankles. His hard dick slapped against her firm butt cheeks. "Look, either I get mine off when I want to, or I'll just lock your trashy ass up for solicitation, attempting to bribe an officer of the law, robbery, and possession of narcotics," he threatened while prying her away.

Baby Girl flopped back onto the bed, laughing. "Damn, boo, I was just kidding with you. No need to get all hostile and shit. You know I always grant your wish."

"Good, then roll over," he commanded.

She looked at him. "Am I still getting paid for two even though Ernest isn't here?"

Adams opened the drawer where she stored the condoms, while she patiently waited on her stomach for him to either penetrate her or answer her question. "One cop, one badge, one payment," he told her as he flipped the short towel onto her back.

She just made a disappointed face while she parted her legs as far as she could for him. "Is this all you want from me today?" she whispered.

"No. We need to talk about the new players I keep hearing about after you clean me up," he said while thrusting deep inside of her.

Then she grabbed the sheets and began to moan as his stubby, uncircumcised penis invaded her loose ass-hole without any lubricant or resistance.

"Oooh!"

215

CHAPTER 27

Deshonne's cell phone alerted him as it moved around in his pocket. Without checking to see whom the incoming call was coming from, he slouched down in the seat to answer it.

"Yo," he whispered.

The man to the left of him cut his eye in Deshonne's direction as if he were disturbing the movie.

"Shhh," Marie playfully whispered with a smile.

"Hey, cuz! Where you at? I'm parked in front of your folks crib now," Kenny informed him.

"Man, I'm way out 202, at Regal Cinema, with my friend, right now. Why, what's up?" he asked.

Marie tapped Deshonne on the shoulder, leaned over, and softly whispered, "Just tell her that you're busy, right now. This is my time, remember."

He covered up the phone to tell her who it was, then just smiled at her for a second.

She then lay on his shoulder to eavesdrop on the conversation.

"Your friend who? You still spending money on them dike broads?" Kenny questioned.

"Nah, I'm with my new friend. And, no you don't need to know her name yet, so don't ask me for it," he warned.

Deshonne didn't want people to know about Marie, so he decided to keep her a secret from everybody, at least until he could get to know her, because to him the past was the past.

"Why you just don't tell him who I am?" she whispered proudly.

"Because if I let him know that I'm on a date with a super model, he might come stalking us for your autograph," he joked.

Satisfied with his make-believe reason, she just smiled at the compliment and returned her focus to the movie.

"Yo, we need to talk about all the shady shit that's been going on the last couple of days," Kenny said, trying to enlighten his friend about the quiet beef that was about to go public on the streets between art and them.

"Can't it wait until after Bad Boyz II is over because I've been waiting a lifetime for this one female to come around," Deshonne said, just loud enough to ensure that Marie heard him.

"Yeah, it can wait. Go ahead and enjoy yourself."

"Cool. And I'll come through the block and holler at you right after I drop her off."

"Noo! Stay off of 23rd period," Kenny barked into the phone.

"Why, what's up?"

"Nothing serious, I just don't want you out there until after I tell you what's up. So just call me after you get back to mom dukes crib, and I'll meet you there."

"You sure?" Deshonne asked.

"Yeah, I'm sure. Just holler back at me when you're done," Kenny said before hanging up.

"So, I'm your little secret now, huh?" Marie asked as soon as he reached his arm around her shoulder and gently rested his hand on one of her soft breasts.

"Nah. You're too beautiful to be my secret, Marie. You're my ultimate fantasy, the prize that everyone wants to win."

"You need to stop it," she said, blushing.

"Stop what? I'm dead serious," he protested.

"Magic, you're not the first man that's tried to sweet talk his way into my pants. I do have a 14 year-old daughter, remember?"

"I would never try to just fuck you, Marie, because you're more special than that. But if that opportunity does

217

arrive, I promise you that I will make love to you like you deserve," he said boldly, catching her off guard.

"Boy, stop lying and watch the movie," she said as she turned his face back towards the screen. "You just say anything out of your face."

"I'm telling you, it wouldn't be me if I didn't put my thing down as best as I could," Deshonne said as he turned back in her direction to continue the conversation. He grabbed the box of extra-large popcorn out of her lap and began to feed it to her. "Besides, I rather watch you smile all night, instead of this movie."

"Whatever. It's your money, Casanova," she reminded him, before turning back to the blockbuster.

I can't wait! he thought.

*****

Art walked up behind his new lady friend and put his arms around her waist, resting his chin on her shoulder as she gazed out the window.

"What you thinking about?" he asked because she was so quiet.

Seeing that she was focused on the people down the street, he asked. "What's wrong? Do you know any of them clowns down there?"

"Yep, as a matter of fact, I know that clown very well. He's my children's father."

Art squinted his eyes, to take a closer look at the potential problem. Whom he saw not only surprised him, but also pleased him. "Pee-Wee's your baby daddy?" he asked, just to make sure that they were both looking at the same person.

Still bitter about his cheating, Tonya said, "Yeah, unfortunately. But I hate that yellow bastard."

And then a devious thought came to mind. She asked him to use the telephone.

"For what? I hope you don't think that you're gonna call that clown-ass nigga from my phone," Art complained. "I don't fuck with that nigga or his sucker-ass boy like that!"

"I wish I would call him. I'm calling my brothers so they can come and fuck him up!" Tonya said as she started to dial one of her brother's numbers. Then another thought popped into her head before she could punch in the last number.

"What's up? What's wrong?" he asked, anxious to see a beatdown.

"Purnell doesn't come outside to hustle without a gun," she said while pointing across the street to the abandoned barber shop on 23rd and Jessup. "It's probably over there in that flower bed he keeps going to or a nearby mailbox." Art then reached for his cell phone. "You sure he got a gun on him?"

"Always. Especially when he's by himself."

"Ah-ight then, I'll handle it later on myself."

"No, don't worry about it. It's not that serious," Tonya told Art, fearing that someone might get hurt.

"You sure?" he asked.

"Yeah, I'm sure. I'm not really worried about the deadbeat, anyway," she assured him.

Art laughed it off. "Ah-ight then. Well, let me go to the bathroom real quick. You can just pick us out a good movie off the on-demand channel," he told her. Then as soon as he closed the door and turned on the faucet, he pressed send to complete the telephone number.

A female dispatcher answered on the first ring. "Hello, Drug Watch. Please hold."

"I sure will," he whispered.

*****

Deshonne's awkward stride was still noticeably slow, as he tracked down Memorial Drive towards the motels. Purnell wondered why.

"Yo, nigga, is them New Balances too small or something?"

"Nah, bitch. My butt still hurts from this shot that the doctors gave me a couple days ago," Deshonne moaned.

"What you get a needle in your ass for? You burning or something?" Purnell joked.

"Yeah." Deshonne answered plainly.

Purnell then jogged forward and stopped Deshonne by putting his arm across his chest. "Stop playing, my nigga."

"Was I just walking like I was playing?" Deshonne asked as he swatted away his friend's hand.

Purnell laughed at first, but when the question of whom he got the STD from came to mind, he suddenly became serious. "Oh shit, cuz! It wasn't none of them bitches from down the motel, was it?" he asked as he began to panic, because he was secretly having sex with Tasty.

"Fuck, no!" Deshonne replied as if the question was a smack in the face. "I get too much ass to be fucking them tricks, fam."

"Well, who was it then? Them dike broads that you keep holding out on?"

"Nah, it wasn't Eve, either. It was the young babe from around Arbor Place, Angel."

"Who the fuck is Angel? I don't think I know that one."

"Well, remember that night that I was supposed to be meeting you down here, and Safe Streets came to my people's house?"

"Yeah, that was the same night that Kasi got hit up, right?"

"Yea, that's the night that I got caught up smutting the babe."

"Well, you still ain't told me who she is yet."

"Man, I can't explain her to you if you don't already know who I'm talking about. Just remember that if you come across a petite, bow-legged, brown-skinned broad with a phat little ass that likes to get drunk on the regular, you might wanna keep walking," he warned.

"See. That's why I don't go raw dog in smuts," Purnell dishonestly stated.

"Me, neither," Deshonne said with his face scrunched up. "I ain't smash Angel raw. I got Gonorrhea from her because she gave me face without a condom on."

Purnell's heart began to flutter at the unfortunate information. His new fear turned to denial and disbelief. "Man, stop playing with my emotions. I know you lying, cause I ain't never heard about nobody getting burnt by a broad giving'em head."

"Man, listen, I'm telling you, the doctor told me that's what happened to me. Because I didn't fuck her raw. My word," Deshonne stated, raising his right hand as if he were taking an oath.

Purnell caught instant chills, causing him to stop dead in his tracks.

Deshonne glanced back to swear again, only to find Purnell with a dumbfounded look on his face. "What's wrong with you, lame?" he asked.

"Yo, do you think Green Eyes burning?"

"Who the fuck is Green Eyes?"

"Tasty, Magic. Now answer my question honestly. Do you think she got something?"

"What you asking me for? I ain't her gynecologist. How the fuck am I supposed to know what's inside that woman's pussy?" he answered sarcastically.

Damn, I'm all fucked up now, Purnell thought as he moped past Deshonne.

Deshonne shook the stiffness out of his leg before proceeding.

"Yo, you know them bitches had got butt-ass naked after you left and put on a show for me, right? So the next thing I know, Tasty and Baby Girl was eating each other out and shit, right? But your snow bunny was in the bathroom getting dressed or something. So, when your snow bunny came back out she told me to join in and that they wouldn't mind as long as I gave them a couple rocks after I got my thing off," Purnell explained. "So I went on ahead and went hard."

Deshonne could hear the worry in his friend's voice, which made him laugh for no apparent reason. "So you stoop to fucking certified prostitutes raw dog, now, huh?"

"Man, fuck, no! I—I let her choke on my python," he said, holding himself.

"So you admitting that you let big titties suck your dick without a condom on, right?"

"Man, I ain't saying shit!"

"Okay, well, don't say shit when your piss gets hot, too, nigga. Keep it to yourself."

"Don't get mad with me because your snow bunny got you walking all funny," Purnell retorted to see if Deshonne had already tapped the exotic white girl who declined all of his advances.

"What snow bunny? I know you ain't talking about Apple?"

"Yeah, I am, cause I know you already smashed her. That's the only reason I can think of that would have that bitch acting like you her man and shit."

"You crazy as hell! You know that I don't get down like that with no fiends," Deshonne protested.

"So you mean to tell me that you haven't tapped that blazing ass white girl's pussy at least one time, yet? But she still brings you every sell, no matter who's in the room and clings to your every word, from the time you get there till the time you leave. Just on the strength that you a nice guy, huh."

"Yep," Deshonne agreed proudly.

"You lying, nigga. I'ma ask her did you smash, watch," Purnell promised as they reached the intersection of New Castle Avenue and Memorial Drive.

As soon as they stopped at the corner to wait for the traffic to slow up, Deshonne noticed a female in a sleazy-looking tube top, extra-short miniskirt, and platform sneakers strutting her stuff like a runway model through the Gulf Gas Station parking lot. "There she goes, right there. You can go right ahead and ask her right now," he dared.

If you didn't smash her, I am. Purnell gladly plotted. "Oh, shit. Yo!" he yelled as soon as he realized that the car beside him was carrying a familiar passenger. "Tasty! Pull over!"

As he looked at Apple from across the street, Deshonne realized that his control over her came simply because of the way that he had played his cards during their first encounter.

He also knew that he could do whatever he wanted to do with Apple for free if he chose to, because she believed that he was the man of their crew, so he vowed to use that to his advantage, every chance he could. It didn't hurt that she was willingly showcasing her enticing assets at him every time he entered the room. He continued to downplay her advances because he had something better awaiting him at home.

CHAPTER 28

After ringing the doorbell for about five minutes, Deshonne finally came and opened the door for Kenny.

"Why you ain't ready for work? It's 4:30," Kenny said as he followed his friend back up to the bedroom.

"Because I switched to the early-morning shift now. That way, I can go straight from the block to work, then home to sleep," Deshonne explained while crawling back into bed.

Kenny sat in the chair at the foot of the bed and turned on the video game. As he waited for Madden football to load up, he noticed that there were even more boxes and bags scattered throughout the room than before. So while making a quick survey of Deshonne's new possessions, he also calculated their value. He realized that his friend's spending habits had increased greatly.

"I see you got a rental car outside," Kenny pointed out, referring to the 03 gold four-door Dodge Intrepid in the driveway. "You still wasting money, huh."

Damn! This nigga don't miss shit, Deshonne said to himself. "I got tired of begging people for rides, so I went and copped it from that Enterprise over on 36th and Market."

"And who kicked out the change for the flick the other night?" Kenny asked, maintaining his line of questioning.

Deshonne sat up and hawkeyed the back of Kenny's head. "What's with the Jeopardy questions?"

Kenny paused the game and candidly turned around to respond. "I'm just wondering if you can see what I see cousin, that's all."

"Man, is this what you interrupted my movie for the other night? You finally realizing that I'm trying to enjoy myself?"

"Nah, that's not what I wanted at all. But I figure it wouldn't be me if I didn't say something, especially since your brother isn't here."

"Ah-ight, well, you said something. And I'm aware of my spending habits. So thank you very much, Dad," Deshonne replied. Then he covered his head back up with a pillow.

Kenny got mad that Deshonne was ignoring his warnings, so he ripped the sheets off of him. "Yo, get up. We gotta talk."

"About what?" Deshonne asked, still lying comfortably in his boxers.

"Art."

"What about him?"

"He's plotting on your block, that's what."

Deshonne laughed it off. "Oh, well, fuck that block." Deshonne blurted. "He can have it if he wants to because I got a new gold mine out this way."

In disbelief, Kenny asked, "Where?"

"The Ave. My nigga, where it's jumping 24/7," Deshonne told him.

"Nigga, is you crazy! Them motels are the hottest spots in New Castle."

Deshonne snatched the covers back. "Oh, well. I'm dumping them joints on time, so who cares?"

Kenny was heated about Deshonne's recklessness, but he still decided to stick with the plan. "What you got left off of the pack, Magic?"

"I don't know. Why?" Deshonne shot back. He then sat up and put on his glasses, as if it made him hear better.

"I need that change when you're done because them last nine I took you to get came from me."

Deshonne looked at him curiously now because things weren't adding up. This made him skeptical because he had already finished the pack that Kenny was referring to and had picked up a fresh batch yesterday. So either his best friend was trying to scam him, or his best friend had already been scammed himself.

"I finished that pack two days ago and got a fresh batch yesterday."

Shit! I need my money, Kenny thought. "Okay, well, what's done so far?" he asked as if it wasn't serious.

"I don't know yet because everything's down Pee-Wee's put-up," Deshonne answered honestly.

Kenny snapped. "How you gonna trust that nigga with 250 grams, Magic? You doing that dumb-ass shit again, huh!"

"Man, I trust that nigga like I trust you, clown. We're all the same. We grew up together, remember?" Deshonne stated in defense.

"No, we not. You must've forgotten how he fucked up pack after pack until you came home."

"So what? You already got your $2,000, didn't you?"

"Yeah, thanks to you."

"Ah-ight then. As long as everybody gets paid on time, it shouldn't matter who I trust, or what I buy. As a matter of fact, it shouldn't be any problems at all."

"You know what? Fuck it, you right. You just make sure that you hit me up when you get the next $6,750. As a matter of fact, you can just drop it off at my party on Saturday," Kenny said sarcastically.

Deshonne couldn't take it when someone talked slick or tried to belittle him, friend or no friend. So since his friend was acting out of character, he decided to do the same by questioning his friend's motive. "I thought that you wasn't getting involved with this part of the game no more. You said don't give you no money, remember?"

"I'm not. But I'm collecting what I put into the partnership, so I can get out completely. I can't beef and get money at the same time."

He could tell that Kenny's voice was beginning to tremble, so he knew that there was more to the story than what Kenny was volunteering. "Don't tell me that them niggas done scared you out of the game because we can go and get at them niggas right now," Deshonne announced, to see what buttons he could push.

"We will," Kenny stated, as if he already had plans for their demise. Deep down Kenny wanted to pop Art for what he had done to him that day in the shop, but he was so close to getting out, he didn't want to get sucked back in so easily. He knew that Deshonne, on the other hand, would move full speed ahead with whatever plan he put in motion because he was loyal to the bone, so he played things to his advantage. "After I collect all my money, Art will get everything that he deserves."

"What, you wanna wait until after the party?" Deshonne asked as if his friend was scared.

"Yeah, after the party," Kenny said reluctantly.

"Whatever," Deshonne changed the subject. "So, are we getting in free?"

"Who's we?"

"Me and my new friend. I'ma bring her, too."

"What? Do you know how many broads come to my parties? Is you crazy?"

"Word. Foreal, though, I ain't thinking about no other broads right now cause I got a real keeper. And, believe me, she's got the whole package," Deshonne stated with his hands to confirm Marie's shape. "I'm telling you, she's not only beautiful, her body's banging, too, cuz."

"Well, what's her name?"

"You'll find out at the party when I introduce y'all."

"Oh, that's how we get down now, huh? You keeping secrets from me." Kenny caught Deshonne off guard and gripped him in a headlock. They started wrestling. "Tell me her name," Kenny demanded as he tightened his grip.

"You'll see on Saturday!" Deshonne laughed.

*****

For three weeks in a row Desiree worked through her lunch breaks to avoid seeing everyone. Little beads of sweat covered her nose, and patches of perspiration soaked her armpits as she transported boxes of unsorted mail to her work station.

"Look who's hiding in the dungeon!" Iyanna shouted out cheerfully as she approached. She brushed off a box next to Desiree's station with the files in her hand so she wouldn't get dirt stains on her new cream-colored Banana Republic pant suit.

"Oh, hey, girl. What's up?" Desiree said as her train of thought was broken. Then she turned her focus back to the work pile that was in front of her.

"That's what I came to ask you," Iyanna whispered. She then placed her hands on top of Desiree's so that she would stop working long enough to answer her next question. "Why am I the last one to find out the good news?"

Desiree stared at her with bewilderment for a second. "What news? Did I get a raise or something?"

"Girl, you've gotta tell me your secret! Because you got to have a helluva sex game to have pulled this one off," Iyanna said excitedly.

Desiree snatched her hands away. "What are you talking about now with your nasty self? What did I pull off?"

"Why you ain't tell me that Alex was getting a divorce? You got a new husband, girl!"

The female in the next station was a gossiping troublemaker. So to avoid any further leaks, Desiree quickly covered up Iyanna's mouth to calm her down. "Shhh! Stop jumping around like you ain't got no sense, girl. The Alex I know isn't leaving his wife and kids for me. He doesn't even have the heart to file his taxes alone."

Iyanna pointed down, then lifted up just enough to pull the top file folder from underneath her bottom. "Then what's this I'm holding?" she asked, fanning the file in front of Desiree's face.

Desire's heart dropped once she realized that her friend wasn't playing a hoax on her. *Shit, shit, shit!* she thought as she held out her hand.

"The ex-Mrs. Emiliano got served with these papers a half hour ago," Iyanna stated as she handed over the blue file. "And, believe me, the way that woman's mascara was running, I don't think that she saw this one coming."

"I don't believe it. He's actually leaving her," Desiree realized while skimming through the bulky packet.

So that's where he works at, huh. She made a mental note about why he knew Deshonne.

"Dee, the big house in North Wilmington, the Mercedes Benz, the extravagant wardrobes, and fancy dinners will all be yours soon."

Desiree closed up the folder and tossed it back in her friend's lap. "How did you get this, Yanni?"

"How do you think I got it? She chuck it, so I took it out of her wastebasket as soon as she left, copied it down to the very last envelope, and brought it straight to you."

"Well, you can just take it back to where you got it from because I don't want it, or him," she stated, annoyed.

"Dee, are you crazy? This man is giving up everything to be with you. You can finally move out of that box you call an apartment and scrap that used car for a spaceship."

"I don't need all that extra stuff, Yanni. I'm content with what little I have now."

"What about having love and good sex, Dee? Those are necessities too. And you can't sit here and tell me that you are completely happy by yourself."

Desiree no longer cared who heard her. "Yanni, love is just a fable that can never be achieved in life. And sex is just a game that people play to pass time. So I could care less about either of them because they don't define who I am as a woman."

"Well, you sure fooled Alex then, because he's throwing his whole life away to chase both of those things that you care nothing about."

"I always told him that our friendship was just an outlet for our built-up stress. And believe me when I say that I do feel sorry for his wife, but that has nothing to do with me."

"Come on, Dee, you've been sleeping with the man for a year now. So who's not being realistic here? I think that this has everything to do with you."

"I didn't ask for this!" Desiree shouted in denial.

"You didn't have to because your actions did," Iyanna told her. She then turned back towards the elevator.

Desiree just sank back down into her chair, covering up her flushed face.

*****

Even in a white tee, basic blue jeans, and wheat Timberlands, Marie's beauty was undeniable. She continuously had to ignore each man who blew his horn until she reached her destination just to stop them from pulling over and talking to her. As soon as she rounded the corner, Shane lustfully
undressed his cousin with his intoxicated imagination.

"They've been missing you at the card games lately," he said as she approached the porch. "Where you been at?"

"Cards have been the farthest thing from my mind, Shane. I've been home with my new friend, chilling."

"Well, what happened to getting money? You don't want none of this free money out here no more?"

"Yeah, why you think I'm out early? I came to see who's out."

"So we doing orders today, right?" Shane asked happily.

"Ain't that the only time that I come outside before 12? Just to get these clowns money," she conceitedly stated.

Shane knew that he would make out good on each order that he got her, so he didn't want her to get away. He swiftly stood up and opened up the front door for her. "Don't worry cuz, I got you. Go ahead on in and visit my mother, and I'll bring you a Christmas list from them niggas over on Pine Street."

Marie poured on her usual persuasion tactics to motivate Shane, pouting and crossing her arms like a spoiled little kid. "I don't got all day, Shane. I have to pick up Kelia from down my mom's this afternoon."

"What's the rush? She's alright. Plus, the mall ain't even packed, yet."

"Shane, my friend is coming over later, so I wanna be done all my running around early."

"Cuz, what's more important, money or some clown-ass nigga?" Shane asked as if he knew her answer.

"My friend," she answered confidently.

Shane was always interested in her personal life because it always benefited him, especially when it came to street dealers. "You must've came up on a baller, huh? Because you don't never put money second to no nigga."

"I don't know if he's a baller. But as far as I can tell, he's not wanting for nothing with the job he has."

"Tell me his name, and I'll tell you if he's making noise on the streets or not."

"Nope," she said flatly. "I'd rather find out on my own this time."

"Huh? Since when did you become so secretive?"

"Never. I'm just going about this one differently for once because I'm feeling this one."

"So I guess that means you already told him what you do up front, then, huh?" Shane jealously asked.

"He already knows that I don't have a job, for your information, Shane. He's known me since grade school, and he's known all about Kelia since she was in pampers," she proudly explained even though she knew that, that wasn't what he was referring to.

"Cuz." Shane said with his hands raised questioningly.

Marie didn't respond, she just walked into the house to visit her aunt. Shane stood there, watching her until her rear end wobble out of sight.

"I'll tell him when I'm ready to. But by then, he won't even   care,"   she   assured   herself.

CHAPTER 29

To Deshonne every day had become a routine that he could comfortably look forward to. But, Apple's outlook on her #1 man had soured once she realized that he wasn't going to fall for her alluring bait. She had come to think of him as nothing more than a nuisance who supplied her with drugs. So, out of disgust, one particular morning she decided to show him how she felt.

Deshonne's normal soft rap came on the flexible window. She just flung the door wide open so that it slammed up against the rubber stopper and bounced back at him. He immediately noticed her combative attitude, her exposed breasts, and her almost invisible G-string. "What's wrong with you?"

"I'm starting not to like you," she told him as he closed the door.

Even though he tried, Deshonne still wasn't immune to her desirable figure. His penis stiffened before she took the three steps it took to reach the bed. And by the time she crawled back under the covers, he was wishing that she wasn't a fiend. "Damn, where'd that come from?" he asked as he sat down on the bed next to her.

"Outta my mouth," she snapped. "I'm about to cut you off."

"Come on, shorty. Don't I come through every morning and check on you?"

"I do bad things for a living, remember? I don't need a babysitter."

Deshonne took her grumpiness as just a sign of a lack of sleep. So he tossed $10 onto the table for her usual McDonald's breakfast, since he forgot to grab it on the way in, and three dimes for a morning blast.

She turned up her face at him. "You can keep your scraps if I can't get paid what I'm worth, then I don't want it."

"Paid, for what? I go out of my way to make sure that you eat and get a wake-up on the strength just cause you good peoples. I don't charge you for none of that."

"You must think that I'm a slow bitch, right? Like I don't know that, one way or another, every dime that you give me, I end up paying for."

Deshonne saw nothing positive coming out of the argument, so he gracefully bowed out before he lost his best customer. "Apple, chill, you win!" he said while slowly wiping her hair away from her eyes. Her clientele far exceeded his, so she was well worth whatever she wanted in the long run. So he compromised. "Look, I'm sorry if you've been feeling disrespected or cheated in any way because those were never my intentions. So, from now on, I'm gonna hit you off better for the time that I spend in here, and the sells that I make. Ah-ight?"

Deshonne tossed two more bags onto the table. "They're on me, shorty. Don't worry about it." Apple shook her head at him because he really didn't know what she was bugging out about. She wasn't beefing over a couple of bags. She wanted the grand prize for herself.

"You can take them back because that's not what I was talking about," she stated with empathy as she released the covers and caressed his unshaven, five-o'clock shadow. "I've never had to beg for anything I've wanted in life, Magic, because men have always offered to give it to me first. But for some reason you're different. So I don't mind having to beg if I have to because for you, I will," she said as she leaned in to kiss his awaiting lips.

Deshonne slipped out of her grasp before their lips could meet and stood up. His hormones were beginning to take over, so he wanted to contain the situation before it got out of his control. "Man, I thought that we were finally past this dumb stuff," he nervously said.

"What's dumb about trying to give you the chance that every man I have encountered has begged me for?" She knew how to entice him. So she scooted out of the bed and stood up close in front of him until their eyes met. "I've only had one real dick inside of me in my whole life, Magic. It's like fucking a virgin all over again, I promise."

He tried to stand his ground by backing up a little as he spoke, but she moved with him until his back was against the wall, and her breasts were pressed firmly against his chest.

"I'm throwing this pussy at you for free, boo. And all I want in return is for us to spend a little more time together."

Deshonne's willpower was deflating by the second. She could feel his dick grow even harder as their bodies touched.

"Control this pussy," she seductively requested as her tongue reached his ear.

Then his cell phone began to vibrate in his pocket. *Saved by the bell*! he said to himself as he dropped his hands to check his phone.

She stepped back, just far enough to wiggle out of her extremely tight panties while he handled his business.

Deshonne covered up the receiver. "It's my soulmate. Shhh, I have to answer this call."

Not now, she won't! Apple said to herself as she yanked away his phone while she still had control of the situation, and tossed it onto the bed. "Magic, it's only sex I'm asking for. I'm not asking you to marry me. I just want you to fuck me real good and hard from time to time. No one will ever know except the two people in this room. I swear," she promised as she stepped back in close to unbuckle his Roc-A-Wear belt.

"You asking me to cheat on my girl, Apple. Even if she doesn't find out, I'll always know."

Frustrated by the way he continuously turned down all her sexual advances, Apple jerked her hands away and flopped down on the bed. "So what! I see how you stare at me every day. And don't you think that's cheating? Every time that I sit on your lap or grab your dick it's cheating, Magic. And you haven't said anything to her about that, I'm sure of it. So I know that you're curious."

"I never said that I'm not attracted to you. But I'm just not on that type of time."

"What are you afraid of? For the first time in my life I'm being completely honest and up-front with you."

"I know, and I appreciate it, I do. But—"

He hesitated so she cut him off. "But what? I'm a whore, right!" she said, finishing his sentence.

"That's not what I was gonna to say. See, you putting words in my mouth."

"Magic, keeping it real with you, every date I get, my whole intention is to rob him blind. That's why I walk around here naked because usually that's all it takes to do what I have to. Now, I am a whore. But I swear I ain't never fuck not one of these nasty-ass men. The only reason they call me the Queen of the Avenue is because I'm the master of hand jobs and oral sex."

Her eyes were sincere when she spoke. And the emotion in her voice touched them both in different ways. But the facts still remained the same as far as Deshonne was concerned. She was still an addict and a prostitute, so no matter what else he felt, she would always be the same woman at the end of the day.

"You don't have to explain anything to me because I already know what type of person you are inside."

Too proud to let any man see her shed a tear for him, she turned her back and dropped her head down into her own hands, and said "I just wanted you to know that I'm not as nasty as you think I am, Magic. My legs stay closed."

If only she wasn't in this business," he thought, as he stood there, speechless.

Someone began to knock on the door, so Deshonne walked over and covered her up with a sheet off of the floor.

"What are you doing?" she asked.

"I'm about to get the door."

"Ooooh, I hate you! Move!" she yelled at him. Then she shoved him aside to answer the door herself.

*****

Gander Hill Prison was a dead end. The building was only built to hold approximately 1,500 inmates, but was now exceeding its capacity by almost 400, year-round. Which made it rough on the underpaid guards and hell on the inmates. Since Delaware was now becoming a police state, probation and parole kept the facility overcrowded with criminals, no matter how minimal their crimes.

As Purnell looked around the room at the scared and restless men, he hoped that he would be gone before the guards could bring him his roll-up bag, which consisted of two sheets, a pillowcase, one towel, one face cloth, and two uniforms.

Booking and receiving was hot and packed with rowdy people. He could see bodies on top of every mattress, filling all eight holding cells, even lining the walls as he made his only allowed phone call.

"I can never sleep in on my day off," Mom Robinson grumbled as she leaned over to answer the telephone. "Hello!"

The computerized answering machine kicked in instantly. "This is a collect call from...Pee-Wee! At Gander Hill Prison. If you wish to accept this call, please dial one now. If you want to know..." the recording continued on while she ran to her son's room.

Purnell listened close to the voice and the background to see who picked up the phone. When he recognized the voice before the recording started, all he could say to himself was, "I know I'm gonna hear it now."

The recording repeated itself a second time. As it was coming to an end, he got a lump in his throat as his only shot at bail seemed to fade.

"Please press one," he prayed.

"If you wish to accept this call, please press one now."

Beep! "Thank you."

"Hello?" she repeated in a frustrated tone.

"Hey, Mom, is Magic there?"

"Purnell, why are you calling my house collect at 8:30 in the morning?"

"I'm sorry Moms, but they locked me up yesterday, and this is the only chance I got to use the phone. This is my only phone call before they send me to the gym or upstairs."

"See. I told you boys that a hard head makes a soft ass, Purnell. Didn't I? Didn't I tell y'all to cut that dumb stuff out?"

"Moms, I swear, I ain't do nothing. I was just walking down 23rd Street to meet some girl, and these two dudes ran up on me and tackled me. So we started fighting. I didn't know that they was the police," he lied.

She knew that there was more to what he was saying because she knew him like she knew her own two sons. "Baby, the police don't tackle innocent people for nothing. It had to be more to it than that."

"Yeah, they trying to say that I had a gun, but they never found one on me."

"Well, what you want me to do, Purnell? Deshonne ain't here. He done snuck his hardheaded ass out of here already."

As soon as he heard that Deshonne was gone, nausea suddenly overcame him. The thought of being back in the system worried him more than being poor on the street. *Aw, man, he's probably down there, fucking Apple*, he thought. "Mom, can you call Tonya for me?"

"Can't you call her after you hang up from me? I don't like calling other people's houses this early in the morning."

"We beefing, so she's just gonna hang up on me if I tell her where I'm at. That's why I need you on the phone. Plus, she won't answer the phone, anyway, if she doesn't recognize the number."

"Well, I'm sorry to hear that, but I can't make her answer the phone or talk to you baby."

"I know, but I just need you to tell her what's happening if she answers. And if she don't, just leave her a message. Please?"

She sighed. "Boy, you know that y'all is a pain in my ass?"

"I know, Mom. And I'm sorry, but you the only person that I can count on."

"Well, what you want me to say to the girl?"

"Tell her that I need her to give Magic all my money. They gave me a $5,000 cash bail for my violation of probation so far, and they might try to be slick and come back and give me a higher bail for the gun charge."

"Hold on. How they violate you in the first place if they never found a gun?"

"Because they said I violated my probation when I fought the police. But I wouldn't of had to fight if they wouldn't of tackled me first."

"You have two minutes remaining for this call," the computerized operator announced.

"Moms the phone is about to hang up on us," he stated as if the world was coming to an end.

"Okay, baby, don't worry. I'ma call that girl until I get a hold of her. Alright. And as soon as Deshonne walks in here, I'ma send him right back out the door to go and get your money."

"Can I call you back?"

"Sure, you can. Every chance you get to call, you call and let—"

The phone went straight to a busy tone for both parties, but Purnell continued to hold it close to his ear for a few extra seconds because he didn't want to go back into holding cell 141.

As soon as the cigar-smoking C.O. closed the door, Purnell began vomiting onto his sneakers.

*****

Deshonne was creeping through the house in the dark, unaware that his mother was shadowing his movements from the living room couch. He nonchalantly sat the balled-up day's earnings on the kitchen table.

As soon as he opened the refrigerator door to put away his usual bag of Wawa goodies, her voice shook him. "It's about time that you finally brought your behind in here!"

"Mom, don't be scaring me like that," he warned her as he slowly turned around. Using the refrigerator light, he found her position. "What you doing down here in the dark, anyway?"

She cut on the 100-watt lamp next to her and stretched out as she yawned. "I was waiting for you, and I must've dozed off."

Deshonne stuffed his money into his bag before she could lay her eyes on it, and pulled out an Italian sub and some orange juice. She sat across from him, put a piece of paper full of information next to her plate, and helped herself to half of his sandwich.

"Well, I'm here in one piece. So you can go upstairs now and get in your own bed with your husband before he gets mad with me."

"We have to talk, Deshonne."

"Mom, can't your lecture wait until tomorrow morning? I'm tired," he told her as he rose up to leave the table.

"Boy, if you don't sit your narrow ass back down and listen to what I have to say!"

He slumped back down in the seat with an agitated expression. "What's wrong? Did my P.O. come through again? Or am I just coming in too late? What? Just spit it out!"

She sat there, amazed for a second by his tone of voice. Then when he was finished, she rose up out of her seat with her favorite if-looks-could-kill expression on her face. "Who do you think you're talking to, Deshonne?"

Just like that, his demeanor became humble, and his eyes dropped to the floor. "Mom, why don't you just tell me what's wrong?"

She pointed at the paper with all his friend's bail information on it, and said "Purnell is over there with your brother."

"For what?!"

"Well, to hear him tell it, nothing. But I called Court #20 on 4th Street, and the stuff on that paper is everything that they charged him with."

Deshonne picked up the paper and read over it thoroughly. *I can cover this*, he said to himself.

The total bail was over $30,000, with the firearm charges and misdemeanors. Deshonne pulled out his cell phone and dialed Tonya's number.

"Who are you calling at this time of night, Deshonne?"

The clock on the wall said 1:30 a.m.

"Tonya."

"You might as well hang up, baby. She's a lost cause."

"Huh? Why you say that?" he asked while he waited for her to answer at the other end.

"Because I talked to that girl earlier, and in so many words she told me that she'd rather let Purnell rot in jail than come home. She told me that all his money was long gone, so he didn't have to worry about calling her no more because she can't help him."

Deshonne jumped up and walked right past his mother. "Man, I'm about to go over there!" *This bitch must be crazy if she thinks that I'ma let it go down like this and don't do nothing! She got all my packs and some of my fucking money*, he thought as he dashed upstairs. Within seconds he reappeared, strapped with a concealed semi auto handgun tucked in his jeans and the number to a bail bondsman he knew who would come through in a rush for Purnell at his request.

"Here," she said as she handed him the paper he'd left on the table. "There's a verbatim message from that girl on the back of that paper, in case you was thinking about bothering her about some dumb stuff."

Deshonne read the reverse side after he read Purnell's information: "Tell Magic that I flushed the drugs that he gave Purnell down the toilet, and I spent the money on me and my kids."

"I'ma kill this bitch!" he mumbled as soon as he finished reading the message.

Before he could get out the door his mother warned him again. "Don't call me if your ass gets locked back up. And don't expect no visits either, because I'm telling you now not to go over there fooling with her."

"Mom, I'm on my way to see a old friend. She has her own bail company now."

"So I guess you got enough to get him out on your own without any help then, huh?" she asked.

Deshonne just closed the door and dashed to the rental. As he turned the ignition, he said to himself, "I hope so."

CHAPTER 30

Deshonne banged uncontrollably on the front door until those inside awoke.

"Who is it?" a male voice asked.

"It's Magic. Open up!"

Deshonne paced outside with his hands clasped behind his head until the door swung open. His mind was racing as fast as the blood pumping through his veins.

"What's up Magic? It's six-thirty in the—"

Before Kenny could finish what he was saying, Deshonne had already dipped past him and was inside the living room, bare chested, pacing back and forth. He was sweating violently as he moved about, wondering what would be the best way to tell Kenny what he had done.

"Yo, where's your shirt, cuz?"

Instead of answering that question, Deshonne just blurted, "I had to drop somebody tonight!"

Kenny flicked on the light and sat on the edge of the couch. Immediately he spotted the splattered blood on his friend's jeans and sneakers.

Deshonne rambled on in a low tone as he paced around the room. "They kept talking slick, and the next thing I know, cuz, I was seeing sparks."

"Magic, slow down! Start from the beginning," Kenny instructed.

Deshonne slowed his pace, locked his hands behind his head, and took a deep breath…

*****

242

The livingroom light was on when Deshonne approached the townhouse, but Tonya wouldn't answer the door. "Bitch, you need to give me what's mines!" Deshonne yelled up to the window filled with watching eyes. Then he picked up the nearest piece of cement and shattered the passenger's side window of her car.

"Motherfucker! I'm calling the police!" Tonya screamed down after the back window found the same fate as the first. Within seconds she came running out of the house with a wooden bat in her hand, barely dressed in an oversized t-shirt. She jumped straight up in his face, challenging him like a man, pointing and poking his forehead. "Your yellow ass is gonna be right with your punk-ass boy before the nights over!" she told him.

Unaffected by her threats, Deshonne gripped her by her wrists and twisted hard until she dropped the bat. "If you don't got everything he left in there, I'ma break this hand first," he threatened, bending the right hand a little harder.

Tonya's rage quickly became harsh screams as he forcefully marched her back into the house.

"Help! Somebody, please, help!" she yelled, alerting the neighbors.

Faces began to appear in the windows, parting curtains and raising shades.

Deshonne shoved her into the house and looked around at the lights appearing around the neighborhood.

"He's gonna kill me!" they heard her say before he got clobbered.

Thwack! An aluminum bat connected with his chest, sending him hurling back out the door, towards the concrete sidewalk…

*****

"**And** the next thing I knew, that bitch-ass nigga art was standing over top of me in his boxers, sizing me up to swing again. So I popped him."

243

By the end of Deshonne's animated narration, Kenny was pacing. The money that he had lost hadn't even registered, yet, but the shooting was so vividly told, that it played out over and over in his head like a CD on repeat.

"Is he dead?" Kenny asked, still in a state of shock.

Deshonne slid down in the far corner of the living room, by the custom-made entertainment center. "I don't know. I ran as soon as he dropped."

"Maybe you missed him."

Deshonne looked down at the dried blood all over his clothing. "I don't think so."

"Fuck!" Kenny yelled at the top of his lungs. "I told you to control your temper. I told you to leave Art to me!"

"Man, I did what you ain't have the heart to do, Kenny. That nigga disrespected us like we were a bunch of bitches or something. And you ain't do shit."

"What you did was stupid, Magic. I told you not to trust Pee-Wee with the caine in the first place. You fucked up!"

With his hands clenching his face and his feet nervously tapping the floor, Deshonne said, "So what? What's done is done. I can't take it back now."

A minute or two passed. they both calmed down a little before speaking again.

"Do you think they called the police?" Kenny asked, trying to assess the consequences.

Almost certain that someone would be the Good Samaritan, he said, "If she didn't, the neighbors did."

"Okay. So we looking at two different scenarios then, Magic. Either the police will be knocking down your people's door within the next 24 hours, or you just started a war with the entire North Side.

Deshonne didn't notice that Kenny had excluded himself from the problems at hand. But Kenny was certain that he wanted no part of a war that could possibly destroy what he was trying to accomplish.

"Fuck them niggas! I'm ready for war."

"No, you're not Magic, because I'm not. We get money, that's what were good at. Not shooting people."

Deshonne listened close to what his friend was saying, he heard what he wanted to hear as his inner rage began to ignite. "Word. We can take it to all them niggas, on they whole team!"

"We—we. Where is you getting this we stuff from, Magic?" Kenny asked, again trying to separate himself. "I didn't tell you to do any of this. As a matter of fact, I told you to stay away from Art."

"Either you with me, or you against me," Deshonne proclaimed with a undeniable fire in his eyes.

Kenny knew how reckless and messy Deshonne could get once he got angry. The butt of his gun was sticking out of his left jeans pocket, so he attempted to take the passive approach. No longer speaking with his hands, he paid close attention to Deshonne's words and actions.

Deshonne knew all about Art smacking Kenny up in the office, which disgusted him. And even though he was mad that Kenny had said nothing nor attempted to do anything about it, he kept it to himself.

"I'm with you. But I ain't going back to jail for nobody. And I ain't built for war no more, either. That's why I'm trying to do different things with my life," Kenny tried to explain, solidifying his neutral position.

I banged that nigga for him, foreal, foreal. And he ain't even with me! Deshonne thought. "So it's fuck me then, huh? Fuck me, right!" he yelled.

"No. I'm not saying that. But you gotta understand that I didn't shoot nobody tonight, Magic. I wasn't even there."

Deshonne turned to leave, because as far as he was concerned, that statement ended their lifelong friendship. He just walked out without saying another word while Kenny curiously watched.

*****

Because of the dangerous rumors that were circulating throughout the streets, Fast-P and his girls began to move

245

around the triangle every couple of days, using the I.D.s of their dates. For some reason, no matter whose name they were under, or which motel they were in, Officer Adams always knew exactly where to locate them.

"Police! Open up!" he called out as he hammered the motel door.

The butt of his flashlight chipped away at the brown paint of the Super Lodge door. His eight-o'clock shift was just beginning, so he wanted to get a good shot of Baby Girl's ass to start off his day.

"I got all day. But if you don't let me in now, I'm going to park a couple of doors down in a plain car and lock up everybody that comes to this door," he promised.

Normally Apple would've stood behind the door and just listened to him all day until he got tired of waiting or his shift ended. But that was before she started working for her soon-to-be man, Magic, the toughest challenge of her life. She knew that he would be coming through soon with a new batch of dime bags for the street and her usual breakfast sandwich, so she had to answer the door, or she would be just hanging him out to dry, like her friends did so many others before him.

Apple pushed down on the handle and opened the door, to the length of the security chain. "Baby Girl isn't here right now. She's laid up on the other side of the Memorial Bridge with another sleazy cop."

Damn! he thought as he slowly reached out and touched the chain. "What is it with you whores and these chains? I thought all dicks were welcome."

She just gave him a fake smile as she thought, *Only paying dicks, you piece of shit.*

"Open up, Apple. I came to speak with the Queen of the Triangle today, not her apprentice."

"I never heard of her," she replied, then she tried to close the door on him, but he hammered it with his flashlight, startling her.

"If you close this door on me, I promise you it's going to be a long day for you."

"What do you want?" she whined, stomping as if she was having a tantrum.

"The bad guys, of course. Have you seen any lately?"

Not knowing that Baby Girl was sharing more than her bed with the cop, she continued to play stupid. But he knew that she was the key to the new dealers.

"No," she answered, annoyed. "I don't associate with real criminals."

"Well, why don't you just open the door so we can converse a little?"

"No offense, officer, but I feel a lot safer with the door between us, you know? It's a lot of sickos running around here, playing themselves off as real cops these days. So you never know who's who."

"You can either invite me in and we have a short conversation about life in general, or I can lock your trailer-park ass up for the trucker you clipped yesterday for his wallet. Your choice."

"Shit!" she mumbled.

"Okay, but real quick because I have to catch the bus in town in a little while, and I still have to get dressed."

Adams smiled at her, revealing his cigarette and coffee-stained chompers. "See how beautiful it is when one hand washes the other?" he said as the door slowly closed.

Apple took a deep breath, looked back at the alarm clock, and reopened the door without the chain. Still holding the door open, she said, "remember, I have to catch the bus in a little while to go grocery shopping, so you have to make this quick."

Adam swiftly forced the door open as soon as it cracked, sending her body flying backwards towards the wall. "You're lucky that you're not shopping from the commissary list over at W.C.I."

W.C.I. was Baylor Women's Correctional Institute. It housed all of the convicted females in the state of Delaware.

Apple walked over to the dresser drawer, got out a homemade busy sign, and placed it on the outside door handle.

Unaware of his intentions, she kept her lingerie on until she felt him out.

"See, I knew that you were the smartest piece of trash on the street. I try to tell my buddies down at the precinct all the time, but they don't believe me because they just don't like you."

Apple sat down on the opposite end of the bed, nervous. She prayed that he wouldn't ask her to remove her undergarments because Deshonne's money and the remaining few bags from his package were tucked within her pink walls.

Adams fluffed up a pillow. "Come, sit over here," he politely commanded.

"Look, I'm sorry to disappoint you, but I ain't Baby, and ain't no kinky shit jumping off up in here! Now, I'ma suck your dick because I don't wanna go to jail. But you gotta wear a condom, and you gonna pay me when I'm done," she said before sitting.

Adams just smiled at her blunt speech. But deep down he hated her and her profession with a passion. He felt as though only black women should be prostitutes, because that is what they were bred for, and any white female who did the same thing, no matter what her reason, was a disgrace to her family and her race. "Hold on, precious. You jumping the gun here," he chuckled. "I only want information from you, nothing more."

Not knowing whether or not to feel disrespected or relieved, she just looked at him for a second. "Huh? You mean to tell me that you got all this in front of you, and you just wanna talk to me?"

"I'm into dark berries. They know what they're doing in the bedroom. Not vanilla trash. So, if you would just answer my questions, I'll let you get back to your stem before it cools," he said as sarcastically as he possibly could.

Adams surveyed the room from the moment he took his first step in. He noticed bent beer cans in the trash can, residue-filled red bags under the air conditioner, and her crack stem, which was mixed in with the hair products on the bathroom counter, without even doing a thorough search. All were enough for a visibility search warrant.

"Okay, well, just give me a minute to put something on, so this visit will feel more formal, and then we can get this over with," she emphasized, as a reminder to him that she wasn't required to perform any sexual acts.

Apple got up and picked a long T-shirt out of the pile of clothes on the floor to cover herself with since she now was feeling disrespected and uncomfortable.

Just as she pulled the T-shirt over her head, he snatched it away. "I always think better around naked women, so there's no need to spoil the vibrant atmosphere. Is there?"

"Whatever," she answered without really second guessing his motives. "Well, what do you want to know?" she asked as she sat back down beside him.

Adams pulled out a pen and a pad. "For starters, what's up with God and his crew of out-of-towners?"

"Nothing, as usual. They're still selling the same bullshit that nobody wants and breaking off pebbles of re-rock that wouldn't melt if you threw it in a volcano."

"Are they still the major suppliers out here?" he asked, knowing that she had a new pot of gold.

"Not for me. If that's what you asking me," she answered proudly. "I'm a true smoker, not a crackhead. I don't recook garbage, or push my choy with a hanger to scrounge up residue."

"So you getting that good shit from somewhere, huh. Which means, you know exactly who got that ear ringer, right?"

"I don't know nothing about—" then her vision went black.

With lightening quick speed Adams mashed the pillow over her face and bashed her covered forehead with his trusty flashlight. Her screams went virtually unheard into the pillow. Holding her face in a daze, she tried to refocus as he climbed on top of her.

"What do you want?" she managed to mumble.

Adams sat down with all his weight on her chest, facing her feet. Then he placed the pillow on her flat stomach. "Apple, I know that crack kills most of your senses. So I'm going to ask you a series of questions, loud and clear, that you can't say that you don't understand. Okay?"

"Yes," she huffed between breaths.

"Now, God and his crew are finished out here, as of today. And it's only a matter of time before I lock up the rest of these petty dealers. So what I'm proposing to you is, if you want to be here in the end, meaning, you'll be free to continue sucking and fucking, I suggest that you cooperate."

As a sign of good faith he lifted up just enough to allow her to breathe and answer, but to his surprise she began to fight back. So he dropped back down hard, knocking the wind right back out of her. "Stop it!"

She lay motionless, trying to think of a way out.

"Now, lets try this again because I believe in giving people second chances. And I've come to notice things—like the fact that the parking lot is filled with the same red bags scattered around your room. So, I need you to tell me, where they're coming from," he asked, despite the fact that Baby Girl had already enlightened him.

"I don't know where it comes from. I get mines from the other girls," she gasped.

"Wrong answer, bitch!" Adams said. Then with force he crashed the flashlight against her belly, causing her dinner to spew onto his back. "Again!"

*****

The Motel 6's parking lot was barren except for two housekeeping employees, who were quietly watching the violent beating through a window, from inside a room on the second floor.

"Help!"

All the energy and strength the defenseless man had, disappeared after he didn't connect on his first wild haymaker, which he shot out to fend off his attackers.

"Help!" Fast-P cried out to deaf ears. "I didn't mean to disrespect y'all. I'm sorry!" he tried to reason as Infinite and Quan stood over him with their guns in his face.

After every sentence Quan administered a punishing kick to his midsection while Infinite kept his eye's on both sides of the building.

"You's a lying turd, Fast. Them hoes cut us off completely because of you and them three country niggas you brung down here," Quan told him. "I should dead you right here, son!"

"No. They're my nephews. They just came to visit," he murmured.

Infinite's Desert Eagle connected with the bone at the top of his nose.

Fast-P just lay half dead in the middle of the parking lot, unconscious and barely breathing.

"Tell them scandalous-ass bitches it's back to business. You hear me?" Quan barked. And then he pulled out his penis and began to urinate all over Fast-P's face.

"Or tomorrow, this'll be one of them," Infinite warned as soon as Quan shook himself off.

*****

Fearing that it was only a matter of time before the police stormed his parent's house looking for him, Deshonne slept in Gander Hill Prison's parking lot until Purnell's trail of bail papers caught up with him. Hauntingly, the reoccurring vision of yesterday's events played out in his mind like a bad nightmare. Every few seconds he caught a glimpse of Art towering over him before the fireworks began. He couldn't even hear his cell phone on the dashboard ringing the first couple of times, because the gunshots in his head drowned out the outside world. The screen saver was programmed to show different pictures when the phone rang. He picked up the ringing phone to confirm the ring tone with the portrait.

"I need you," she whined as soon as he answered.

"Apple?" Deshonne asked, not recognizing her broken voice.

Apple tried her best not to move an inch because her body was aching from head to waist. Her throbbing head made it difficult to focus, so other than reaching for the phone, she remained balled up in the fetal position, just as Adams had left her. "Magic, can you please hurry up and come straight here? I need your help."

"I can't right now. I'm over at G-hill waiting on Pee-Wee to come out."

"Can you come as soon as you're done?" she begged.

Deshonne began to talk in their own personal code. "I haven't been in the house yet shorty, so you might have to wait until after I make a stop, and then I'll be right there, okay?" he told her because he assumed that the reason she wanted to see him was because she was done.

"No! I need you to come here first. Alone."

"Apple, I'm not for no bunch of games today. And I'm still not fucking you if that's what you banking on happening."

"Baby, the way I feel right now, I couldn't take you fucking me. Just come by yourself, please. And bring a bottle of Tylenol."

It must be that time of the month, Deshonne assumed. "Ah-ight, I got you."

"Boo, please don't take all day because I'm in some serious pain."

"Okay, okay, I won't," he said and hung up.

"Lord, please help me!" she moaned after she fished her arm out to hang up the phone with her eye's closed.

I hate being around cramped up broads, he said to himself as he redialed the bail bondsman's office to see what the holdup was.

252

CHAPTER 31

Deshonne and Purnell still couldn't believe what they had just seen, and the story of what went with it made things even more unbelievable. The world that Deshonne was growing accustomed to was crashing down around him. as he and his friend drove on I-95 North towards Wilmington, he contemplated his next move.

As they approached the Maryland Avenue exit, the sight of the Bluerocks Stadium made Purnell open up. "Did you see the bruises that cop left on your snow bunny's face and stomach?"

"Why you keep calling her my snow bunny?" Deshonne asked out of irritation.

"Hey, she took a helluva ass whipping for you, my nigga," Purnell told him, childishly rubbing his head. "So that definitely makes her yours."

"Pee-Wee, you know damn well I don't fuck with fiends. It's against my code. So this is a waste of good conversation. Talk about something else."

"Come on now, Magic. So you mean to tell me that you still turning down that sexy-ass broad, even when y'alls alone?"

"Yep. Especially when we're alone," Deshonne reiterated. She didn't look too sexy today, he thought. I should've took her to the emergency room or something. Deshonne felt her pain. And now he had found a new level of respect for her. But he still wasn't willing to cross that line even if she was a ride-or-die broad.

"Yeah, right!" Purnell said in disbelief. "And I'm not titty fucking Tasty every chance I get, either. I hate the way she lets me nut in her mouth," he lied. Lying-ass nigga. I know you gotta be balling her up. Cause I would, he told himself. I know she ain't just get tortured for nothing.

"Hey, if you ain't want the truth, you shouldn't of asked," Deshonne said as he braked at a light on Fourth and Adams Streets.

"Whatever," Purnell said, not wanting to debate. "Just be glad that those face bruises on her face don't look like the ones under her shirt."

The statement went over Deshonne's head. "Why?" he asked. "She's still in pain."

"Because as long as she keeps them clothes on, she can still get us that money," Purnell replied.

Deshonne let that statement go. He was just glad she was alive. As he turned left onto Fourth and headed up the hill to the bail bondsmen's office, he changed the subject. "Do you think it was any truth in what Baby Girl said about Fast and them New York boys?" Deshonne asked. He was skeptical about the validity of her story.

"She said he got rushed to Christiana Hospital," Purnell agreed.

"Pee-Wee, I can't put my finger on it, but I don't think both beatings were a coincidence."

"You think?"

"Yeah. And I think we should be prepared for the weather to come because it's about to rain."

"Yeah, well, I'm ready to make it rain on Tonya's fat ass!" Purnell said vengefully. "I can't believe she had that nigga up in my shit."

"In due time," Deshonne told his friend calmly. "We have to get our money right first."

"Ah-ight, well, what you working with?" Purnell asked, anxious to return the favors.

"I got six grand in the bank. And the other hammer I got from them bitch-ass niggas. Everything else went down the toilet."

Damn, Tonya set me back nine thousand! Purnell worried to himself. And she fucked that nigga in my bed. "That's your personal stash. We can't fuck with that."

Deshonne pulled over on the corner of Fourth and Union Street, in front of a office, and parked. "Pee-Wee, do you got my back?" he asked as sincerely as possible.

"You motherfucking right I do! You've had mines since we was this high," Purnell gestured to measure the size of a baby.

"That's all it is, then," Deshonne said. As he spoke, he pointed at both of them. "We got six grand."

"But what we gonna do for a connect?"

"I guess we gotta take a trip up top."

New York City was considered the drug capital for Delaware dealers because of the quality and price differences. Most dealers feared the turnpike because of how state troopers targeted minorities, but Deshonne had already been down that road, so he didn't mind taking the chance.

"When we going? I'm ready now!"

"I'll let you know. Patience cuz."

"I hope it's gonna be soon because we need to keep that flow coming," Purnell reminded him.

"I know. Don't worry about that. Just go ahead inside real quick so they can take your picture cause I'm tired."

"You can sleep at my room if you want," Purnell volunteered.

"Nah, that's okay. I'm gonna go over to Marie's spot to take a nap."

"You smashing her, yet?"

"Why?"

"Cause y'all been spending a lot of time together, and I wanted to know was she worth that change you've been spending on her."

"Get out the car, Pee-Wee. You starting to sound like that faggot Kenny."

Deshonne's whole attitude changed without warning. Purnell just looked at him oddly as he walked through the office door.

*****

The sound of two mistreated toddlers screaming in the next room broke up Deshonne's well-needed nap. As he stretched and yawned, a heavy pillow hurled playfully across the room hit him in the stomach like a sandbag. He quickly picked up his glasses off of the nightstand to stare at his goddess, as she combed her silky long hair in the mirror, in just a bra and pair of loose fitting jeans.

"I guess you gonna act like you really came here to see me," Marie stated over her shoulder as she twirled her hair into a bun.

"I did," Deshonne told her with a smile. "I wasn't sleeping, I was just resting my eyes."

Marie turned around, with her arms crossing her voluptuous chest, and walked over to the bed to retrieve the Ralph Lauren button-up she had pulled out for the day. "Can you hand me that, please?" she asked with one hand out.

Deshonne cursed himself for not having X-ray vision as he gave her the shirt. She turned her back to put on the shirt, and he reached out as if he wanted to touch her soft skin.

"While you were drooling on my pillow, I made those two phone calls for you."

Deshonne was anxious to hear what was going on with art because he knew that his future depended on Art's life or death.

"Which do you want to hear first, the good news or the bad?"

"I don't care. The good news, I guess," he answered as if neither bothered him, but deep down he prayed that the man lived.

"Okay, well, Trigg said that Art is gonna make it. So you won't have to worry about getting a murder charge, Mr.

256

Shoot-First-And-Ask-Questions-Later," she said while poking him in his forehead.

Deshonne smiled inside at the good news. You can't pay a dead man off, he thought. "What's the bad news?"

"They wouldn't say who, but I heard him tell someone crying in the background that whoever shot Art won't have to worry about the police because they're gonna keep it in the streets."

That's what it is, he gladly thought.

Marie could tell by the arrogant look on his face that he wasn't worried about the empty threats, but a part of her was growing fond of him. "Magic, they're gonna try and kill you!" she warned.

He laid back on the pillow and propped his head up with his hands. "Listen to you, sounding all concerned and stuff."

"Why shouldn't I be? You're my buddy, right?"

"Oh, that's what I am? Your buddy, huh?"

"Magic, I'm just calling it like I see it. We're not in a relationship that I know of. We've just been enjoying each other's time."

"I guess Marie, if you say so."

Her statement wasn't what he wanted to hear, and it showed on his face, so she toyed with him. "Why? Did you think there was more than that between us because you've been occupying a majority of my time lately?"

Marie sat down beside him, and flirtatiously guided her hand under his T-shirt.

"Not really. But buddies just sounded so distant."

"Well, if you want to close the gap between us, just come correct," she challenged. Then she gave his belly button a quick peck and hopped up.

"Wait!" Deshonne said as he grabbed her hand. "Sit back down."

Marie smiled at him. But on the inside she was planning out her game, play by play. "Nope, because my daughter could come back here at any time, Magic. And besides, we're not the only ones here, remember?"

"We can lock the door," Deshonne suggested." "I won't moan if you don't."

"Sorry, sweetie, not today. Me and my baby are about to go to the mall."

"Come on, Marie," Deshonne pleaded." You just got my hopes all worked up for nothing."

"No, I didn't. I just gave you something to work for," she told him.

Marie walked over to the door, opened it, and hollered for her daughter to get ready to go. Then she turned back. "If you're good, then maybe next time I'll tell you how to get past our buddy stage," she teased.

Deshonne soaked up every word. "Can't you see that I'm on my best behavior now?"

"Now doesn't count cause I'm about to leave."

"I could take y'all," Deshonne offered. "That way we can pick up right here when we come back." He wanted her bad, and he wasn't trying to give up easily.

"Magic, its girls day out. Sorry. But you can stop by later on if you want to."

Deshonne hugged her sideways and just kissed her on the cheek once he realized that she wasn't giving in. "Okay, call me later."

"Aren't you forgetting something?" she asked with her hand out.

"What?"

"We need money to shop," she stated. Marie knew how to manipulate men, and she used every tool that she had as a vixen to do it.

CHAPTER 32

Purnell had the car's cruise control set at a even pace of 69mph as he and his partner ventured north on the New Jersey turnpike. P.I.M.P by 50 Cent was in heavy rotation on both power 98.9 and hot 97, as Deshonne played the D.J.

"Why am I the designated driver?" Purnell objected.

"Because it's your fault that I haven't had much sleep in the last 48 hours."

"I thought that was the whole purpose in you ditching me at the mote to babysit your bunny yesterday."

"It was, but me and Marie went out to dinner and talked half the night," Deshonne explained.

"Did y'all talk?" Purnell asked with a sly grin." Or did y'all talk?"

"Why is you so worried about my sex life?" Deshonne asked, annoyed. He was discouraged that his night didn't end the way he had planned, between Marie's legs.

"I'm just trying to keep you awake, that's all."

Purnell had made numerous propositions to Apple yesterday, hoping that he would succeed in sexing her now that she was in need of comfort and support. But as she had done every other man, since the breakup with her baby's father, she turned down all his advances.

"Yeah, well, remind me to buy a porno from the Trading Post when we get back."

Deshonne reclined his seat and put his hand towel over his eyes.

"Which exit do I take?" Purnell asked because he was basically driving blind.

"Don't worry about it, dummy! Just keep straight, and wake me up when we reach the George Washington Bridge toll booths."

"Well, what part of the city is we gonna cop from? Because I got some peoples in the Bronx," Purnell inquired. He was trying his hardest to keep Deshonne awake for the duration of the ride so he wouldn't have to be alone. Deshonne lifted the cloth and peeped at his driver.

"Spanish Harlem, why? Do your people got a connect for us?" he asked, hoping for a better alternative than he already had.

"Nah, they in church."

"So what the fuck you brung'em up for, then?" Deshonne said, then he laid back again.

Purnell reached into the door panel of the Intrepid and pulled out 50 Cent's Get rich or Die trying. Then he put it on track number four, and hit repeat. The volume was all the way up when the song came on...

*****

God never felt secure when he picked up and dropped off with his connect because it was a public spot, and everyone around him had a gun, except him. As always, the two bodyguards frisked him at the door, and confiscated everything, except the briefcase. The Riverfront warehouse was completely empty except for an antique desk and leather office chair.

I should kill him right now, the arrogant, Cuban cigar smoker thought.

Even though it was a hot summer day, the well-dressed professional looked calm and collected in his crisp Brioni tailormade suit.

"Here's the cheddar from our last shipment, Big Al," God said, placing the steel case onto the desk.

"You're a week late," Al answered coldly. "And I've been hearing that some nickel-and-dime dealers are quietly, but effectively, taking over."

"You've been misinformed," God said in a professional manner. "Them niggas I called you about should be relocating as we speak."

God stood at ease, with his hands clasped behind his back, in his Lacoste shirt and Polo jeans.

"I thought I told you to get your hands dirty?"

"No," he calmly contested. "You told me to handle my B.I., and that's what me and my crew have been doing."

"Do you actually think beating up a weak crackhead is enough persuasion?" Big Al asked, as he put out his cigar, and took inventory of his profits.

How the fuck do you know what we did?! God wondered. "If not, then Infinite is ready to dead them all."

After quickly counting, Al placed the case on the floor beside him and replaced it with a similar case. "You know, you're not as smart as I thought you were, God. Perhaps I picked the wrong crew to help me prosper."

"Don't disrespect my gangsta, son," God told him as he leaned forward aggressively on the desk. "I make you money."

Big Al's hands were already in his lap, so he raised both of them to the taped up handguns under the table.

"And you've been late on two payments too," he reminded him.

"It won't happen again. That was my fault."

"I know it's your fault, Paul," he pronounced God's government name in a belittling tone. "That's why your case is only one kilo short, instead of two."

"What!"

God popped open the case, and found only two duct-taped kilos instead of the normal three. "You fucking with my livelihood, son. Our agreement!" he protested.

"No, I'm not cause I still want my agreed-upon payment. But I am penalizing you for your mistakes."

"How the fuck we supposed to eat, son!"

"Lower your voice when you speak to me, Paul."

God knew how calm his connect was, and the fact that his posture hadn't changed, was ominous. "This shits twisted, Al."

"Hey, if you can't survive off of what you have, I'm suggesting that you take back that cute little toy out front that you're leasing."

"We make you good money, son, so you might want to rethink this bullshit."

"Listen, as far as me and my associates are concerned, we can cut all ties right now if you don't agree with how you're being compensated for your services," Al warned.

"You need us, son. You need our workers," God reasoned. "We've dug in the trenches."

"I need that block,"Al corrected. "You and your friends are dispensable."

"This is bullshit," God said under his breath.

"No, this is your reality, God. Either you accept my arrangement, or you can start looking for legal employment."

God picked up the case and turned to walk away. Big Al stood up and grabbed the new wood and steel shovel that lay concealed beside him.

"God!" he called out.

God nervously turned, and Al tossed the shovel to his feet. "What's this?" he asked, not understanding the meaning.

"Your third option," he answered with a grin.

*****

Christiana Mall was packed with shoppers, as always, which made merchandise ripe for the taking. As Marie paced nonchalantly back and forth from the dressing room unnoticed, she'd wished that she had come alone.

"Why are you taking so long, Kelia?" she mumbled angrily at the dressing room door.

"Mom, I'm trying the clothes on him as fast as I can."

Baby Wali was sleep in his stroller as Kelia diligently worked. Marie could hear the store alarm beepers popping off as Kelia continuously squeezed down on the wire cutters.

Paranoid that someone else might also hear, she went in to supervise.

"Damn, you make me sick!" Marie told Kelia as she snatched away the tool. "I should of left you at Zenda's and came by myself."

"Mom, it's not my fault," Kelia explained. "They wasn't cutting right."

"Just get out. Move!" Marie commanded. "I'll do it myself."

"I don't know what you mad for."

"Kelia, get out of my face before I hurt you," she warned." And go get the other outfits that I stashed behind the bookbags."

"After we done, are we still gonna get me stuff out of The Limited?"

"No, cause you took too long. I have to take back the car in a hour."

"I hate you," Kelia mumbled as she reached for the door knob.

"What you say?! Don't mumble."

"I hate when you act like this," Kelia told her mother as she began to push the baby out.

"Leave the stroller in here, stupid!"

"But you told me to go get the stuff."

"Take Wali."

"But he's heavy," Kelia protested.

"You plucking my nerves. Don't make me knock you silly."

Kelia picked up the baby and continued to backtalk as she backed out. "I hope you get caught," she mumbled with a hurt expression as the door closed.

CHAPTER 33

The farthest north Purnell had ever traveled to before this day was to the Statue of Liberty on a school field trip. So from the moment that they got out of the car, on the side of a brick cemetery wall, he was astonished. The first block they passed by was abandoned. But as soon as they turned right and walked down 149th and Amsterdam, summertime in the city was obvious.

Deshonne spotted a dark-complexioned Latino man, who looked to be in his mid-fifties, make two swift, hand-to-hand sales before they could walk up on him. "Hey, Papi, you working?" he inquired.

Without hesitation, the Dominican answered, "Yeah, What's up, papa?"

"We need-" Purnell got out before his partner cut in and finished the sentence.

"A 20 cent piece," Deshonne added. "Work with me."

Purnell looked at his counterpart oddly because of the numbers he blurted out. But papi didn't catch it.

"You can either get two grams of rock or one gram of soft."

"Is the soft good?" Purnell asked.

The Dominican looked surprised after that question. His conceit kicked in. "Y'all must not be from around here huh?"

Deshonne looked scornfully at his friend because of his lack of patience. "Why you say that?"

"Because nobody questions my products, papa. It's against my religion to sell Basura."

A patrol car coasted down the block, and the three of them walked back towards the car until it passed them by.

"Money is money, comprendre, wait right here."

"Make it quick, yo. We not trying to be standing around here long," they told him.

"Walk around the block. When you get back, it will be here," the Dominican informed them.

"Why we ain't tell him what we was working with, so we could bounce?"

Deshonne continued to walk on with the $6,000 taped to his inner thighs, in silence.

Purnell complained after every block they went to until his friend finally let him get involved. After four blocks and four different testers, they decided together to backtrack, to 131st and Broadway.

*****

As Marie color-coordinated all of the stolen Children's Place clothing, the paying customer looked on in disapproval over her shoulder.

"Marie, this isn't everything I asked you for," Cookie told her as she skimmed through the items, shaking her head.

"Girl, I'm sorry," Marie convincingly fibbed. "But the mall wasn't too crowded today, so I didn't get to go into all the stores I normally hit." She had already sold most of her merchandise to her other associates on Concord avenue. This was her last stop since her aunt's house was only around the corner. "I'll probably go back tomorrow."

"Well, can you make sure you get my twins some more Baby Gap jeans? Because I would rather keep paying you, not the store."

"Honey, I am the store!" Marie boasted.

"I know that's right," the full-figured, stay-at-home mom agreed.

As Cookie counted out the money from a white bank envelope, Marie counted with her.

"Um, do you get women's clothing, too?" Cookie asked as she handed over the $150.

"Only if you're spending one-fifty or better. Because in adult stores they watch like hawks, so I don't go in for just a couple things," Marie explained.

"Well, my boyfriend is giving me $200 for food tomorrow. But if you can get me some cute stuff, I'll spend one-fifty of it with you, plus the kid's stuff," she added. "He'll just have to be mad."

Marie hadn't even gotten the money, yet, and already she had it counted out and spent. "Just call me in the morning and I got you."

Marie kept looking at her watch, hoping that Kelia didn't sneak out of Zenda's.

Cookie noticed that she was preoccupied and decided to let her leave. "Well, thanks again."

"No problem. Just call me tomorrow!" Marie reminded her. "But even if you don't call, don't worry, I'll be here."

*****

Deshonne and Purnell walked into the Hispanic restaurant searching for the same guy whom everyone else was going to, but he refused to serve them because they weren't buying weight. They looked around and acted out of place as they sat down at the diner-style counter.

"Hey, Papi!" he called out to the man behind the register. "Where's your peoples at with the Volvo out front?"

The cashier waited until his paying patrons walked out before responding. "My store is about to close in 15 minutes," he said in fluent English. "Buy something."

Purnell repeated Deshonne's question. "Yo, do you know where the dude that was sitting on that Volvo went?"

"Beef patties cost 600 a piece, fellas. How many do y'all want?"

"Ten!" Purnell answered as soon as he calculated.

Deshonne put out his hand, advising his friend to shut up. The cashier noticed the lack of communication and cut in to bargain before they could change their minds. "I'm only making my brother make one trip, and y'all ain't got all night to decide, either."

"It's soft, right?" Deshonne asked.

"You seen the waiting line earlier, didn't you?"

Without consulting his over-rebellious friend, Deshonne gave him a cautious number. "We'll take four patties, Papi. That's all we can afford."

"Magic," Purnell whined as if he was making a bad decision.

"Pee-Wee, would you just stop confusing the man so he can make the phone call."

Deshonne didn't trust the man behind the counter. He was way too fidgety. "My man, we sell blazing coca. And this is our place. Trust me, messing with us y'all will prosper off our product."

Deshonne stood up and tapped his friend. "I'm sorry we wasted your time, Papi. Maybe we'll come back tomorrow."

Papi didn't want to lose a potential ten-ounce sale, so he pulled out his personal showcase. "It's scale, papa. Guaranteed to bounce back everytime."

Purnell picked up the quarter ounce of powder and unknotted the baggie. The aroma was strong and distinctive. "It looks official."

"Looks can be deceiving," Deshonne warned.

"It's top-notch, believe me." the cashier said. "And I rock, too."

"Five-fifty a pattie," Deshonne tried to bargain.

The middleman laughed in their faces. "You can't even get good garbage around here for that price."

"Jump on it, Magic."

"Yeah, jump on it, Magic," the peddler agreed.

"You gonna weigh it in front of us?" Deshonne asked as he sat back down.

"If that's what you want. As a matter of fact, since you spending good money, I'll even break it straight off the brick, and cook it up for you," he offered as a token of good faith.

"Ah-ight, we'll take the four, then. And if it's as blazing as you say, we'll be back tomorrow."

The cashier picked up a cell phone and began to talk in Spanish. Deshonne sat, second-guessing himself. Purnell was just glad that they hadn't come all that way for nothing because he was broke and in debt.

After a half hour of consuming an unlimited supply of very greasy patties, Deshonne's patience wore thin. Purnell was flirting with the cleanup girl, and the cashier would disappear into a back room every five minutes.

"Pee-Wee, it's taking too long," he said, only loud enough for his friend to hear. "Something ain't right."

Purnell waved it off, as if the wait was worth it. "He's on his way now. So we might as well wait a couple more minutes."

"You can wait. I'm bouncing."

"I know you ain't trying to go back empty-handed, Magic. We've been up here all day."

"My brother will be here in a minute. He's always late," the female told them as she continued to sweep up.

Deshonne turned around in the stool and walked towards the door. "We'll be back tomorrow if your brother wants our business," he said over his shoulder.

Purnell was still sitting at the counter, trying to plead for a few more minutes so they wouldn't have to take that two and a half hour trip back empty-handed.

Something ain't right! his conscience kept telling him, so he didn't respond to either of them like they had hoped. "You better be in the car before I pull off," Deshonne sternly recommended, "or you'll be hitchhiking back to Deli."

As he opened the chiming door, Purnell reached out as if he could touch his friend 20 feet away while the dark shadows passed low and fast by the window sills.

Oh, shit! Purnell thought, too late to forewarn Deshonne.

The cleaner and cashier disappeared without hesitation as the first gun touched Deshonne's temple. "Magic!" he called out.

EXCERPTS FROM DIRTY LIVING 2

Kenny walked into the hospital room with hateful intentions as Art's peaceful nap triggered bitter memories of their last encounter...

*****

Kenny laughed at Art's threat as if it was empty, and Art slammed his fist down on the desk, demonstrating his rage.

"If you ain't with us, you against us!" Art warned. He was all amped off of pills and liquor.

Each word of warning from Kenny went unheeded as Art reached for his gun Kenny grabbed for the arm holding the chrome-plated .45, but Art crunched his balls with a swift knee.

"Ooooh!" Kenny groaned as he felt a streak of terrible pain roll into his stomach. Then, in a wild swing, the gun smacked his cranium.

*****

"How you feeling this morning, Art?" Kenny asked with an unforgettable sneer on his face as he stood at the foot of the bed.

"What the fuck do you care!?" Art asked in a worn-down, tempered tone. "For all I know you could've sent that nigga."

I wish he killed you! Kenny thought. "I try to prevent these problems, not create them," he reminded him.

Art used the remote to raise the bed as high as it could go without hurting his wounded stomach. Kenny stood with his arms defiantly crossed, as if to say, I told you so.

"What do you want? Visiting hours are over."

"You know, that's funny cause the nurse at the desk said that visiting hours had just started."

"Yeah well, that's only for welcome visitors," Art pointed out. "And you're not welcome."

Kenny felt amused by the tortured look on Art's face. As he slowly walked to the chair by the window, he enjoyed the bedridden man's pain.

"Well anyway, me, the unwelcome visitor, just stopped by to see if I could smooth everything over before somebody really gets hurt, or worse."

A cold smirk touched Art's face, as he gritted his teeth to consume the pain. "Because of your peoples, I got a shit-bag strapped to my leg until my stomach heals and a tube in my dick. So I can promise you," he emphasized, "promise you that he'll feel worse than this."

"Art, I think that you need to think about your next move carefully, because believe me, it's not promised that the end result will be in your favor."

Kenny leaned forward, clasped his hands, and rested his elbows on his knees.

"What, you threatening me, now?" Art asked domineeringly.

"Never that," Kenny said sarcastically. "I'm only making a suggestion."

"You can keep your suggestions to yourself. And get the fuck out of my room before I forget that we used to be friends!"

Art had raised his voice, so Kenny figured it was time to go.

"Well, since I'm not welcome, I'm just gonna be the bigger man and leave you with one more suggestion."

Art had a ferocious, murder-one, look to him as he listened to Kenny. He wished he could reach out and strangle him.

"As you can see from the position you're in now, it's getting real messy in the streets. So I can promise that if you don't come home with a new attitude, you're gonna need life insurance."

After Kenny finished his statement, he pointed both hands at Art as if they were real guns and imitated a gun going off.

"Your threats don't hold no weight, bitch!" Art yelled. "Wait until I get outta here."

Kenny walked out, satisfied about what he had just done. He also planned for deadly repercussions.

*****

Marie answered the door in an oversized Larry Bird throwback jersey that came down to her knees, some black Polo jeans, and a pair of green and white Bo Jacksons.

Deshonne couldn't even muster up a smile at her early morning radiance.

"Hmm, what happened to you and our dinner date last night?" Marie asked with a frown as she walked off, leaving him to follow her.

It was a first for her to look forward to something and get stood up, so she jealously assumed that his absence involved another female.

"It's a long story, boo. Can you not walk away from me so I can explain why I couldn't make it last night?" he appealed.

Marie sat on the couch Indian-style and picked up her daughter's new poetry book as if she was about to read it.

"There's nothing to explain. I understand that we're still buddies," she said as if she didn't mind.

What is she talking about? Deshonne wondered. "Huh?" he murmured as he scratched his unbrushed waves, and sat down beside her.

Deshonne tried to lay his head on her shoulder, but she shoved him away. "You're still wearing the same clothes from two days ago. And your zipper is down. Don't touch me!"

He looked down and fixed his zipper without saying a word.

"Was she good?" Marie asked, still with her eyes focused on the cover of the book.

"Marie, I don't know what you talking about. But the reason I ain't make it was because I was way up New York, in jail."

"What? What happened!?" she asked in shock.

"You won't believe this shit, but fucking with Pee-Wee..." He began to relive last night's disaster.

*****

"**Magic**!" he screamed too late.

Deshonne was caught off guard as the first DEA officer smashed the muzzle of his assault rifle against his temple.

"Get on your knees! Down, now!" the masked officer ordered. "Get down, now!"

The rest of the officers rushed the restaurant.

Purnell threw his hands into the air and kneeled down to surrender when he realized that it wasn't a robbery.

"Get the fuck off me!" Deshonne barked as two cops kneeled on his back to apply the plastic restraints...

*****

When Deshonne finished the story, Marie got up and walked into the kitchen.

"That was a lame excuse, Magic. I know you could of came up with something better than that," she told him as she poured two bowls of Fruity Pebbles.

He dug the paperwork out of his pocket. As soon as she returned with their breakfast, he handed her the copies. "What's this, an apology letter?"

Read it," he told her.

Marie sat the plastic bowl on the floor after reading the police report and stopped chewing after reading the amount of money confiscated. "Ouch, boo. They took a lot of money from you." I guess this confirms your second occupation, she said to herself.

"That's a lot of money to give away for an excuse, don't you think? It would have been cheaper for dinner and a movie," he said as a poor joke.

Marie studied the papers until the last word and looked at the $6,940 lost twice. "Can't you get this back with pay stubs?" she asked as she handed the papers back.

"Nope. Because I was in a known drug area with money strapped to my legs. And while I was on the ground, the dogs sniffed out the money."

"Well, how much did they take from Pee-Wee?"

"He ain't have nothing for them to take. I'm the only one that got raped last night."

"Why you say it like that? You should be happy you're free."

"Marie, I got swindled. I know it!" he told her as he smashed his fist into his palm. "Them Puerto Ricans and those cops was in on that shit together. I know they split up my little change."

"And what makes you believe that?" she asked, paying attention to every detail.

"Because the boy I was waiting for never came."

"Well, you should be glad he ain't come cause then you would have had a drug case, dummy."

"I told Pee-Wee to come on, but nooo. That clown didn't want to leave with nothing. Now I have nothing," he said, upset with himself. Then he flung the useless papers at the ancient TV.

Marie moved in closer and let him rest his head on her stomach as she rubbed his head in comfort.

"All I got now is $200 to my name. I wish I had left his ass in Gander Hill."

"Don't say that. That's your friend."

"I know, I don't mean it. But because of him and Tonya, I'm constantly strapped and watching my back. Plus, I'm out almost fifteen grand," he confessed.

"Well, at least you still got your job."

"Man, I'm mad right now. I feel like quitting and just saying, fuck everything!"

Marie smiled at him and her thoughts. She stepped back and held out both of her hands invitingly. "I guess you came to talk to the right friend this morning then, because I'm about to cheer you up."

"No offense," Deshonne said as he held her gentle hands, "but I don't think you should waste your time trying to cheer me up. I feel like crawling into a hole and dying."

She pulled at him and led him down the hallway to the bedroom. "Come and see what I got for you boo. I'm about to bring you back to life."

"Unless you got fifteen grand back here stashed, I don't think its gonna happen."

"Watch my magic, boo," Marie said encouragingly. I love challenges, she told herself.

*****

Purnell was banging on the motel door. Before he could bang again, the door opened up.

"What are y'all trying to do, put me on a crack diet?" Apple asked cynically. She stepped back and allowed him to enter.

"You gonna be on one if you was waiting on us to get you high," he said as he sat down in the chair.

The whole room was clean, to his surprise. But even more surprising to him was Apple's new attire. She looked like a professional woman in her pantsuit and heels and even more sexy in her intellectual eyeglasses.

Damn! I wish she'd just let me smash once. I know she got that snapper, he fantasized. "Who was you expecting, all dressed up?" Purnell asked curiously.

"Not you," she said as she folded her arms. "Where's Magic?"

"You know he had to go to work," he reminded her.

"Well, where's the rocks at? I've been missing all types of money."

"We don't got none. We fucked up."

"Is my baby okay!?" Apple asked as she sat on the dresser.

"Physically, yeah. But financially and emotionally, it's real messy."

"Well, stop talking in riddles and tell me what's wrong!" she said as she began to panic.

"Are we alone?"

"Yeah. Everybody walked over to the Sunoco. Why?"

"Because what I'm about to say ain't for everybody."

Apple cut off the TV so she wouldn't miss a word.

*****

Deshonne was exhausted and depressed as he stripped down. All he wanted to do was lay down and forget about the whole past week. As he climbed into his bed and peeled back the homemade quilt his mother made in her spare time, she screamed on him.

"Don't you get your nasty behind in that clean bed! I didn't raise you to be no bum."

"Mom, I just got off from work, and I'm tired. Can you please leave me alone?"

He just laid on top of the sheets and rolled over towards the wall. Mom Robinson stood in the doorway and continued her verbal chastising.

"Deshonne, I just finished making that quilt. Go get your butt in the shower."

"Mom, close my door, please?" he mumbled without moving.

"You don't own no doors around here, mister," she said with her left hand on her hip. "This is my house, remember?"

How can I forget when you keep reminding me," he told himself.

When Deshonne didn't respond, she walked over and tickled the bottom of his foot. "You need to get your own place, Mr. Man," she said playfully.

He kicked her hands. "Stop!" he whined. "I will as soon as I save enough money."

"Good. But until then, bring your butt in here at night. Or at least call."

"My fault. I stayed over Marie's last night," he lied.

276

"Who's Marie, your new girlfriend?"

"Yeah, something like that." After this morning, she wifey! he told himself.

"Well, is Purnell home, yet?" she asked as she picked up his dirty laundry.

"Yeah, he's out," he answered as if he didn't care.

She wondered why he answered like that. "Is he okay?"

"Mom, nothing's wrong. I'm just tired, and you won't let me go to sleep."

"I'm about to turn the shower on for you on my way to work. So get up."

"Please, don't touch anything. Just go to work and have a nice day."

"Okay, dirty gurt!" she said and closed the door.

"Thank you, Mom," he mumbled and closed his eyes.

About five minutes later the door reopened. "Baby, I almost forgot. Kenny called yesterday afternoon. He said call him at his mother's."

"Okay, Mom, I'll call him later." Fuck that clown! he thought. "Why are you still in the doorway?" he asked without looking back.

"Because I'm trying to remember the boy's name that stopped by here last night for you. What's that boy's name that picked you up in the truck that time?"

Deshonne rolled over and sat up, "Trigg?" he asked with a confused expression.

"Yeah, I think that is what he said. Everybody else in the truck waved."

"What did he say?"

"He said to tell you that his brother was sick in the hospital and to tell you that he was gonna make it."

"Is that all?"

"Yeah, why? Was he supposed to leave you a number or something?"

"Nah, Mom, thanks." I'ma have to kill these dudes now. They came to my mother's spot, Deshonne told himself.

"Oh, and the rental car people called and hour ago," she said before walking away again.

"Shit! I don't got $489 for them now. They beat," he said as he lay back down and wondered how things would end.

Street Knowledge Publishing LLC
1902-B Maryland Ave
Wilmington, DE 19805
TOLL FREE: **1.888.401.1114**
www.streetknowledgepublishing.com

Date: _____

Purchaser _____

Mailing Address _____

City _____ State _____ Zip Code _____

Qty.	ISB Number	Title of Book	Price Each	Total
	978-0-9822515-6-0	Bloody Money	$15.00	
	978-0-9822515-9-1	Bloody Money 2	$15.00	
	978-0-9799556-4-8	Bloody Money 3	$15.00	
	978-0-9799556-0-0	Tommy Good story	$15.00	
	978-0-9822515-0-8	Tommy Good Story II	$15.00	
	978-0-9746199-1-0	Me & My Girls	$15.00	
	978-0-9746199-0-3	Cash Ave	$15.00	
	978-0-9822515-1-5	Merry F$$kin' Xmas	$15.00	
	978-0-9799556-0-7	A Day After Forever	$15.00	
	978-0-9822515-3-9	A Day After Forever 2	$15.00	
	978-0-9746199-6-5	Don't Mix the Bitter with the Sweet	$15.00	
	978-0-9799556-9-3	Playing For Keeps	$15.00	
	978-0-9799556-3-1	Pain Freak	$15.00	
	978-0-9799556-5-5	Dipped Up	$15.00	
	978-0-9799556-6-2	No Love No Pain	$15.00	
	978-0-9746199-4-1	Dopesick	$15.00	
	978-0-9799556-7-9	Lust, Love & Lies	$15.00	
	978-0-9746199-7-2	The Queen of New York	$15.00	
	978-0-9746199-8-9	Sin 4 Life	$15.00	
	978-0-9822515-4-6	A Little More Sin	$15.00	
	978-0-9746199-5-8	The Hunger	$15.00	
	978-0-9746199-3-4	Money Grip	$15.00	
	978-0-9822515-7-7	Young Rich and Dangerous	$15.00	
	978-1-944151-26-3	Street Victims	$15.00	
	978-1-944151-28-7	Street Victims II	$15.00	
	978-1-944151-30-3	Street Victimes III	$15.00	
	978-1-944151-32-4	A Small Wonder	$15.00	
	978-1-944151-45-4	Coup De Grace	$15.00	
	978-1-944151-47-8	Burton Boys (May 2017)	$15.00	
	978-1-944151-56-0	Burton Boys 2	$15.00	
	978-1-944151-58-4	Burton Boys 3	$15.00	
	978-1-944151-00-3	Dirty Living	$15.00	
	978-1-944151-65-2	Watch What You Say	$15.00	
		Total Books Ordered	Quantity	
			Subtotal	

SHIPPING/HANDLING (Via U.S. Priority Mail)		
$7.20 for 1st book, $2.00 for each additional book		
Institutional Check & Money Orders ONLY	Shipping	
(No Personal Checks Accepted)	Total	

Total $

Sierra

Street Knowledge Publishing LLC
1902-B Maryland Ave
Wilmington, DE 19805
TOLL FREE: **1.888.401.1114**
www.streetknowledgepublishing.com

Date: _____

Purchaser _____
Mailing Address _____
City _____ State _____ Zip Code _____

Qty.	ISB Number	Title of Book	Author	Price Each	Total
	Butterfly Collection				
		Beautiful Demise	K.D. Harris	$13.99	
		Scarred	K.D. Harris	$13.99	
		Pressure (Coming April 2017)	K.D. Harris	$13.99	
		Dying to Fit In (Coming June 2017	K.D. Harris	$13.99	
		Legacy (Coming August 2017)	K.D. Harris	$13.99	
		Classy Clique (Coming Sept. 2017)	K.D. Harris	$13.99	
		Caged Secrets (Coming Nov. 2017)	K.D. Harris	$13.99	
		Messy Media (Coming Dec. 2017)	K.D. Harris	$13.99	
	SKP Erotica				
	978-1-944151-04-1	Beyond Measure	K.D. Harris	$15.00	
	978-1-944151-06-5	Beyond Measure II	K.D. Harris	$15.00	
	978-1-944151-62-1	Beyond Measure III (April 2017)	K.D. Harris	$15.00	
	978-1-944151-08-9	The Games We Play	K.D. Harris	$15.00	
	978-1-944151-02-7	For The Love Of It	K.D. Harris	$15.00	
	Eric B Crime Novels				
	978-1-944151-20-1	That Was Dirty	Wasiim	$15.00	
	978-1-944151-22-5	It Gets Dirtier	Wasiim	$15.00	
	978-1-944151-24-9	As Dirty As It Gets	Wasiim	$15.00	
	978-0-9799556-8-6	Money and Murder	Fred Brown	$15.00	
	978-1-944151-35-5	Money and Murder II	Fred Brown	$15.00	
	978-1-944151-39-7	Money and Murder III	Fred Brown	$15.00	
	978-1-944151-49-2	Scandalous Ties	Jermaine "Ski" Buchana	$15.00	
	978-1-944151-51-5	Scandalous Ties II	Jermaine "Ski" Buchana	$15.00	
	978-1-944151-52-2	Scandalous Ties III	Jermaine "Ski" Buchana	$15.00	
	978-1-944151-55-3	Scandalous Ties IV	Jermaine "Ski" Buchana	$15.00	
	978-0-9799556-2-4	Courts in the Streets	Kevin Bullock	$15.00	
	978-0-9822515-5-3	Courts in the Streets II	Kevin Bullock	$15.00	
	978-1-944151-43-0	Courts in the Streets III	Kevin Bullock	$15.00	
	Total Books Ordered			Quantity	
				Subtotal	

SHIPPING/HANDLING (Via U.S. Priority Mail)
$7.20 for 1st book, $2.00 for each additional book
Institutional Check & Money Orders ONLY
(No Personal Checks Accepted)

Shipping Total

Total $

www.ingramcontent.com/pod-product-compliance
Lightning Source LLC
Chambersburg PA
CBHW031149270326
41931CB00006B/204